Dependence and Exploitation
in Work and Marriage

Dependence and Exploitation in Work and Marriage

by Diana Leonard Barker and Sheila Allen

Longman
London and New York

LONGMAN GROUP LIMITED

London

*Associated companies, branches and representatives
throughout the world*

Published in the United States by Longman Inc., New York

© British Sociological Association 1976

First published 1976

ISBN 0 582 48673 4 Cased
ISBN 0 582 48674 2 Paper

Set in IBM Theme 10 on 12 point

Printed in Great Britain by
Whitstable Litho Ltd., Whitstable, Kent.

Library of Congress Cataloguing in Publication Data

Dependence and exploitation in work and marriage.

Bibliography: p.
Includes index.
1. Women—Employment—Addresses, essays, lectures.
2. Housewives—Addresses, essays, lectures. 3. Sex
role—Addresses, essays, lectures. I. Barker, Diana Leonard.
II. Allen, Sheila.
HD6053.D46   331.4   75-43517
ISBN 0-52-48673-4
ISBN 0-582-48674-2 pbk.

Contents

Notes on Contributors

Sheila Allen. Professor of Sociology at the University of Bradford. Author of *New Minorities Old Conflicts: Asian and West Indian Migrants in Britain* (Random House, 1971), editor with Diana Leonard Barker of *Sexual Divisions and Society: process and change* (B.S.A. Explorations in Sociology 6, Tavistock, 1976) and a contributor to *Race* and *Sociological Review*.

Diana Leonard Barker. Lecturer in Sociology in the University of London Institute of Education, member of the Executive Committee of Women's Research and Resources Centre. Editor with Sheila Allen of *Sexual Divisions and Society: process and change* (B.S.A. Explorations in Sociology 6, Tavistock, 1976), author of 'Women in the Anthropology profession' in Leavitt (ed.) *Women cross-culturally: change and challenge* (Mouton, 1975) and 'A Proper Wedding: an essay in the meaning of ritual' in Corbin (ed.) *The Couple* (Penguin, forthcoming). Also author of articles and reviews.

Richard David Barron. Lecturer in Sociology in the Department of Social Science and Humanities at the City University.

Colin Roy Bell. Professor of Sociology at the University of New South Wales. Author of *Middle Class Families* (Routledge, 1968), *The Disruption of Community* (H.M.S.O., 1970), with Howard Newby *Community Studies* (Allen & Unwin, 1972), ed. with H. Newby *The Sociology of Community* (Cass, 1974) and *Doing Sociological Research* (Allen & Unwin, 1976). Contributor to *Sociology, Sociological Review, Human Relations, Sociologia Ruralis* and *New Society*.

Richard Kemp Brown. Reader in Sociology at the University of Durham. Author with Parker, Child and Smith of *The Sociology of Industry* (Allen & Unwin, 1972), editor of *Knowledge, Education and Cultural Change* (B.S.A. Explorations in Sociology 2, Tavistock, 1973), contributor to Hurd (ed.) *Human Societies* (Routledge, 1973), Smith *et al.* (eds.), *Leisure and Society in Britain* (Allen Lane, 1973), and Bulmer (ed.) *Working Class*

Notes to Contributors

Images of Society (Routledge, 1975). Also contributor to *Sociology, British Journal of Industrial Relations* and other journals.

Leonore Davidoff. Lecturer in Social History in the Department of Sociology at the University of Essex. Author of *The Best Circles: Society, etiquette and the season* (Croom Helm, 1973) and articles in the *Journal of Social History* and the *Bulletin for the Society for the study of Labour History*.

Anne de Winter. Freelance graphic designer.

Jean Gardiner. Tutor in Economics, London University Extra-Mural Department. Author of 'Women's Work in the Industrial Revolution' in *Conditions of Illusion*, ed. Allen, Sanders and Wallis (Feminist Books, 1974) and a contributor to *New Left Review, Bulletin of the Conference of Socialist Economists* and *Red Rag*.

Emily Hope. Community worker. Formerly Assistant Lecturer in Social Anthropology at Birkbeck College, University of London.

Mary C. Kennedy. Lecturer in History in the Extra-Mural department of the University of London. Author of *Revolution in Perspective* (Peter Lowe, 1972) and several articles, including contributions to the *New Statesman* and the *Times Educational Supplement*.

Jane Marceau. Research Fellow at the Institut Européan d'Administration des Affaires and lecturer at the Université de Paris X (Nanterre). Author of *Class and Status in France* (Oxford University Press, forthcoming), 'Education and Social Mobility in France' in Parkin (ed.) *Social Analysis of Class Structure* (Tavistock, 1974). Contributor to *Public Opinion Quarterly*.

Howard Joseph Newby. Senior Lecturer in the Department of Sociology at the University of Essex. Author with Colin Bell of *Community Studies* (Allen & Unwin, 1972) and editor with Colin Bell of *The Sociology of Community* (Cass, 1974). Also author of several articles on farmers and farm workers.

Geoffrey Michael Norris. Lecturer in the Department of Social and Economic Research at Glasgow University.

Verity Jane Saifullah-Khan. Research Associate at the Research Unit on Ethnic Relations in Bristol. Author of 'Asian Women in Britain: strategies of adjustment of Indian and Pakistani migrants' in de Souza (ed.) *Women in Contemporary India* (Manohar, Delhi, 1975) and 'Pakistanis in Britain' in *New Community* (Winter, 1975-6).

Notes to Contributors

Roger Frederick Smith. Lecturer in the Department of Sociology at the University of Essex.

Ann Whitehead. Lecturer in Social Anthropology in the School of Social Sciences at the University of Sussex.

Introduction:
the interdependence of work and marriage

The papers in this volume are concerned with the themes of work and marriage. These have frequently been treated as quite separate fields of sociological enquiry, with the consequence that systematic inter-relationships have been neglected.[1]* Indeed the two are more usually distinguished and contrasted.[2] The dichotomy drawn between a sheltered, affection-based, organic group and the rude, commercial, aggressive world overlaps with the dichotomy between the rural golden age of the gemeinschaftlich village community and the gesellschaftlich city (Nisbet, 1967; Williams, 1973; Davidoff, L'Esperance and Newby, 1975). It finds popular expression in, for example, the advertising image portraying the man returning from the dirty, rushed, crowded, disorganized and exploitative outside to the clean, tidy, leisured, caring and warm household, complete with a cup of drinking chocolate prepared by his wife (see Davidoff, *et al.*, 1975: 34):

> The more the wider society grows in centralized corporate and state power, in size of institutions and in alienating work environment, the more the home becomes fantasized as a countervailing haven. Home-baked bread, French farm-house cookery, wine-making, organic gardening — the whole gamut of 'creative home-making' have become the suburban substitutes for the fully fledged return to the self sufficient small holding, only made real by a tiny minority.

Views of masculinity and femininity are bound up with this dichotomy between 'the home' and 'the world'.[3] The wife/mother/housemistress has become merged with the physical symbol of 'the home' to such a degree that a separate reality for adult women is difficult to achieve or maintain. The following (Higgins, 1974: 15) illustrates well the kind of ideology supporting masculine/feminine divisions:

> Women are not only different, but have kept what men have lost: a special capacity for intelligent feeling, for interpreting and handling emotion, for articulate intimacy and for what I can only call *waiting*.

---

*Notes applied to these superior numerals can be found at the end of chapters.

Sheila Allen and Diana Leonard Barker

> They have the power, especially, of particular, close-focused love. They live closer to human realities, and less urgently. Paradoxically, women's historic subjection to men may have helped to preserve these capacities. Certainly it is just these which men have been largely induced to neglect by the demands — and temptations — of our industrial culture. Man has become too cerebral, driven by ambition and material 'needs': cool above all, and distrustful of instinct and feeling. [our italics]

Such ideas are also prevalent in sociology, owing much in recent decades to the crude and literal application of the Parsonian dichotomy between instrumental and expressive roles. Pahl and Pahl (1972: 14) commented on their own work:

> This tension between the two approaches perhaps provided the dialectic out of which our particular approach developed. Frequently, R. E. Pahl argued for the man, his career and the needs of the company against the more expressive and affective approach of J. M. Pahl who argued for particularistic, familial views. Both of us felt our individual identities and values were bound up in the stances we adopted

We would stress that it was not felt necessary for anyone to argue for the woman: she was seen as inextricably and totally part of the family, in which she is not doing but being.

Emphasizing affective ties and consensus within the family has directed attention away from the material relationships which bind the family and from the differential distribution of power as between individual members of family groups.[4] We see not a domestic *group*, but a domestic *unit*. The domestic idyll ideology denies the reality of calculative relationships between family members. Further, since 'work' and 'home' are contrasted, housework is typified as non-work, women's paid work is regarded as marginal and temporary, and working wives and mothers are 'problems'. In consequence alternative structures are less viable — e.g. families without male 'heads', or where the father wishes to care for the home and children, or where the wife can earn more than the husband. By suggesting that existing divisions are intrinsic to the differences between men and women, the dominant ideological apparatus denies the possibility of change.

The division between home and work has been more or less faithfully reflected in academic sociology, but the papers which follow reject this approach. Some stress that in addition to sexual and affective ties the family must be viewed in terms of the economic and power relations which are crucial to its functioning.[5] Others show how these are connected with the positions of men and women in the labour market.[6]

Questions are therefore raised which bear directly on the problem of causality. These concern how the institutions of work and marriage are interrelated; what are the limits of integration; and what areas of autonomy exist. For instance, what effects does the division of labour in the market, with all its connotations of women's work, women's wages and so on, have on the institutions of marriage and the family? Does it result in the modifying of domestic and marriage relationships to accommodate the world of outside employment? And how far are such accommodations effective in altering the opportunities and experience of marriage partners? What are their effects inside the family and what conditions (social, economic and cultural) underlie them? What are the differences between work in the home, the unpaid servicing of family members, which has not as yet been prominent among the concerns of the sociologists of work, and that outside the domestic group which is paid and has been studied for many decades by industrial sociologists? If we seek social change, at what points in the structure can we most effectively 'insert a lever'?

Some of the papers confront, as a central question, the relation of domestic labour to the system of capitalist production. Interest in this question in recent years has produced different interpretations, but the crucial bearing of this relationship on major areas of sociological explanation can no longer be ignored. It is of important theoretical interest, and relates directly to the likely effectiveness of policy proposals, both in consciousness raising and political action and in legislative attempts to reduce institutional discrimination in work and training.

The first four papers consider paid work — usually, but not always located outside the home. Richard Brown examines the studies of industrial sociologists in relation to women employees — both in order to understand the position of women in the workplace and how their paid work relates to their overall position in society; and with a view to suggesting how, by giving consideration to this group of workers, new light can be thrown on the traditional concerns of industrial sociology. He argues that a better understanding of 'orientation to work' and collective action in the work situation could be achieved. He makes specific suggestions as to how a start can be made on this task, or in a very few cases carried forward. If his suggestions are followed, we can anticipate a very different kind of industrial sociology in future.

In the meantime, his paper critically assesses what we have. He considers textbooks on the sociology of industry, and finds that in only one is there an adequate recognition and discussion of the distinctive characteristics of the situation of women as employees. His selection of research on shop-floor and routine non-manual workers reveals that the occupations studied were often wholly 'womanfree' (and there was no

Sheila Allen and Diana Leonard Barker

questioning of why this should be); or the employees were treated as 'unisex' — as if their sex was irrelevant; or women employees were treated as problems. He is not arguing, nor would we want to argue, that women employees should be seen *qua* women, but that explicit consideration should be given to when and how 'latent' social identities of employees (men and women) are of consequence in the industrial situation.

He quite rightly takes to task those sociologists who have seen the problems of employers, male employees, unions, or husbands and children as the problematic of women's employment in our society. This approach has been used to obscure the problems of women workers and to attribute *to them* the responsibility for their work situations (i.e. it is said that it is women themselves who do not want training, who chose to stop work to care for children, etc.). It is now becoming recognized that the majority of women receive low pay, have little security of employment and few prospects for advancement, but it does not make it easier for those in routine, boring and badly paid jobs to be told that this is suited to their needs or characteristics. The use of women in 'part-time temporary' employment (even where this is lifelong) serves important functions for society as it is now, both from the point of view of industry and from the conventionally accepted status of married women. It is to a consideration of these aspects that more of the time and expertise of sociologists should be given.

Brown's paper draws attention at several points to the importance of labour market studies to industrial sociology and Barron and Norris take this as the theme of their paper, arguing that in Britain there is a dual labour market which cuts across firms, industries and the manual/non-manual division. The primary sector consists of relatively well-paid, secure jobs with promotional ladders, fringe benefits and better working conditions, while the secondary sector lacks all these features. The vast majority of women are confined to the secondary sector, along with such groups as the young, the old, the handicapped, black and immigrant workers.

They make an important distinction between the characteristics of labour markets and jobs within them, and the characteristics of those who fill the jobs. This seems a simple and rather obvious analytical distinction, but one all too rarely made. Thus secondary sector workers are seen as less reliable as individuals — with higher absenteeism and turnover — when, in fact, they are restricted to jobs which offer no possibility of training or reward for experience, which are boring and badly paid, and where a high labour turnover may be necessary to allow for fluctuations in demand for the product. Barron and Norris suggest that the core elements in a secondary labour force are dispensability, social difference (normatively defined inferiority) from the primary sector worker, low investment in training (human capital), low pay, and lack of solidary organization. They attempt to show how most women, through a combination of the structure of opportunity and expectations derived from socialization within a sexually divided society, fall into the workforce characterized by these attributes.

The authors point out, however, that over time the characteristics of jobs do tend to become the characteristics of job holders — i.e. job histories and attitudes towards jobs come to reflect the jobs. Indeed, expectations about work may well be formed before young people leave school, in terms of the market situation they know they will shortly find themselves in (see Shaw, 1976). Thus the job market is both cause and effect of women and men's overall social position. Many previous researchers in both industrial sociology and the sociology of the family, by ignoring the structure of labour markets, have seen inequalities rather than major structural barriers, and thus have stressed women's *choice* of marriage and the domestic sphere, rather than its economic necessity (see Delphy, 1976, and Marceau, Ch. 10, and Whitehead, Ch. 9).

Barron and Norris's labour market model calls attention to the relationship between the primary and secondary workforce. The levels of earnings and job security in the two are *interdependent*. The differentiation of the labour force provides 'key workers' with relatively high wages and stability, but requires that others receive low wages and little stability of employment. This reduces class solidarity. It presents considerable problems for trade unions in representing the interests of all their members, and for inter-union relations. Further, women workers in the secondary sector may well be married to, and thus to an extent share in the standard of living of, primary sector workers, so that the potential for women's organized action is reduced.

By calling attention to the relationship between the primary and secondary workforce, Barron and Norris bring out a crucial structural element in labour market theory which has a bearing beyond the question of women's employment. But in terms of the relationship between work and marriage, because it is assumed that men are breadwinners and women work for pin money, the overall differential position of men and women has too often been merely alluded to and then ignored.[7] The fact that the *typical* secondary worker is a woman passes unremarked. Only by analysing the causes and the consequences of dualism which are embedded in the divisions between the sexes can any adequate understanding of the conditions of low pay be achieved or the formulation of policies to remove inequities be begun. Legislation for equal pay and equal opportunity, though necessary, are likely to change very little, except to make clearer the way in which the processes of dividing the workforce operate.

Brown's and Barron and Norris's papers form an excellent

Sheila Allen and Diana Leonard Barker

background against which to look at the two following papers, which give accounts of particular occupations – elite journalism and homeworking.

Roger Smith looks at 'secondary dualism' within Fleet Street journalism. Here women are very largely confined to jobs which are necessary to the continuation and functioning of the enterprise but which are low in prestige and effectively dead ends. He rejects the common approach which sees women's participation in careers as *determined* by their socialization or their domestic life-cycle, and looks instead at the processes of discrimination in the work situation. These operate so that very few women get into Fleet Street in the first place and those who do are either pushed sideways on to the women's pages, or denied promotion and generally discouraged. Many opt out. Smith makes the important point that rather than assuming that 'wastage' is due to women dropping out to become housewives and mothers, we should actually observe women who quit careers. While accepting his critique that women's 'life-cycle' is often simply a legitimation for discrimination rather than a cause of failure, there is no doubt that the different domestic situations of men and women do hinder women's achievements.[8]

Smith explores the structure and ideology of journalism so as to locate the mechanics of the continuance of sexual differentiation and stratification over time. He concludes that:

> women are cut off from many key-learning situations and contact with important occupational roles, and the resultant differential distribution of knowledge (and expertise) is the major mechanism whereby sex differentiation and stratification are maintained.

This suggests a useful analytical framework for studying many other occupations. It also suggests the key points on which women's caucuses and the unions might press for change.

He does not enter into much consideration of *why* women are discriminated against; his data simply show that men journalists do become part of a male subculture from which women are excluded. The strength of the cultural value that intimate groups, at work or leisure, should be of one sex is mentioned in Brown's paper and is a key point in Whitehead's paper (Ch. 9). Informal groups will remain untouched by the current anti-discrimination legislation, and, as Smith says, this is not an area in which the union would be willing to intervene.

Smith challenges the notion put forward by some sociologists (e.g. Becker and Strauss, 1956) that groups that recognize their situation as inferior and exploited will develop a rationalizing ideology. He rightly points out that consciousness of exploitation may also lead to militancy and change. The relation between consciousness and structure which is raised at the end of Brown's paper is central here: under what conditions is consciousness of exploitation raised and in what circumstances does it lead to collective organization and change? Smith approaches these questions obliquely but his account should help all those interested in explaining why women, 'no matter what sphere of work they are hired for or select, like the sediment in a wine bottle . . . settle at the bottom' (Epstein, 1970: 2), for he suggests ways of identifying what obstructs women's consciousness and what obstructs change.

Homework presents a stark contrast to even the lowest of Fleet Street jobs. The small project on which Emily Hope, Mary Kennedy and Anne de Winter base their paper (Ch. 5) highlights some of the crucial features of homeworking, which has been ignored for over half a century by social scientists and politicians. It is secondary sector work *par excellence;* appallingly badly paid, with many homeworkers making less than 10p per hour.[9] The level of insecurity is extremely high: there is no contract of employment and many homeworkers are left without work for weeks at a time and expected to work very long hours when the market is booming. There is no promotion, not even a slight increase in rates of pay for long service. There are no fringe benefits, no sick pay, no paid holidays or pension provisions. The trappings of homework, the boxes of crackers awaiting collection, the fishing rods laid out to dry, the industrial sewing machine and rail of completed dresses, may take up as much as a quarter of the family's living space, added to which the dirt, smell and noise may fill the home. The North London study estimated one household in eight in their area had someone doing homework, almost all of them women, and 250,000 is given as a minimum figure for people engaged on this kind of work.[10]

Homeworkers are truly captive women. They may have dependent children or be housebound with elderly parents or disabled husbands, or themselves be disabled. They are ethnically diverse and include women living in *purdah.* Some are isolated in the country. Some of those interviewed in North London had children of school age, but they were unwilling to go out to work for better wages because they felt an extreme form of obligation to serve their husband and children (see Maher, 1975 and Barker, 1972). Many of these women are encapsulated in a contradiction between the good wife and mother ideology and the sheer material necessities of day-to-day living. Hope *et al.,* stress that their informants' money is spent on food and children's clothing, or sometimes on such things as household repairs, or to help with high mortgage repayments or rents, and is not 'pin money'. The husbands of homeworkers are frequently on very low wages (see Brown, 1974).

One of the findings from their study concerns the women's evaluation of their time and their attitude to their pay for working at home. Their income is not considered in relation to the time it took them

Sheila Allen and Diana Leonard Barker

to do the work, nor in terms of the market value of their skills as machinists or coil winders, etc., but in terms of the amount paid for each garment and the total which comes in each week. By doing homework the woman is able to earn something in her moments of 'free-time', in between serving the needs of other family members.[11]

These sweated labourers are certainly unprotected. Hope *et al,* point out that there were no homeworkers on the wages councils and union officials were 'not unreservedly sympathetic' towards homeworking, since they thought it should be abolished.[12] The profits made by the employers have recently been shown to be extremely high.[13]

The interest of the women's movement in the forms of oppression involved in homeworking is a stimulus not only to reform, but also to a reassessment by sociologists of the social and economic relationships involved in this form of production, in which domestic and paid work are integrally related. It is unlikely for several reasons that large-scale survey methods would be applicable to teasing out the nature and extent of these relationships. The small-scale projects already completed provide us with a beginning and more work on similar lines is badly needed.

Jean Gardiner's contribution (Ch. 6) makes an analysis of domestic labour performed within the family and, like Hope *et al.,* she sees the world of work and family as a totality, explicitly breaking down the conventional boundaries erected between sociological specialisms. She emphasizes the economic advantages which accrue to the capitalist mode of production from the domestic work of those who maintain and reproduce labour power. She suggests that surplus labour produced outside the capitalist mode of production (i.e. not productive for capital in Marx's sense) may nonetheless be appropriated by capital as an additional source of profit.

It could be argued that Gardiner gives too little attention in her paper to the indirectness of the means by which the wives' surplus labour is appropriated: i.e. that the wife has a relationship with her husband; and he has a relationship with capital. (The husband appropriates his wife's surplus labour and some of this is in turn appropriated by capital. The husband receives a wage from his employer and the wife receives upkeep from her husband.[14]) If, as Gardiner at several points suggests, marriage could be analysed as a distinct mode of production, then it can be argued that relations between husbands and wives have class-like properties. Gardiner maintains that housewives should not be viewed as a class, but that there is a serious argument for looking at them as being in the same class position, that of domestic labourer. The appropriation of the housewife's labour is indirect, it is appropriated individually, and (as it appears) voluntarily 'on the basis of personal, familial ties', and it is a permanent commitment throughout married life, with no set hours. This is in contrast to the direct extraction of labour from the wage labourer, with the hours and the price of labour stipulated.

Gardiner does not argue that this kind of analysis of domestic labour supposes a recognition of the common position of housewives, though it could be used as the basis for those who seek to organize them. Nevertheless she suggests that questions of consciousness and organization on a class basis are incomplete without consideration of the forms of dependence and exploitation inherent in domestic labour; for the majority of women domestic labouring is part of their class position whatever other relationships of production they are also engaged in. The identification of the wife with her husband's class position is therefore necessarily ambivalent.

A radical rethinking of many of the most cherished frameworks used by sociologists, political scientists and economists is called for if we accept such an analysis. It demonstrates the need for a critical re-examination of some of the basic ideas which have been built into economic theory and adopted by social theorists. For example, the sociology of social stratification must no longer practise *couveture:* the doctrine that husband and wife have one socio-economic/class position, and that one is his.

Whereas Gardiner concerns herself primarily with the political economy of domestic labour, Leonore Davidoff (Ch. 7) examines housework as part of culture, providing an historical account of the material structure and ideology of household management since the seventeenth century. She links in her analysis the separation of the household from public concerns and the cash ethos; the emphasis on the purity of women and the 'double standard' of morality; the stress on classification and segregation, order, pollution and cleanliness in the nineteenth century; changes in the hierarchical structures of society; and pressures towards a rational economy. The main body of her paper uses materials from the nineteenth and early twentieth century, but she also draws out the relevance for our present situation.

One point she develops is that of the contradiction between the pressures towards rationalization which operated (and still operate) in the wider economy and were sought in the domestic economy, and the factors within the household which frustrate the application of rational calculative methods — viz: the small scale of the units and the goals of maintaining hierarchical boundaries and the personal servicing of superiors. This has resulted in the home remaining labour intensive and it has also affected the general evaluation of all women's work.

Davidoff's mastery [*sic*] of the available material allows her to make observations and associations which become obvious once stated, but which hitherto taken-for-granted approaches have kept hidden. The subtlety of the processes by which generations of women have become

Sheila Allen and Diana Leonard Barker

enmeshed in social relationships which define their main activity, and thus them, as not only less important than men, but trivial, is well worth exploring further. Davidoff points out that there are considerable difficulties in collecting the relevant historical information, but she shows the possibilities which are opened once the data are recognized as important.

It is no doubt a reflection of the fact that the world of professional sociology, economics and history has been overwhelmingly peopled by men that it has not questioned the assumption that the task of servicing the present and future generation *should* be attributed to women. The arduous, boring, low-status work of 'boundary maintenance' in cooking and cleaning and childcare may occasionally be shared, or delegated, or rejected by women in our society, but it remains their primary responsibility (supported by the appropriate moral, financial and physical coercive sanctions). The cross-cultural uniformity of the attribution of such responsibilities has led to speculations such as those of Ortner (1974) and Brown (1970) — to which Davidoff refers. However, the suggestion that women are seen as 'closer to nature' or weaker and dependent because of their physiology and part in reproduction, whilst initially appealing, must in fact be seen rather as a legitimation for a pre-existing power relationship.[15] One could, after all, argue that men are closer to nature because of their 'unrestrained sexuality' and 'aggressiveness' and that they are physically more vulnerable because of their external genitalia. Rather we would follow Davidoff in pointing out that colonial powers delegate domestic work to the 'natives', and suggest that being provided with protection from pollution and disturbance: having clean, quiet rooms, punctual meals, warm, tidy houses, washed, ironed and mended clothes *provided* for one is a privilege of the powerful. It comes with power and helps to maintain it: it does not produce power.

Bell and Newby (Ch. 8) leave aside the historical development of power relationships between men and women and look instead at how these are maintained and stabilized today. They concentrate on the relationship between husbands and wives and look at the relational and normative means of ensuring male authority in marriage. They presume men's acceptance of their own position and suggest that the problem is rather women's consciousness:[16] why do women accept and support sets of values which endorse their own inferiority? Bell and Newby dismiss the suggestion that women are passive and deferential *qua* women; stressing rather that it is the relationships between men and women (specifically in marriage) which are characterized by deferential behaviour. Thus we must look at the relationship, not at one party to the interaction.

They argue that stratification within the family has been overlooked partly because those interested in stratification theory have regarded the family as the unit of analysis, though their analogies of hierarchies frequently use the family. Drawing on the general sociological discussion of hierarchical relationships, they stress that while these are based on power (in marriage on the husband's power of the hand and of the purse), coercion is a potentially unstable basis of power, whereas the *right* to hold might (i.e. to have legitimate superior status) provides greater stability. Might need only come to the forefront when 'ideal' subordination threatens to break down and real subordination is necessarily revealed.

Study of other deferential relationships suggests that the conditions of marriage and the home gives rise to deferential relationships *par excellence*. This sort of relationship is most marked when continuing face-to-face interaction occurs within a particular location, and where the subordinate has more limited access to the outside world than the superordinate and thus depends heavily for his/her interpretations of reality on the superordinate. This casts a new light on what is going on in the middle class marital discussion described so favourably by Berger and Kellner (1964) and generally taken as indicative of marital equality.

By inhibiting the development of consciousness of subordination and the possibilities of action to change it, deferential relationships are unusually stable. This has obvious implications for sexual stratification inside and outside the family. We need to document in some detail deviant marital relationships where deferential relationships break down or are minimal; to analyse the conditions under which this takes place; and to look at what are the limits to such change. The effect on marriage relationships of a deliberate 'raising' of women's consciousness, for instance, could be examined.

The stability of marriage is supported by the inherent contradictions in the relationship. The spouses are differentiated from one another (in terms of power and division of labour), yet they share an identity of interests against outsiders (for example, in the husband's success in his job, which is a source of cash and prestige for them as a couple, in their affective ties, and in their concern for the children's well-being and success). Bell and Newby discuss the management of this contradiction in the processes of on-going interaction between husband and wife; for instance, in asymmetrical gift giving. However, they rather understress the male hegemony in definitions coming into the deferential dialectic from outside. The 'male defined' nature of the 'going rate of exchange' of rights and duties, the effects of socialization, and the media all work with the husband, not against him. Men hold the ring outside as well as inside marriage. Where there are children, this is especially the case: the husband acts as a mediator of the external controlling agencies over the wife. Ann Whitehead's paper (Ch. 9) brings out women's powerlessness clearly; and it is not unrecognized by spouses within a marriage, particularly women in bad marriages who would like to get out. Erin Pizzey quotes one husband

Sheila Allen and Diana Leonard Barker

who, as he beat his wife, taunted her with 'Where can you go? What can you do?' (Pizzey, 1974: 43).

Bell and Newby are concerned with the relationship between husband and wife, but it seems possible that their analysis applies particularly to the husband and wife-with-children situation. Others have stressed the importance in understanding the power of men of the attribution to women of the responsibilities for childcare (Delphy, 1976; Abrams and McCulloch, 1976). It is useful therefore to look at recently married couples without children to see how far Bell and Newby's account holds.

Jane Marceau's paper (Ch. 10) deals with couples where the husband is attending a prestigious business school in France. The object of her research is to explore middle-class strategies to prevent downward social mobility among their sons — such as occurs when the value of previously obtained degrees or training is lowered or where the sons cannot be placed in the family business. She has investigated the extent to which the marriages contracted by these young men are such as to maintain or improve their social and economic position, by exploring the forms of economic, social and cultural capital contributed by their wives.

The wives' personal wealth is considerable and, further, their earned income in at least half the marriages makes possible attendance at the business school, where the fees are heavy and life style expensive. The wives' social origins (in terms of their fathers' occupations) is on a par with or higher than their husbands' and their kin networks provide links with significant political, industrial and professional spheres. The 'cultural capital' which they bring to marriage is not, in this sample, weighted towards intellectual pursuits; but rather comprises the varied characteristics of upper middle-class leisure activities, competence in foreign languages and the practice of religion backed by the appropriate religious, moral and sex-appropriate education. Though these are less tangible or quantifiable than economic assets, they are important if not indispensable status-conferring qualities. They include encouraging their husband to attend the school, and taking an intelligent interest in and being a discussant of his career.

Most of the wives moved with their husband to the locality of the school, despite the fact that most had jobs or were studying, and the course lasted only for 1 year. The investigators felt they could take for granted that little could be learned about power relations between husbands and wives by examining the division of household tasks, since these young wives with husbands who were studying would automatically shoulder the household duties.

More fruitful as indices of marital power were the control of financial resources and decisions concerning the husband's job. Marceau argues that her findings reveal considerable equality and independence in financial matters. Certainly these wives are as well placed to exercise power as any can be. Only two did not have an income of their own and at the time their husbands were not earning; and the companionate, egalitarian view of marital relations is probably most accepted in the early stage of middle-class marriage. However, we would stress more than Marceau does that, while the marriage contracts were such as to restrict the rights of the husband to the wife's property in the event of death, divorce or bankruptcy, the husband benefits from it during the marriage and *'may well be involved in the management of it'*. Some wives with dowries were *helped in their administration* by their fathers or brothers. That is to say, we are not clear as to quite what 'control' these wives exercise over 'their' money.

Certainly, their earned income is not likely to be a permanent basis of power. Most were in 'feminine' jobs, which have low initial salaries and little by way of career ladders. Those in less sex-typed jobs would almost inevitably meet with discrimination if they continued working. Thus their earnings would be low compared to those of their husbands. This, combined with marrying ambitious men likely to be geographically mobile, their conventional upbringing, and parental expectations, result in almost all of them expressing the intention to stop work when they have children. It is perhaps to be expected that those wives who were likely to have the highest earnings in their own right were the ones most determined to continue working.

For the rest, as Marceau points out, neither their potential earnings nor their private incomes would allow them to maintain their accustomed life-style unless they married. Their high involvement and interest in their husbands' careers is rational in terms of the effects on their *own* standard of living. In terms of the cultural hegemony it is not surprising either that *all* the wives said that their husband's career was 'of far greater importance than their own'. 'Even the wife with her own flourishing business emphasized that if her husband's career demanded it, she would give up her professional life, although they would try hard to combine the two.' 'Most underlined the predominance of the husband's career *when asked about their own* . . .' [our italics]

While at this particular point in marriage the wife's material contribution makes her relatively equal in some decision making, this is within a limited sphere and does not, for example, involve her considering what sort of work she would like to do, or whether her job or her marriage 'should come first'. She expects to do such domestic work, entertaining and child rearing as her husband's career and their marriage shall require. As her husband's market position improves and hers declines, so will her power in decision making decrease.[17]

Sheila Allen and Diana Leonard Barker

Ann Whitehead's paper (Ch. 9) describes a very different marital situation: a rural village with little geographical mobility, where the barriers to women entering the labour force (except as part-time domestic cleaners) are almost total, and where there is little if any possibility of private income or inherited property till late in life. Women must therefore marry, or work as housekeepers for kin. Kin, work and friendship networks overlap, making 'strategic presentation of self' difficult. In addition, there is marked sex segregation, and an ideology which holds women in contempt.

Her paper is a significant contribution to the sociology of the family in Britain. Detailed information on relationships between marriage partners is scanty and Whitehead's material is based on participant observation over many months, supplemented by interview material on marital norms. She also places marital relationships within the context of other social relationships, both inside and outside the home.

She suggests that the view put forward by many sociologists that the relationships between men and women in the family are becoming increasingly companionate, love-based and home-centred is attributable to men having been looked at in their work situation and women in the home, and to reliance on replies to questionnaires. There has been a lack of observation of how men and women *behave* towards each other at work or in the home. On the basis of her own work she stresses the absence of shared interests and talking between husband and wife, and in general the paucity of time actually spent together. Nor is she convinced that the same-sex network fulfills for women the companionship, help and support functions lacking in marriage. Whitehead asserts that in this village there is minimal corporate female solidarity to act against the men as a whole, or against particular husbands, in the way that the male group acts against women and against particular wives. The 'women's trade union' in Ashton or Bethnal Green, when seen from the women's point of view as opposed to that of male sociologists, might produce similar doubts about its solidary nature.

Whitehead emphasizes the (often overlooked or unmentioned) consciousness of sexuality as a dominant aspect of the behaviour of men and women; and the use made of women to symbolize, express and maintain both solidarity and ambivalent rivalry between men. The joking behaviour between the sexes which she observed ranged from reciprocal banter between men and women, through hostile and boisterous teasing between groups of opposite sex, to overtly hostile and physically abusive attacks on individual women by groups of men. She draws attention to the need to look not only at the *use* of joking abuse at work and leisure as a distancing mechanism between the groups and as a control on thhe behaviour of women, but also at the *content* of joking. Three features were evident in the joking among the men at the pub. First, that the stereotypes of women were contemptuous or degrading. Second, that the language was obscene, and treated women as objects 'to be screwed'. And third, that control over particular women was a counter in the competition for male standing. The more a wife stayed in and cooked and cleaned and did not look at other men, the better for her husband's prestige.

She argues that these attitudes are not changing and that they must inevitably influence the marital relationship. Nor are they restricted to rural working class 'backwaters'. It is not that virility is a source of competition for those who have nothing else with which to compete, for comparable behaviour is to be found in all areas and all classes: in medical schools and rugby clubs, on homebound commuter trains and in senior common rooms, in the Houses of Parliament and Working Men's Clubs. The attitudes are, in brief, an integral part of the normal male sub-culture.

Brown's paper quoted Caplow's contention that two of the core values of our culture are that intimate groups outside the family should be of one sex, and that men should not be subordinate to women. If we add to this Whitehead's stress on the awareness of sexuality in heterosexual relationships in totally 'inappropriate' situations, the processes which underlie women's inferior position become clearer. By and large until recently women have tried to make their way individually against these cultural disadvantages.

Against this background we must agree with Verity Saifullah-Khan (Ch. 11) that those who instantly see *purdah* as bizarre and deviant and inhuman are being arrogant. In many areas of our society unrelated men and women very rarely come into contact in work or leisure; a pronounced double standard of sexual morality still exists; and also many presume that if a man and a woman are alone together, sexual intercourse is the inevitable cause or result. The distinction between *purdah* as practised by Mirpuris, and segregation in many groups in Britain seems to be largely that the latter form of segregation is produced by informal intersex antagonism, while the former it is achieved by formal, ritualized mechanisms. Indeed, Saifullah-Khan's account of the 'relaxed conviviality' of the women's and men's domains, and the possibilities of corporate female action against a husband who transgresses the mores of appropriate behaviour, compares favourably with rural Herefordshire.

She points out that the system she describes is now a part of British society. She compares the forms of social relationships found in traditional village society with their variants in the British industrial situation; and in so doing she illuminates both the adaptive mechanisms at work and the strengthening of tradition often resulting from the pressures exerted by the 'host' society.

Moving to the urban industrial city has made life more difficult and

Sheila Allen and Diana Leonard Barker

hence *purdah* more constricting for women. (This provides interesting comparisons with experiences in England during the eighteenth and nineteenth centuries, and between rural and urban-industrial Africa.) In many cases the women are alone with their small children, carrying out more burdensome household tasks with no female kin to help. The wife may have more areas in which she exercises control both because of the absence of her mother-in-law, and because of the increasing financial and family decisions which she undertakes when her husband works long, unsocial hours. But the sexes are *perceived* as less mutually interdependent; and the husband-wife relationship is one of greater dependence. The wife's supports against her husband are reduced and with the absence of constraints on him from his father and kin he may be more autocratic. The situation is full of dilemmas and Saifullah-Khan brings out the continuing interactive processes by which these are, if not resolved, at least coped with by the groups.

In the latter part of her paper Saifullah-Khan stresses that modern British society has virtually nothing to offer to replace the support of the traditional kin network. The costs of this network are high — especially for women in *purdah* — but this should not lead us to advocate the imposition of a substitute which also oppresses and exploits women and their children in the family and the labour market. She rightly points to the confusion which exists amongst central and local policy makers and administrators as to whether and in what form cultural pluralism is acceptable (though a politics stressing self-determination does not seem to be part of their intention); and poses the problem of whether the aim of a multicultural society may contradict in part attempts to get rid of racism and sexism.

Saifullah-Khan's suggestion that it is arrogance to assess cultures other than one's own in terms of the levels of consciousness of groups within them is to our mind too simple a notion. We follow her in not wanting to encourage the particular forms of ethnocentric condemnation met with in European social science, to say nothing of the more popular prejudices. Nevertheless, to preclude the possibilities which comparative analyses offer of sought and directed social change, involving changing the consciousness of the participants, seems to be a negative approach. For the Mirpuri women and their families change can not be avoided, even if they were all now to return to their rapidly changing home villages. We would argue that the more they understand the situation the greater the possibility that they can participate in the making of relevant choices. We would not, however, want to suggest that these choices are not severely constrained by the minority position of the whole Mirpuri population of Britain, and indeed by their political and economic position as part of the long-standing Kashmiri situation.

We hope that this volume will contribute to changing the way in which questions are posed about the divisions between the sexes in our society. We began by pointing to the cultural values which stress the separation of 'the home' and 'the world' and to the way in which the dichotomy between loving home life and rational, aggressive, urban industrial capitalism has become elided with the dichotomy between femininity and masculinity. By and large sociology has supported this ideology, taking masculine behaviour as the norm and as unproblematic outside the home, while seeing the family itself mainly in terms of its 'functions' as a unit. Women have been occluded time and again by encapsulating them within their fathers' or husbands' social persons.

The papers in this volume stress that women live, move, and have their being outside as well as inside the family; that the household is a group of individuals, having economic as well as emotional relationships with one another, being divided in some contexts while united in others; and that the relations between the sexes outside and within the family are inter-related. Their argument requires that sex should no longer be dismissed as a 'status attribute' (cf. Parkin, 1971 : 14-17) by those concerned to develop sociological theory. Rather, the sexes should be seen as social collectivities, whose class-like inter-relations need to be considered in any half-way adequate theory of social differentiation and inequality.

Notes

1. This separation has been questioned from time to time by some of those examining the interrelation of work and leisure or 'central life interests' (for example: Dubin, 1956; Wilensky, 1969; Parker, 1973; and Pahl and Pahl, 1972) and by those concerned with the 'problems' of women working outside the home (see: Brown's paper in this volume; Fogarty *et al.*, 1971; Rapoport and Rapoport, 1971a). We maintain, however, that the structural inter-relations of home and work are not systematically incorporated in sociological analysis.

2. The growth in the contrast between 'the home' and 'the world' has recently been commented on by: Laslett, 1965; Middleton, 1974; Gray, 1973; Rowbotham, 1973; Davidoff, L'Esperance and Newby, 1976; and Comer, 1974; among others.

3. This has been identified as the Solveig Syndrome. 'An extreme and according to some critics even deliberately exaggerated statement of (women's power to save men from their baser selves and the outside world by their general good example and passive influence) can be

Sheila Allen and Diana Leonard Barker

        seen in Ibsen's very influential play, *Peer Gynt*' (see Davidoff, L'Esperance and Newby, note 60, 1976).

4.   See: Young, 1952; Oren, 1974; Delphy, 1976; Delphy and Barker, forthcoming.

5.   Like most sociologists who say that they are talking about 'the family', we are in fact concentrating upon relations between husbands and wives. The power and economic relationship between parents and . children are also commonly occluded by talk of 'affective' versus 'instrumental' bonds, and in general children are treated as objects not as actors within the domestic group.

6.   Nine million women are in paid employment — about 36 per cent of the total work force of *c*. 25 million in Britain. Four-fifths of these women work full time; two-thirds are married (Department of Employment, 1974). Since the 1930s, adult women have earned 45–55 per cent of adult men's weekly earnings (Social Trends, 1975; Department of Employment, 1975).

7.   As Land (1976) points out, this attitude — and the associated social insurance and tax systems — ignore the fact that 2 million women workers are the chief supporters of their households and that in 1970 the number of poor, two-parent families in which the father was in full-time work would have *trebled* if the father's earnings had not been supplemented by the mother's.

        The *locus classicus* of the neglect of women's earnings is Eric Hobsbawm's comment (1964: 346):

> No initial problem of wage determination arose for the unskilled or those in abundant supply. They had to take (if men) a subsistence wage, or one fixed so as just to attract them away from (say) farm labour. (Women and children of course got less than subsistence, but since their rate was normally fixed in relation to the male wage, we may neglect them).

8   A normal day's work as currently defined, is that of someone who does not have to do domestic work for him or herself (see Delphy, 1976). Some domestic services can of course be purchased, but there is no substitute for a wife (see Syfers, 1971). And women (single or married) cannot have wives. Conversely, men are perceived as needing to have jobs or promotion more than women because they have wives to support. For jobs which call for 'fitting in' to the male work group, being able to give 'full commitment', and 'needing' the job, men will be evaluated more favourably.

9.   See also Brown (1974). Her evidence is based on 50 (white) women contacted via the Jimmy Young programme on the radio. She found

that more than half of the women earned less than 16p per hour; 22 per cent less than 6p.

Average hourly rate for homeworkers		*Average hourly rate for industrial women workers*	
Full-time (30+ hours per week)	12.5p	Full-time (30+ hours per week)	56.4p
Part-time	22.6p	Part-time	52.3p

Source: (Brown, 1974: 10)

10. Brown cites Peter Townsend's survey of Poverty in the UK, which relates to 1968/9. Owen (1974) believes the numbers of homeworkers are increasing and relates this to the rag trade in particular. The increase is seen as due to 'the declining labour force, industrial rents, and the great cheap fashion boom ... which saw a mushrooming of small dress firms' (Owen, 1974).

11. Brown's study showed that the women were not unaware of their exploitation, 'the term slave labour was referred to by almost everyone, and the homeworkers' comments ranged from anger ... to bitter resignation'. They say that 'beggars can't be choosers,' and they recognize the *competition* for this sort of work (Brown, 1974: 17).

12. None of the sixteen in Brown's sample whose work was covered by a Wages Council were aware of this and one-third of the homeworkers were paid less than half (often much less than half) of the statutory minimum wage laid down by Parliament; but a visit from a wages inspector is extremely unlikely.

13. 'Normally she gets 30p or so for making dresses which are sold on Oxford Street for up to 16 gn. or more. Rates which accord ill with the recently published analysis (by N.E.D.C.) of profits in the industry which show an average return on net assets of 29 per cent in dressmaking, where outwork is most common. "It's quite extraordinary to find a sample of 64 firms in an industry making profits so high," said an economist. Contrary to manufacturers' common complaints they're doing very well. It's the kind of return that gets monopolists sent to the Monopolies Commission' (Owen, 1974).

14. This line of argument has developed from earlier writings from the women's movement which focus on the relations of production between husbands and wives (Benston, 1969; Delphy, 1970). It seeks to explain the effect on marriage (and other male—female

Sheila Allen and Diana Leonard Barker

relationships) of their present location in industrial capitalism, rather than focusing on the usefulness of the family for capital.

15. For example, the suggestion that women need men to protect them because, in the event of an attack, women can't run fast when carrying babies. But who says that it is women who should carry the babies?

16. This is a common presumption, but one which needs to be questioned (see Pleck and Sawyer, 1974). It can lead to men's behaviour continuing to be seen as the norm and women's as problematic, and to a neglect of men's socialization.

17. The Pahls, after all, see as a significant divide in 'marital consultation' whether or not their middle-aged managers discussed their career changes — including changes of job which might involve the whole family moving house — *before or after the husband had made up his own mind*. (Pahl and Pahl, 1972: 59–60)

Women as employees: some comments on research in industrial sociology

In the majority of cases where they have not been ignored altogether, women employees have been regarded by industrial sociologists in one of two ways: on the one hand as indistinguishable from men in any respect relevant to their attitudes and actions at work; and on the other as giving rise to special problems, for the employer and/or the families or communities from which they come.[1] Both approaches are inadequate and the adoption of either means that the possibilities of comparative study of the expectations and actions of men and women in industry are generally lost — possibilities which could aid the analysis of some of the central problems of industrial sociology, as well as provide a more adequate understanding of women's position in the labour market and at work.

In this paper I shall provide a critical review of the ways in which women employees have been featured in accounts of social research in industry. I shall concentrate on studies of shop-floor workers and routine office workers; the position with regard to studies of qualified professional and managerial women employees is probably rather different. Inevitably with such a large volume of literature my discussion will be selective and the selection will be arbitrary rather than systematic.[2] Nevertheless I think it likely that the generalizations I do make, even though they are of course subject to some exceptions, would also apply to the literature which I have not covered.

'Women' in introductory textbooks on industrial sociology

The most common approaches can be illustrated first of all by considering the variety of ways in which women employees have been treated in a number of the general introductory and text-books in industrial sociology and closely related areas. There is a range of approaches, each of which is represented in one or more texts.

In the first place, some writers do appear to treat employees as 'unisex', so far as I can discover making no reference to the significance of sexual divisions in industry. Most writing on the sociology (or the 'theory') of organizations (with the notable exception of Gouldner, 1959, to which

Richard Brown

I shall return later) is based on the assumption that one can safely generalize and 'theorize' about organizations without giving any significance to the sex of their members. This is true of a number of introductory texts on work and organizations by psychologists (e.g. Schein, 1965; Tannenbaum, 1966), even though studies of women workers are quoted. Similarly Fox (1971) appears to make the same assumption in his *Sociology of Work in Industry,* though he too cites various studies of women workers in the course of his argument. I shall discuss this approach further in the next section.

Secondly, there are those who include explicit reference to women at work, but as a special category of employees who give rise to certain problems. Discussion is focused on the extent to which married women go out to work, on their motivation, and on the problems they and their employers face as a consequence (Parker *et al.,* 1972: 51-4; Schneider, 1957: 439-43); or on women as the objects of special protective legislation (Schneider, 1957: 469-70). In their treatment of sexual divisions in industry these texts incorporate the sort of research findings which I shall discuss in the third section, but fail to transcend what I believe to be their serious limitations.

Thirdly, mention may be made of the sex of workers in a particular situation or case study, but the significance of this characteristic for the overall argument, or for any generalizations which may be made, is not explored. Women as employees are not exactly ignored — there is acknowledgement that their sex is a possible source of variation in responses to incentive payment systems (Eldridge, 1971: 30-1, 54-5); or that relations between women and men at work in certain circumstances may differ from those between men and men, or women and women (Miller and Form, 1964: 152-3, 237) — but when the point has been made, no further use is made of it. In the last part of the paper I shall try to develop the potential this sort of approach contains.

Finally, there are those works which concentrate on an analysis of the labour market and do attempt a description and more rarely an explanation of women's position in the world of employment in terms of the way in which the labour market operates.[3] The most thorough example of this sort is Caplow's *Sociology of Work* (1954: 230-47), which contains a whole chapter on the 'Occupations of Women'. He goes beyond the listing of women's occupations which is also to be found, for example, in Miller and Form (1964: 58, 517), to develop a powerful explanation of women's occupational inferiority to men. This is based on an enumeration of the special conditions of women's employment (discontinuous careers, secondary breadwinners, residential immobility, a large reserve of employable women) and on the assertion of what he regards as two central cultural 'themes' (Caplow, 1954: 238):

1. That it is disgraceful for a man to be directly subordinated to a woman, except in family or sexual relationships.

2. That intimate groups, except those based on family or sexual ties, should be composed of either sex but never both.

As a result Caplow (1954: 244-5) argues:

> a woman's job must be one in which employment is typically by short term, in which the gain in skill achieved by continuous experience is slight, in which interchangeability is very high, and in which the loss of skill during long periods of inactivity is relatively small ... a woman's job must be one which does not involve the subordination of adult males, or any close participation with male workers doing parallel jobs ... women's occupations ... cannot be effectively monopolised ... occupation by occupation, unorganizability appears both as the cause and the effect of a preponderance of women.

However much one may dislike his conclusions, or even regard them as a form of self-fulfilling prophecy, Caplow draws attention in a way few other social scientists have done to the relationship between the situations of women in society at large and the dominant values of that society (presumably, in his case, America), and the market and work situations of women employees. His tendency to dismiss possibilities of any change in this state of affairs is perhaps too easy, at least when seen from 20 years, and the Women's Liberation Movement, later; but his analysis at least provides some basis for understanding the resistance to pressures for such changes.

Thus, in only one of a fair selection of introductory and general books in industrial sociology is there anything approaching an adequate recognition and discussion of the particular characteristics of the situation of women as employees. Not surprisingly, perhaps, in that the general books are based on it, the specialized literature is for the most part not more illuminating.

Employees as 'Unisex'

In the literature of industrial sociology there are a large number of studies which make no mention of women as employees for the very obvious reason that virtually no women work in the industry in question. This includes many of the industries which have attracted a lot of attention from social scientists for one reason or another: their propensity to strikes; the rate of technical, organizational and/or market change; unusual conditions of work; the existence of large (and perhaps more accessible to research) plants and firms; or some other circumstances making employment in them more problematic than elsewhere. Thus studies of coal mining (Scott *et al.*, 1963; Trist *et al.*, 1963), fishermen (Tunstall,

Richard Brown

1962), dockworkers (University of Liverpool, 1956), lorry drivers (Hollowell, 1968), printers (Cannon, 1967), steelworkers (Scott *et al.*, 1956; Banks, 1960), navvies (Sykes, 1969), process workers (Wedderburn and Crompton, 1972), seafarers (Fricke, 1974), affluent workers (Goldthorpe *et al.*, 1968) and shipbuilding workers (Brown *et al.*, 1972) — to name but a few — can throw no light on the expectations and actions of women as employees. At the most researchers in such situations have extended the scope of their study to consider the implications of work for family and community life, and vice versa (see, for example, Tunstall, 1962, Fricke, 1974, and Hollowell, 1968). They have not acknowledged that the absence of women in many cases is due not to the nature of the work but to either the tight control of the labour market exercised by men through their unions, and/or the policies of employers. For example, women worked successfully at many jobs in shipbuilding during the Second World War in this country and in the USA (see Archibald, 1947), but were excluded from all production work afterwards. It may seem rather unfair to complain about the lack of such a reference when the dominance of men in such industries is so widely taken for granted, but as is the case with respect to some other aspects of the context of the employment relationship, questioning the taken-for-granted is essential for a more adequate analysis.

However excusable the neglect of women as employees may be in these cases, one must be more doubtful about the way in which some social scientists have tried to provide a general account of certain social processes in industrial situations and have apparently assumed implicitly that it would be valid for situations in which either sex were employed. For example, in his penetrating analysis of *Piecework Bargaining*, based on studies in ten factories including some with women employees, William Brown (1973) provides an account of 'non-negotiated' processes of collective bargaining and their determinants. The implication of his study is that the sex of those employed under piecework does not affect whether or not these processes take place, but if this is the conclusion it requires justifying in the face of the argument to the contrary (e.g. Lupton, 1961: 20-3).[4]

A possible defence of these studies might be the claim that their 'models' must necessarily be subject to modification in the light of further research, and sexual divisions in the industry may be one factor which will give rise to such modifications. I doubt whether such a defence could be entertained for the studies in the Human Relations tradition, from the Hawthorne Experiments onwards, which have put forward generalisations — for example, about the relationship between supervisory style, productivity and morale — without considering adequately how far such generalizations are equally applicable to workers of each sex. The consequences of treating workers as 'unisex' have been particularly far reaching in this case because of the widespread influence of Human Relations thinking for the development of industrial sociology, and for managerial ideologies.

In some ways the failure to pay attention to the significance of sexual divisions in industry is particularly surprising in the case of the Hawthorne Experiments, because of the striking contrast between the findings of the Relay Assembly Test Room group of experiments and those of the Bank Wiring Observation Room. In the former situations all the employees were women and as a consequence of the changes, intended and/or unintended, introduced by the investigators these workers increased their output, at least temporarily, and gave evidence of increasingly cooperative attitudes towards management. In the Bank Wiring Observation Room a cohesive work group of men 'restricted' their output, contrary to management's intentions and interests, and the investigators appear to conclude that there was very little the supervisor or anyone else could do about it. Yet the significance of the relay assemblers being women (who in addition had a male supervisor in the test room) and the wiremen being men is not discussed (e.g. Roethlisberger and Dickson, 1939: 559-62). This is despite the fairly full discussion of the personal background of many of the employees in question; and despite the authors' clear comments on differences between male and female attitudes as expressed in the interviewing programme (Roethlisberger and Dickson, 1939: 251)

> It is interesting to note that men and women differ markedly with respect to urgency in two of the three groups of subjects ... In the second group, women have much more to say than men about *hours of work* and *fatigue*. In the third group women are much more articulate than men in their praise of the company's employee relations activities. There is very little evidence to suppose that actual conditions of work for men differed from those for women as greatly as these differences in urgency might indicate. It is more plausible to suppose that differences in sentiment between men and women, because of differences in social situation, account largely for the differences in urgency of these topics.

Landsberger (1958) has argued that the Hawthorne Experimenters cannot be blamed for the ways in which subsequent investigators misused their findings. But with respect to their consideration of the significance of sexual divisions in industry, at any rate, the direction given to subsequent research by the work reported in *Management and the Worker* was particularly unfortunate; and the social—psychological nature of much of that later research meant that more general questions of the influence of

Richard Brown

the social 'roles' in the wider society of those being studied were rarely raised. Thus the body of research which attempts to explore the relationship between such factors as supervision, participation, informal social groups, and productivity, morale and acceptance of change, does not really consider, though it does report, the sex of the workers who were the subjects of the investigations as being any sort of limitation on the generality of the conclusions. In the case of certain important and much quoted studies, for example Coch and French (1948) on overcoming resistance to change, and Morse and Reimer (1956) on the consequences of a reallocation of decision making, the employees were women but the findings are taken as having general applicability. This same assumption, that it is valid to generalize about the determinants of all employees' attitudes and behaviour from studies which may have considered only men or only women (surprisingly often the latter, given the ratio of men to women in the labour force), is also embodied in the general accounts of this whole series of studies (e.g. Viteles, 1954; Kahn, 1958; Tannenbaum, 1966). It is one example of the more general failing for which the social—psychological 'branch' of the Human Relations 'movement' has often been criticised: that they show insufficient awareness of the significance of the organizational and societal context of their investigations — with the added emphasis that the distinction between male and female is more visible than that, for example, between union member and non-unionist, or between 'farm reared Protestant Republican' and 'city bred Catholic Democrat'.

My argument at this point is not that men and women are so different that no generalizations, no accounts of generic social processes in industrial situations, can possibly be true for both sexes; rather that the possible significance of the different social situations which men and women are in, by virtue of their gender, both within and outside the factory (and these can change), must always be considered in evaluating any research which it is argued has general implications. The point has been put very clearly by Gouldner (1959: 412) (see also Acker and Van Houten, 1974).

> It is obvious that all people in organizations have a variety of 'latent social identities' — that is, identities which are not culturally prescribed as relevant to or within rational organizations — and that these do intrude upon and influence organizational behaviour in interesting ways. For example, there is usually something occurring between people of opposite sexes, even though this is prescribed neither by the organization's official rules nor by the societal values deemed appropriate for that setting. Yet many sociologists who study factories, offices, schools, or mental hospitals take little note of the fact that the organizational role-players invariably have a gender

around which is built a latent social identity. One does not have to be a Freudian to insist that sex makes a difference, even for organizational behaviour.

Failure to insist on this is not only misleading but also loses the researcher the opportunity to make any contribution to increased understanding of men's and women's position in industry or society.

In the case of the Human Relations approach, in particular, some of the most influential studies were of women employees; the extrapolation of these 'findings' to all employees can of course be criticized on many grounds, but the absence of explicit consideration of the significance of sexual divisions in society is one of them.

Women employees as a problem

The largest category of studies of women *qua* women as employees is that which regards the employment of women as in some way giving rise to problems — for the women themselves in combining their two roles; for the employer in coping with higher rates of absence and labour turnover, and demands for part-time work; for the social services in providing for the care of children of working mothers, or in coping with the supposed results of maternal neglect; for husbands and other kin in taking over part of the roles of wife and mother; and even for the sociologist in attempting to discern the 'motivation' of women in paid employment. As this list suggests, the focus of attention has been on the employment of married women, but, as has been pointed out often enough, in a society where the great majority of women marry, and at younger ages than in the past, women in employment now more often than not means married women (Stewart, 1961).

The foci of these investigations vary. In the absence of adequate official statistics a good deal of effort has been expended on trying to establish the facts of women's employment, their occupations and conditions, often combining this with other questions such as the factors which influence women's decision as to whether or not to seek employment (Thomas, 1948; Klein, 1960; Hunt, 1968). Some studies have been concerned with international trends and comparisons (Leser, 1959), or have combined such a discussion with comparison of conditions of employment in different societies (Klein, 1965a). A number of investigators have focused on particular categories of women employees — mothers of (young) children (Thompson and Finlayson, 1963; Yudkin and Holme, 1963) or older women (Le Gros Clark, 1962). Others have been concerned with the situation from the employers' point of view (Klein, 1961) or have considered the situation from both employers' and employees' viewpoints in one particular factory and/or locality (Jephcott

Richard Brown

et al., 1962; Brown *et al.*, 1964). And a few writers have provided fairly comprehensive accounts of several of these issues (Myrdal and Klein, 1956; National Manpower Council, 1957).

It is apparent that these studies result from the assumption that there is something problematic about women (and especially married women) in employment, which is not problematic in the same sense in the case of men. In one sense this represents a realistic assessment of the situation (at least in Western societies). In so far as common-sense understandings of the world do include such differentiations between men and women workers in any society, the sociologist must take account of them. To do this, however, does not mean taking them as *his* problem; this is likely to lead to an acceptance of the *status quo* and serious restrictions on the questions which are raised and the answers which can be given.

I think it is fair to say that most of the studies I have mentioned are mildly critical of the existing state of affairs and indicate that some changes in policies and practices are needed: changes in the policies of employers and government and in the accepted conventions of family life. Yudkin and Holme (1963: 174—82), for example, conclude with a list of proposals (mostly directed at the government, but also at employers and trade unions), as does Klein (1965b: 87—8). Smith (1961: 21—2), Klein (1961: 37—9) and Brown *et al.* (1964: 40—1) are all critical of the employers' reluctance to recognize the special needs of a group who have become an essential part of their labour forces, and also make recommendations. Thompson and Finlayson (1963: 166-7) conclude:

> Quite apart from the issue of working wives, the whole pattern of family life has been changing in recent years as roles become less rigidly defined and more dependent on the interests and personalities of individual family members. It may be time to enlarge the concept of 'the needs of the child', if such can indeed be isolated, to include the needs of the family as a whole. In so doing it is not necessary to assume that the role of 'homemaker' cannot be shared nor that it is incompatible with external responsibilities.

In some cases questioning is rather more penetrating. Myrdal and Klein (1956: 87—8) entitle one section 'A Question Which is Never Asked', in which they refer to the 'idle women' who do not work outside their homes; and Le Gros Clark (1962: 107) suggests, 'Men will need to make their own adjustments in the female—male relationship. It is not so unimaginable as it once was that men should share more or less equally with women in running the home and family', and goes on to discuss desirable changes in education.

Nevertheless the framework of these investigations was one which emphasized the special social problem-creating nature of women's employment in a way which meant that different questions were to be asked about it from those asked about men; most obviously, for example, about why they worked at all, rather than why they preferred one job to another. Also, in spite of the criticisms of employers, there has been very little recognition of the especially exploitative nature of the relationship between them and their women employees, in particular the mothers of children. Several studies report a reluctance by employers to cater for the domestic needs of such employees, for example by providing child care facilities, because they do not wish to encourage mothers to work outside the home. Yet they are increasingly dependent on this source of labour, while the women themselves are both paid less than men and left to carry the burden of ensuring that their domestic responsibilities are met.[5] The possible wider economic consequences of the employers' stated preferences for fewer married women in the labour market — higher labour costs and reduced consumer demand — are conveniently ignored by the employers, and unfortunately too often by the investigators as well.

As with so much else, this general issue is put very forcefully and well by Rowbotham (1973: 83–4), who writes:

> The use of the labour of married women in advanced capitalism is part of complicated changes in the structure and organization of work, as well as the need always to find new markets and to effect continual changes in the nature of demand. Despite the dependence of capitalism now on married women as a permanent and essential part of the work force, employers are still apt to behave as if they were doing women a favour by employing them. They still act as if women should somehow be grateful for the chance to be exploited. This is particularly ironic in view of the actual nature of the jobs which are categorized as 'women's work'. The only factor these jobs really have in common is low pay, which means the profit capitalism takes from women is direct and crude. The cheap labour of women is an alternative to investing in machinery.

It is probably true to say that some (but by no means all) of the more recent studies have been much more prepared to question the inevitability or rightness of the existing situation (e.g. Fogarty et al., 1967; Pinder, 1969), and that this change has been in part at least a response to the way in which members of the Women's Liberation Movement have redefined the issues. This is welcome, but does not meet my final comment on this category of research: that it contributes very little to an understanding of the sociological problems raised by the employment of women in societies like our own (indeed, many such studies are probably better considered as part of the sociology of the family rather than of industry). These problems can be stated as: in what ways do sexual

Richard Brown

divisions in society affect the social consciousness of workers who otherwise have in common that they sell their labour power in the market; and how far can comparisons between men and women increase our understanding of the nature and determinants of workers' orientations towards and actions in the work situation? Some useful information about attitudes to work is to be found in the social problem-oriented studies, but for a more comprehensive attempt to deal with these sorts of issues research with a quite different emphasis is needed, such as that which characterizes Barron and Norris's discussion (Ch. 3) of the dual labour market in this volume.

I will therefore now turn to a consideration of some of the existing studies of women employees which are relevant for the discussion of two such substantive areas — orientations to work, and collective action in the work situation — and will suggest some ways in which research on women employees might be made even more useful for the analysis of problems in these areas.

Women as Workers

Orientations to work   As a result of the extensive discussion during the past 10 years or so I think a number of areas of agreement have been established about the notion of 'orientations to work' (see R. K. Brown, 1973; Daniel, 1973). The work of Goldthorpe and his colleagues (1968), and of various successor studies, has established the utility of some such notion to express and emphasize the ways in which social, economic and technical aspects of a worker's market and work situations are mediated by his definition of their significance; and the ways in which his actions must be seen as the outcome of his perceptions of the various options open to him and of which alternative best meets his priorities at the time. There appears to be more disagreement, however, about the answers to certain further questions, though the questions themselves are admitted as important by writers who might answer them quite differently.

These questions include: how far can clarity and stability be attributed to 'orientations to work'? Do the difficulties of determining such orientations empirically indicate lack of clarity, limitations in available vocabularies of motive, or incompatible objectives among respondents? How far do the same priorities hold in different contexts? What are the determinants of an actor's, or a set of actors', 'orientations to work'; in particular are they related to characteristics of the work situation, the non-work situation or both? Does homogeneity of 'orientations to work' in a particular workforce result from self-selection in a labour market characterized by full employment, or from socialization in the locality or the workplace? It is doubtful whether existing studies of women as employees can make any decisive contribution to resolving these questions, though some of them are of relevance; but it seems likely that the additional comparative 'leverage' which taking account of sexual divisions in society can provide could be of considerable value.

For these possibilities to be realized involves stating, however tentatively and hypothetically, in what ways one would expect women to differ from men in our society at the present time with regard to 'orientations to work'; and how sexual divisions in society are related to other sources of differentiation or change in such orientations. Attempting to do this raises rather different questions from those just mentioned and forces consideration of some issues which have on the whole been taken for granted in existing approaches to the study of 'orientations to work', in particular the nature of primary socialization and the influence of the labour market on orientations.

In the following discussion I have assumed that 'orientations to work' can most usefully be seen as the outcome of processes over time, and that they must therefore be seen as likely to change as a result of new social experiences and changes in social situation. This assumption has the advantage of drawing attention to the way in which a category such as 'women employees' must be differentiated in terms of life-cycle situation and experience.

The first of these processes is that of primary socialization. Socialization for girls differs from that for boys in our society and for the majority leads to lower levels of ambition, a lesser likelihood of staying on at school, less interest in a career and a tendency to regard marriage as a terminal state which it is more important to achieve than any occupational goal. Thus the job priorities of girls leaving school, especially at the minimum school-leaving age, are likely to be different from those of boys — less concerned with training, and with career opportunities and, although financial expectations are likely to be modest, less prepared to sacrifice them for some future benefits.

For example, in the United Kingdom in 1972, boys aged 18 and over and still at school represented 8·2 per cent of the 18 years age group, as compared with 5·8 per cent for girls; at age 17 the figures were 21·2 per cent and 20·2 per cent; the same sort of differential occurred in previous years as far back as 1961, though of course the tendency to stay on at school has increased over this period (*Social Trends*, 1973: 143). Results in 'O' level GCE examinations are approximately the same for both boys and girls, but markedly fewer girls obtain 'A' levels. Fewer girls than boys go to university even when they have the same number of 'A' levels, though this is partly compensated for by the larger number going to colleges of education (*Social Trends*, 1973: 147–9: for similar findings in an earlier period see Committee on Higher Education, 1963: 50, 59).

Richard Brown

Further, three studies of school leavers/young workers provide very similar findings with regard to ambitions, careers and marriage. In a study of 700 boys and 600 girls attending grammar, technical and modern schools in two counties in southern England it was found that girls were less likely to seek success through occupational channels, and mentioned expectations of promotion less often than boys; they ranked very low on a scale of 'ambitiousness'; secondary modern school girls were at the bottom of the scale, with grammar school girls just above them, followed by secondary modern school boys (Veness, 1962: 161—4, 94—5). Of the same sample of girls, nearly half recorded 'marriage' as the answer to a question about their probable job at age 25, and only half said they would take up work again (full-time or part-time) when their children 'were old enough to be left' (Joseph, 1961: 179—80).

On the basis of his research on 100 girls and 100 boys from secondary modern schools in Sheffield, Carter (1963: 49) commented:

> Security was not a matter of importance for girls, and nor, on the whole, were prospects. Work for girls was not a career, as they did not aspire to positions of power and responsibility.

Similarly, Maizel's study of young workers in firms in the London area employing under-18s, found that girls were more likely than boys to want to leave school and less likely to consider staying on; and girls rather less frequently than boys expressed the wish to earn money (Maizels, 1970: 27, 33, 78). She made the following comparison (287):

> As in the Veness and Wilkins's inquiries, references to marriage and children dominated the replies of girls to the question of what they hoped to be doing by the age of twenty-five ... two in three referred exclusively to their hope for a family life. Those who commented on their future employment tended to assume that this meant remaining in the same kind of work, few assuming that any kind of promotion was likely. ...
>
> By contrast, boys' hopes were almost exclusively vocational, and their references related chiefly to specific jobs or positions of higher skill and responsibility. . . . Over one-half of the boys expressed the hope that by the age of twenty-five they would be in more skilled and responsible work than at present.

Thus, on the one hand, girls are socialized to want and expect a quite different pattern of life from boys. On the other hand the opportunities in the labour market available to them, certainly as they are perceived by them and by most others, are very much inferior to those for boys: very few apprenticeships, lower rates of pay — especially in the long run — fewer long-term opportunities for promotion or upward mobility of any sort, and a tendency even for clerical work to be increasingly routine and demanding little skill (Seear, 1968: 2–8; Pinder, 1969: 545–84). As a result the choice, even if girls were ambitious, would be much more restricted, and the experience of the process of moving from school to work is likely to reinforce rather than change 'orientations'.

Thirdly, life-cycle changes must be considered to have more significance for women, in our society at present, than they do for men. Changes in life-cycle situation — for example, marriage, the birth of a child, the youngest child starting school, children leaving home — are likely to have considerable impact on women's orientations to work. There is a good deal of evidence of such a relationship.[6]

Fourthly, relatively few women doing manual and routine clerical work are actually employed in work situations which are identical to those of men. This makes qualitative comparisons between them difficult; and when tasks are the same, other factors, such as men working shifts, may make for differences. It is obviously impossible to generalize about the differences (women's manual work may be less heavy physically, and is often less interesting and more repetitive), but it is probably true to say that the majority of women are employed on jobs whose demands on them and rewards for them are not such as to increase their involvement in the world of work at the expense of their 'central life interests' in the home and the family. In so far as work is an essential part of their lives, substitute satisfactions — friendly workmates, a considerate management, convenient location or hours — are likely to be sought and emphasized.

The processes (socialization, 'choice' in the labour market, the life cycle, and adapting and reacting to work experiences) are of course closely connected. Girls' socialization in our society reflects and reinforces the structure of work opportunities for women; the work experience of women is the outcome of the interaction between the priorities and values which result from socialization, and the opportunities which exist (or more often do not exist) in the labour market; and by its nature work experience contributes to the greater significance which life-cycle changes have for women than for men; life-cycle changes affect the position of women in the labour market in a way which they do not affect that of men — and, because of the reactions of employers to the knowledge that a woman is married, or has children, they have these consequences regardless of the woman's own priorities; and so on. 'Orientations to work' of women employees must be seen as the outcome of the way in which these various processes combine over time. The significance of any individual factor is dependent on its place in such a configuration, rather than as a unique determinant.

In contrast to existing studies of 'orientations to work', therefore, what is needed is an extension of enquiry beyond the conventional

Richard Brown

dichotomy of work and a limited range of non-work factors to include, in particular, patterns of socialization and the nature of the labour market.[7] Consideration of the ways in which 'orientations to work' for the majority of women might be generated, and sustained or changed, also draws attention to the constraints on their possibilities of action — constraints which for many are so restrictive that the explanatory value of the notion must be called into question. Job 'choice' or behaviour at work would be much the same whatever the 'orientation to work'.

Social consciousness and collective action   There are two questions to be considered with respect to collective action by women employees: whether they are less likely to take such action than men in comparable employment situations; and if they are, what explanations can be offered for such differences in patterns of action. These questions arise given the assumption that in our sort of society all employees have conflicting interests with their employer and must act collectively to protect and further their interests (see Allen, 1971). Consideration of the actions of women employees may help identify the conditions which affect whether or not such action occurs. I shall discuss the evidence with regard to three areas of collective action: 'regulation' of output under payment by results schemes; trade union membership; and strikes.

As we have already seen, the Hawthorne Experiments showed very different patterns of behaviour under incentive schemes between the girls in the Relay Assembly Test Room and the men in the Bank Wiring Observation Room. An apparently similar finding resulted from Lupton's study of two workshops: women in a waterproof garment factory accepted management definition of their role, emphasized the norm of hard work and 'looking after number one', and did not exercise any 'will to control' even when management was unable to provide the appropriate conditions; men in a transformer assembly workshop had a clear conception of what represented tolerable effort and fair pay, haggled with rate-fixers over the bonus prices, regulated their output to prevent rate-cutting and operated an elaborate 'fiddle' to compensate for management shortcomings in the planning of work, and to stabilize their weekly earnings (Lupton, 1963). Although he does not rule out altogether the possibility that in general women differ from men in their likely reactions to payment by results schemes, or indeed management controls more generally (see Lupton, 1961: 30–3; 1963: 91), his explanation of these two cases discounts the importance of the sex difference. This is because the expected reaction to the incentive payments system appeared to characterize each factory as a whole: the men in the garment factory behaved in much the same way as the women Lupton observed; and in the engineering factory 'in general the women had, so far as I could ascertain, accepted the standards set by the men. They haggled with the rate-fixer about prices, and employed methods similar to those employed by the men when booking in work, to minimise the effects of waiting time, and so on' (Lupton, 1963: 191).

Lupton's interpretation is reinforced by Cunnison's (1966) discussion of another waterproof garment factory where men and women worked on the same tasks in the same workshop, and both sexes shared the prevailing norm of militant individualism. In the history of the industry this tradition appears to have been passed from men to women rather than the opposite. Klein (1964: 42), who studied an engineering factory where a minority of the operators were women, reported that all of them set a ceiling to output and earnings on the incentive scheme. As we have seen, W. Brown (1973) did not feel it necessary to consider sexual divisions as a factor in piecework bargaining situations.

The studies cited cannot be regarded as conclusive, but if the suggestion is right that women as such do not differ from men in their willingness to regulate their output according to group norms and in opposition to management's expectations, the problem arises of accounting for the widely held conventional view 'of the woman industrial worker as a "sucker", easy to exploit, and with no capacity for collective action, or as women would perhaps say, "women are more conscientious than men" ' (Lupton, 1963: 191). This may of course merely be part of male ideology serving to justify men's claims to superiority. It may arise because women follow the lead given by men whatever that lead may be. If may, however, reflect the very different occupational and industrial distribution of women manual workers. Lupton's studies suggested that collective action of this sort on the shop-floor is more likely to occur given certain technical, economic and social conditions. It is possible that women employees are to be found predominantly in situations which lack these conditions. The operation of the labour market would then become a central part of the explanation.

The occupational and industrial distribution of women employees is central to any explanation of the patterns of trade union membership. During the post-war period trade union membership in the United Kingdom has increased from over 9 million in 1948 to 11 million in 1970, and after declining slightly from the 1948 peak of 45·2 per cent 'density' (proportion of total employees), the 1970 total of union members represented a density of 46·9 per cent. Within these totals women employees have consistently been less strongly unionized than men; only 24 per cent in 1948, and only 25 per cent of a considerably larger number of women in employment in 1970, were members of trade unions. This difference between men and women remains when manual workers and white collar workers are considered separately; indeed female manual

Richard Brown

workers are less likely to belong to a trade union than male white collar workers. However, the absolute and relative rates of growth of women's trade union membership have been higher over the whole post-war period, and especially in the years since 1964 when most of the increase in white-collar union density has occurred (Bain and Price, 1972: 378-9).

It is not possible, however, to conclude from these figures that women employees as such are necessarily reluctant to join trade unions. Writing on the growth of trade unions in the cotton industry, for example, Turner (1962: 24—5) comments: 'Until the First World War, indeed ... the cotton unions remained the only ones to organise women workers effectively. And that they did in a large way.' But he also goes on to comment on the lower levels of participation by women members in union affairs (1962: 293—5). Clegg and his colleagues make the membership claim even more strongly, though in a footnote: 'In cotton, women were almost as well organised as men. In 1910 the proportion was 39 per cent compared with 44 per cent for the whole industry.' (Clegg *et al.*, 1964:469—70). More recently Blackburn has shown that women bank staff are less likely to join the union but has pointed out that the sex difference also corresponds with differences in the status of the work done (1967: 122, 125, 196—7, 257—8). Lockwood (1958: 151) is more emphatic in dismissing 'feminization' as a factor in the unionization of clerical workers:

> It was Bernard Shaw who said that the two groups most resistant to trade unionism were clerks and women. Women clerks, therefore, might well be considered a most formidable obstacle to the development of blackcoated unionism ... The generalisation is not in accordance with the facts. A high proportion of women in a clerical occupation is not universally associated with a low degree of unionisation, nor does unionisation necessarily proceed farthest when women are in a minority. Indeed, if a generalisation is to be made, it is that the proportion of women in clerical unions is usually roughly equal to their representation in the field of employment which the unions seek to organise. Differences in the degree of unionisation are therefore to be attributed to something other than the differences in the sex ratio of the group.

Thus there are suggestions in both historical and contemporary studies that whether or not women join trade unions is to be explained not in terms of their sex, but in terms of the nature of their work situation. The industrial distribution of women employees, as it results from the operation of the labour market, becomes a crucial part of the explanation. Women work predominantly in industries, such as clothing and footwear, and distribution, where firms and plants are small; trade unionism is strongest where large numbers are employed. On the basis of regression analysis Bain (1970: 41-3) argues that:

> The fact that a low degree of unionization is associated with a high proportion of women and that women generally are not as highly unionized as men can be accounted for by differences in the way males and females are distributed across firms ... Density of unionization is higher in areas where the average size of establishments is large and employment concentrated than in areas where the average size of establishments is small and employment diffused ... The proportion of women is highest in the smaller establishments and lowest in larger establishments ...
>
> The proportion of women has not been in itself a significant determinant of the pattern of manual or white collar unionism in Britain.

This finding is based on aggregate data and would not necessarily apply in all situations. It also leaves unexplained the persistent belief that women are more reluctant to join trade unions than men, a belief which can become a self-fulfilling prophecy when it is acted on by male shop stewards or union officials as Beynon and Blackburn (1972: 115-17) described in their discussion of the way the trade union became 'the men's affair'.

Indeed, any adequate explanation of levels of union membership must include consideration of what it means to the actors involved to belong to a union, as well as reference to structural factors such as size of plant. The links between the ways in which the labour market operates, women's actions as 'potential' trade unionists, and women's and men's perceptions of trade unions and of women as possible union members, are probably complex and interrelated. Do men, for example, oppose the employment of women in certain occupations and industries in part because they see them as difficult to organize, and consequently likely to depress pay levels or worsen the effort bargain? If they do, does this help perpetuate the very situation of which they disapprove? Do the different priorities at work held by women as compared with men (e.g. hours and conditions) mean that their main concerns are given second place to men's (e.g. overtime) in male-dominated workplace union organizations, which thus continue to fail to attract their interest and support? Does women's experience of being excluded from certain areas of work by male trade unionists encourage them to see union membership as not for them — and thus reinforce the men's prejudices? The labour market operates as it does partly because of the choices and preferences and definitions of the situation of the actors involved, but these in part reflect experience of the way it operates. Exploration of such interconnections might not only

Richard Brown

provide a more complete explanation of the pattern of union membership among women, but contribute to our understanding of union membership in general as well.

In the case of strikes there are, so far as I am aware, no statistics of the actions of women employees as compared with those of men, not even approximate figures like those of union membership. The most strike-prone industries in Britain, however, in the post-war period — the docks, coal-mining, motor vehicles, shipbuilding, metal manufacture, construction, and so on — are industries in which women are not employed in any numbers. In addition one of the best-known attempts to explain inter-industry differences in strike proneness appears to assume that women are less inclined to strike (Kerr and Siegel 1954: 195):

> If the job is physically easy and performed in pleasant surroundings, skilled and responsible, steady, and subject to set rules and close supervision, it will attract women or the more submissive type of man who will abhor strikes.[8]

Such assumptions about women employees' strike activity cannot go entirely unquestioned. In a review of strikes in the inter-war period and in the years before the First World War, Knowles (1952: 182-4) certainly denies that women as such are less inclined to strike:

> Although there is no quantitative evidence here, it is clear that women — having regard of their numbers in industry — have played an important part in strike movements. True the relative youthfulness of women workers and the other consequences of their 'mortality by marriage', as well as the hostility of the established men's Trade Unions to the organisation of the exploited minority, did for a long time inhibit the large-scale organisation of women, but it is doubtful how far these things have restrained women from striking.

> Possibly their very lack of economic opportunity and responsibility has influenced them in the opposite sense. Women, wrote Barbara Drake, have never been backward in strikes: 'They are, on the contrary, more often accused by their officials of being too forward, so that they "down tools" for frivolous reasons and often drag the men after them. It is a fact that the courage and loyalty of unorganised women in supporting organised men have been among the principal factors in deciding the latter to organize them.' The authoress had in mind, of course, the great women's strike movement of the late 1880s and of 1911-13, which opened and closed the sweated trade agitation.

In his study, Hyman (1972: 54, 119) cites some more recent examples of strikes in which women have been involved. He argues that although industrial conflict among women workers may manifest itself in alternative ways (e.g. high labour turnover), 'This does not mean, however, that women are never prominent in industrial disputes'. But he, in some contrast to Knowles, concludes, 'Women tend to be employed in industries and occupations where collective organization is least strong, and they strike far less frequently than men.' In a study of the motor industry, Turner and his colleagues (1967: 32) could find no relationship between the proportion of women employed in motor car factories and their relative strike proneness. More recently the night cleaners' campaign, the Ford machinists' strike in 1968, the Leeds clothing strike and the work-in by women in Fakenham have been well publicised examples of women employees' willingness to take strike action; and the fifth issue of *Red Rag* (n.d.) was able to include a long list of strikes in which women employees had been involved during 1972 and 1973.

Thus, as in the case of other forms of collective action, the situation appears to be one where it is not possible to claim that women employees as such are unwilling or unable to strike. But women do work predominantly in industries and occupations which are less strike prone (and may be part of the reason for this?); and they do share characteristics like lower levels of union membership and higher rates of labour turnover which are associated with a lesser propensity to strike. What might be most illuminating, in terms of the more general question of explaining manifestations of industrial conflict, would be research which studied in comparison with other situations those where women have taken collective action. In such situations one could perhaps see more clearly than elsewhere the ways in which changes in conditions of action and changes in 'consciousness' are combined and interrelated and lead to collective action.

Conclusion

I hope that this discussion of some of the relevant literature on women, and men, as employees has been able to establish my initial claim that many existing studies in industrial sociology are not entirely satisfactory in their consideration of the nature and implication of sexual divisions in industry; and to support, too, the suggestion that research which was more adequate in this respect would contribute to the understanding of both social relations in industry and the position of men and women in society.

There are two further points of importance. More attention must be given to the ways in which the labour market operates than has been the case in many studies in industrial sociology. The contributions of Mann

Richard Brown

(1973), and of Barron and Norris (Ch. 3), are two of a number of recent studies which indicate that this area is beginning to receive the attention it warrants. Indeed the nature of the labour market for the workers in question is likely to be of importance in any situation, and in some circumstances it obviously sets very narrow constraints on the posibilities for action. To study 'orientations to work', job satisfaction, the presence or absence of collective action, and so on, without considering these constraints is likely to give a very misleading picture. Secondly, in considering the position of any disadvantaged group, such as women (or ethnic minorities) in our society, it is essential to look not just at their conditions of action nor at their, and others', perceptions of the situation, but at the ways in which the three are related and interact. The relationship between 'structure' and 'consciousness' is a key issue in sociology, and it is crucial for the understanding of the position of women as employees.

Notes

1. This point has also been made recently by Beynon and Blackburn (1972: 144-5)

   > It is unfortunate, therefore, that industrial sociologists have paid such little attention to women workers. True, there have been studies of women but these have, in the main, been either human relations experiments or studies concerned with the particular problems created by 'women's two roles'. 'Women' have almost become a separate subject area. Composite pictures of manual workers, and studies of the working class invariably deal solely with men. Where sociologists have attempted to compare the attitudes of men and women workers they have tended to present descriptive generalisations, without theoretical content, raising questions such as whether women are more satisfied than men. Not surprisingly, different studies get unexplainable contradictory results.

2. I must stress that I have been looking at these works in industrial sociology from the sole perspective of whether and how they discuss women as employees. I have been critical of many of them on this score but this should not be taken to imply any general criticism of what I think are, in many cases, very valuable and valid analyses of other sociological issues.

3. See, for example, the discussion in Florence (1964: 34-7, 52-4). The labour market is also of interest to economists, who do appear to

acknowledge the distinctive position of women, though sometimes with a 'problems' emphasis; see for example Phelps Brown (1962) where the appropriate entry in the Index reads:

> Women workers: exclusion from jobs; extension of opportunities; lack of mobility; protective legislation; as reserve of labour; wage differentials; waste of abilities.

For a discussion of the situation of women in the labour market which in many respects parallels that by Caplow, but has the advantages of being more up to date, concerned with the British situation, and supported by a good deal of empirical data, see Seear (1968).

4. In a similar way Sayles (1958: 68) puts forward a general explanation of the *Behaviour of Industrial Work Groups* which, on the basis of data from a number of industries, relates their level and type of grievance activity to their position in the job hierarchy and to the type of work roles they perform. Interestingly he comments:

> ... there certainly seemed to be some tendency for work groups with a high proportion of female employees to be more passive and restrained than their male counterparts. Nevertheless those female groups that we expected, on the basis of the other criteria, to produce high activity, often fulfilled the prediction. Where they did not, it could also be due to a greater preponderance of short service, temporary employees within the female group.

One study of the shop floor which does explore the implications of sexual divisions for social relations in an illuminating and important way is that reported by D. H. J. Morgan (1969).

5. This general finding is reported, for example, by Klein (1961: 26-30), who found that only 1 in 6 of the 120 employers in her sample made any special allowances for the domestic commitments of their married (and other) women employees. In a small survey of the care of children while their mothers are at work, which was carried out in Leicester in 1961 by C. E. Ashworth, G. A. Drew, M. G. Godivala, M. P. Hayes and P. J. Rushton under the supervision of J. M. Kirkby and the writer, we found that few firms had a clearly defined policy on employing women with young children, though many of them did so; and with the exception of varying working hours they did very little to make it easier for these women to work for them. The typical ambivalent attitude — 'We believe it is not good for the children, but owing to the shortage of labour must term

Richard Brown

it a "necessary evil" ' — illustrates the way in which conflicting economic and moral interests are conveniently reconciled.

6. Several writers have argued that the expectations and priorities of women employees must be differentiated with reference to their position in the life-cycle, and there is enough research of relevance for some general categories to be outlined.

For *young single women*, Lupton (1963: 191) suggests industrial employment is:

> ... a temporary phase between school and marriage ... earnings from industrial employment enable these women to make a contribution to family income for a while, and to buy the clothes and cosmetics which will make them attractive to men, and to attend places of entertainment when they will meet men.

Similarly Mumford and Banks (1967: 21) state:

> Women — or rather girls, for the great majority are under twenty-five — will, at present, accept routine jobs that are unlikely to lead anywhere. For most of them matrimony is their principal objective or interest and work is regarded as temporary and incidental, rather than central in their lives. Because of this they are willing to put up with tasks that seem intrinsically dull and for the same reason they are not unduly anxious for promotion. ... This passive acceptance by women of low grade, routine work may, of course, not continue in the future.

In considering a more heterogeneous group, though the majority were single and aged under 30, Beynon and Blackburn (1972: 149) give the following description:

> Most of the women who worked full time did have to support themselves, however, so good pay and security were quite important to them ... their interest in security lay between that of the part-time women — mostly older and married — and that of the men. Pay is a basic expectation from any employment and their personal circumstances could lead to them putting some emphasis on this reward, but in general their expectations were not particularly high ...
>
> They had little experience of factory jobs, and did not much care for the type of work they had to do ... they did not have high expectations of the intrinsic job ... Where they did expect some satisfaction from their work was in the social relationships. ...

Their main attachment to their jobs lay in friendships with workmates. Not only was this the chief source of social reward, but not having the family responsibilities of the part-time women, they were more likely to develop close friendships.

Some of these studies provide a basis for thinking that orientations towards work change quite quickly with age and/or the likelihood of getting married. Lupton (1963: 91) continues: 'Earnings also make it possible for young women to save towards a contribution to the setting up of a home, and many continue to work for a while after marriage, and before they start to bear children, to contribute towards the furnishing of a home'. Cunnison (1966: 84) comments about a similar factory: 'In the case of the younger women, income was earmarked for the large items of domestic expenditure'. Millward (1968) has described how the family status and the work behaviour (though not orientations as such) of girls change when they go 'on board' and suggests that, — among other reasons, this is likely to happen when a girl becomes engaged, starts saving money to get married, or more vaguely reaches some significant age (commonly 18). Beynon and Blackburn (1967: e.g. 114) suggest that as single girls get older 'they begin to think less of the day they get married and give greater significance to their employment relationship'.

There are some differences from this in the outlook of *married women with family responsibilities*. Cunnison (1966: 83-5) describes the situation she observed as follows:

> In many respects the position of women workers at Dee was similar to that of men, yet there were significant differences arising from their different family roles as defined by their social class and culture. The women carried on the work of running their houses and looking after their families, cleaning, washing, shopping and cooking, the married ones with little or no help from their husbands. Such matters were considered to be the responsibility and duty of women regardless of their position as wage earners. Because of this, women did not work such long hours as men, nor with such consistent application. . . .
>
> Wage-earning differed for married and single women. Married women thought of their paid job as an addition to their main job of home-keeping, and their income as a supplement to that of their husbands ... The money was important. . . .

Richard Brown

> Even so, for the married women, unless they were breadwinners, there was not the same sense of the inevitability of working that there was for the men. Three married women told me that they came out to work 'for the company'. No man ever said this. Yet these women were very interested in their wages and complained just as loudly as the others if they had bad work. . . .

In the biscuit factory studied by Jephcott and colleagues the situation was described somewhat similarly (Smith 1961: 20-1):

> What most women wanted was opportunity to earn money to raise the standard of living of the family as a whole, and provided the firm paid some attention to the claims of home life by adjusting its traditional rules and regulations, and afforded the opportunity to earn this money, they seemed to have very little to offer in criticism. A 'satisfactory' job, therefore, was one in which the importance of domestic duties was recognised and which also provided the opportunity to earn 'good money'. For this reason piece-work was on the whole preferred. A well-run department was appreciated as it was realised that this was essential for the steady flow of work on which high earnings depended. . . .
>
> What these women asked and expected from their job was a steady flow of work which would enable them to make the best use of their limited hours in the factory; in short, they wanted a really well organized department. They did not want . . . opportunities for participation or a fuller life inside the factory. . . . but on the other hand they did expect to be treated with respect and consideration due to a woman combining the duties of the job and home.

Discussing a group of married women who worked part-time Beynon and Blackburn (1972: 147-8) outline their expectations in comparable terms, though with rather more emphasis on the importance of 'company' at work:

> Their reasons for working were typically a combination of economic and social considerations, viewed from a distinctive married women's perspective. Their economic interest was to some extent based on fundamental necessity but even here the problems of job security and the actual level of income were less important for the women than for their husbands. They worked to supplement the family income but within the range open to them the actual amount was not so

important. The other main reason for working was escape from the loneliness at home to the companionship of work. Once friendships were established at work there was, therefore, a reluctance to change jobs to maximise earnings.

After emphasizing the importance to these women of convenient hours of work, they conclude:

This group of women had low commitment to work which was, for them, very much secondary to being a wife and mother. They were glad of the opportunity to fit in a few hours in a job, providing extra money and company. Beyond this their expectations were very low. Consequently they were well disposed to the firm and relatively uncritical of their experience at work.

On the basis of interviews with married women in a Leicester hosiery factory we reached the following conclusions about their expectations about work (Brown *et al.*, 1964: 34)

Primarily, they wanted a job which would satisfy their desire for a worthwhile addition to the family's income. At the same time they wished it to provide them with social contacts — the opportunity to make friends and to work and talk with them each day. Such contacts, however, were generally confined to the factory, most women emphasizing that they kept home and work separate. They also expected that physical working conditions should be pleasant, and conditions of employment fair and considerate of their home responsibilities. As decisions and comments about hours of work showed, work for most of those interviewed took second place to their commitments to their homes and families.

In the case of both the biscuit and the hosiery factories, married women were not in general interested in promotion possibilities (Jephcott *et al.*, 1962: 81; Brown *et al.*, 1964: 35-7; see also Beynon and Blackburn, 1972: 88).

After reconsidering the hosiery factory data, however, I am certain that there are significant distinctions within the 'married women' category; that, for example, there are important differences in 'orientations to work' between women with young or school age children, older married women without such responsibilities, and older single, widowed and separated women; the emphasis on financial rewards is greater for the first and last category than for the middle one, whilst it was among older women that there was any interest in supervisory posts. I do not have the appropriate evidence

Richard Brown

at this stage, but can quote in support that there were significant differences in labour stability and turnover, absence and output as between young single, young married with children, older married and widowed or divorced women, from which — given that tasks and conditions were similar for all — one could infer differences in expectations and priorities. Even without such evidence, however, I think the studies quoted so far in this note have demonstrated the relevance and importance of considering stages in the life cycle.

7. Recent studies have also emphasized the importance of the labour market in influencing 'orientations to work'. Beynon and Blackburn (1972: 159) conclude their discussion of women's 'orientations to work': 'It was their position within the labour market in combination with their position within the family which produced their particular and distinctive orientation toward the workplace'. Mann (1973: 40-67) develops a sophisticated and important argument (which has not been assimilated for this paper) about the relationship between different models of the labour market, and 'orientation to work' and 'employment dependence'. In this volume the paper on homeworkers by Hope, Kennedy and de Winter (Ch. 5) illustrates similarly for the case of workers employed at home how their expectations about work and a very weak labour market situation combine and interact to perpetuate conditions of extreme exploitation.

8. I am not clear how many women's jobs Kerr and Siegel (1954) consider have these characteristics!

Sexual divisions and the dual labour market

To begin to understand the reasons for sex-related occupational differentiation in the labour market, which is the object of this paper, it is necessary to consider both the sexual norms which define the place of men and women in the household and outside it, *and* the forces which operate in the labour market itself. The emphasis in this paper is on the structure of the labour market, and the question of men and women's place in the family — the household sexual division of labour — is relegated to the status of an explanatory factor which contributes to, but does not of itself determine, the differentiation between the sexes in their work roles. The structure of the labour market is seen as one cause among several of women's overall social position, albeit an important one. Ideological factors are, in this view, both cause and effect of women's inferior position in the labour market and within the family.

In the last few years studies of the labour market in the developed capitalist societies have begun to recognize the importance of the stratification of the labour market into a primary sector — containing relatively well-rewarded and stable jobs; and a secondary sector — containing lower paid and insecure occupations. The investigation of the causes of poverty in the advanced societies, particularly in deprived urban areas, has increasingly directed the attention of economists and sociologists towards the reality of significant barriers to upward mobility for the less skilled in the labour market and away from the 'human capital' emphasis on individual deficiencies as prime or sole causes of economic deprivation. In colonial and neo-colonial economies dualism is an obvious feature of the labour market, since modern, highly capitalized industries co-exist with a primitive, labour-intensive economy, and industrial workers in the primary sector are clearly separated from traditional rural and craft workers. Dualism in Western labour markets is less obvious, however, except in those areas where salient social divisions have highlighted the distinction between the two sectors as well as reinforcing their intensity. Thus it was the reality of the work experience of black people in the United States which awakened academic interest in labour market dualism in that country.

R. D. Barron and G. M. Norris

In Britain, the secondary labour market is pre-eminently a female labour market if low earnings levels are taken as an indicator of the secondary status of a job. If, for example, we calculate a combined mean for all men and women of gross hourly earnings,[1] then in 1972 only 7.8 per cent of full-time manual men and 2·8 per cent of full-time non-manual men were paid less than two-thirds of this figure. The comparable figures for full-time women were 70·3 per cent and 38·6 per cent. Seventy-five per cent of part-time women were paid less than two-thirds of the combined mean. This means that in the low paid sector,[2] women outnumber men by more than 5 to 1.

The striking difference between men's and women's earnings levels, which produces a tendency to bimodality in the national earnings distribution, has of course been recognized by researchers (for example, Lydall, 1968; Thatcher, 1968). But it has become almost an orthodoxy to set aside the implications of this finding by treating the earnings distributions of men and women as separate phenomena. This leads, typically, to different definitions of 'low pay' for men and women (N.B.P.I., 1971; Field, 1973) and thus to a general tendency to overlook the fact that the *typical* low paid worker is female.[3]

Bimodality in the national pay structure is associated with pronounced occupational segregation. Women are concentrated in certain occupational groups where average pay tends to be low, though there are one or two groups (e.g. senior clerical workers) in which women are represented in proportion to their numbers in the labour force and where earnings are average or even above average. Sexual divisions in the labour market are shown by the fact that nearly two-thirds of women work in occupations in which they are either highly over-represented or highly under-represented. In manual work they are under-represented in all skilled work, with the exception of skilled textile operators, and they are over-represented in jobs like packing. In non-manual work they are over-represented in nursing, in secretarial work, in hairdressing, as shop assistants and as cashiers, and in lower level catering jobs. Although there are no high-paying occupational groups in which women are highly represented, there are one or two low paying sections of the labour market which are male preserves — agriculture being the chief example.[4]

Thus it is clear that in Britain the vast majority of women occupy the lowest paid jobs and, conversely, that most low-paying jobs are occupied by women. This in itself does not prove that the British labour market is a dual one; in fact, there are several other attributes of a dual market which need to be considered.

Dual labour market theory

There are, of course, many ways of characterizing a labour market; for example, as a disaggregated, amorphous system in which isolated workers sell their labour to competing buyers, so that the price of labour is determined by pure market forces (the basic economist's model). The market may also be characterized by various kinds of segmentation, all of which produce more or less non-competing groups of workers. For example, the *local* labour market approach emphasizes the importance of geographical or monetary barriers to mobility which give rise to localism in job search behaviour. Or, again, a labour market may be seen as a series of separate industrial or occupational markets, with different means of disseminating information about job opportunities and different skills restricting inter-industrial or inter-occupational mobility by individual workers. All of these models have some explanatory value, but this paper concentrates upon one type of segmental model; the 'dual' labour market.

A dual labour market is one in which:

1. There is a more or less pronounced division into higher paying and lower paying sectors;
2. Mobility across the boundary of these sectors is restricted;
3. Higher paying jobs are tied into promotional or career ladders, while lower paid jobs offer few opportunities for vertical movement;
4. Higher paying jobs are relatively stable, while lower paid jobs are unstable.

This model also emphasizes the extent to which pay inequalities between the primary and secondary sectors are reinforced by other factors; primary sector jobs, it suggests, will also provide good fringe benefits, better working conditions, and so on. Some writers would probably stress the particular form which the division between primary and secondary sectors takes — for example, racial lines of cleavage may be an obvious institutional barrier between the two sectors; or the secondary economy may characteristically contain certain sorts of industry. But these versions of the dual labour market model are merely special instances of the general model outlined in the above four propositions.[5]

In our view, not shared by some authors (e.g. Bluestone, 1970), dualism in a labour market can cut through firms, industries, and industrial sectors. Although some firms or industries may be mainly primary employers, it is possible for a single employer or industry to contain both primary and secondary labour markets provided that the four conditions are met. Furthermore, dualism is essentially a matter of degree. Some labour markets are more dualistic than others, but probably most labour markets are neither wholly dualistic nor entirely unsegmented. To establish the extent of dualism in a national labour market would be a formidable methodological task, probably requiring a cluster analysis

R. D. Barron and G. M. Norris

technique to establish inter-correlations between pay, conditions and promotion prospects of jobs and mobility behaviour of job holders.

Such an exercise, which is beyond the scope of this paper, has yet to be undertaken,[6] and in seeking to establish whether or not a labour market is a dual one many researchers have fallen back on observations based on individuals. This can lead, however, to an inferential problem; it is very easy to confuse properties of jobs with characteristics of job holders, because individuals who are confined to a particular sector of the labour market will acquire histories and attitudes which reflect their jobs and which mark them off from workers who do not share the same experiences. These characteristics may then be seized upon, both by employers in the labour market and by researchers looking for explanations, to justify or account for the confinement of certain workers to a particular sector of the labour market. This circular process operates both in the real world and at the level of explanation.

In the real world jobs not only confer upon individuals a biography which they find difficult to escape from, one which reinforces the attitudes of employers and of agencies which serve the employment market, but, through secondary socialization, jobs also help to create or at least strengthen attitudes and outlooks which in turn may confine the horizons of the individual to particular kinds of work and to particular ways of behaving in the job market.

At the level of explanation there is a danger that the properties of jobs may become so closely associated with alleged characteristics of individuals that any explanations become entirely circular. For example, it is often said that women 'have higher turnover rates' as though this were a property of women and not of the jobs which they occupy. Of course, it may be true to say that women are, as a group, more likely to want to leave jobs more frequently than men, but this should not be confused with the existence of higher *involuntary* turnover rates for women (a property of the job), nor should we ignore the possibility that higher *voluntary* turnover rates can also reflect properties of the job — like low pay and poor work conditions. A failure to unravel the different strands of 'individual' and 'structural' causation can lead to a crude reification of individual characteristics and an unwarranted emphasis upon those characteristics as causes. In this paper we are in no sense suggesting that women are 'innately' suited to secondary jobs.

The task for research then is, first, to examine the forces that make for labour market dualism and, second, to attempt to determine those features of a workforce which, within given structural constraints, help to determine its status as either a primary or a secondary workforce.[7] The fullest discussion of the process of labour market segmentation is found in Gordon (1972). He argues that the primary sector has increasingly separated from a basically secondary labour market, particularly during the past 70 years, partly because of employers' need to promote employee stability in jobs which require extensive manpower investment, and partly because of its utility in reducing class conflict potential at the workplace by weakening the unity of the working class.[8] These points have been made before, of course, but chiefly in relation to the significance of white collar employment and the special relationship of non-manual workers to the industrial enterprise (Lockwood, 1958). There is, arguably, an equivalent to the segmentation of manual jobs in the white collar sphere, which takes the form of a 'de-skilling' of some areas of non-manual work, leading to secondary status for a section of the workforce. Thus the primary/secondary division cuts through manual and non-manual work — a phenomenon which is reflected in the extensive mobility of women workers between lower grade clerical and office jobs and the semi- and unskilled manual sector.

The important point about this process of primary—secondary differentiation is that employers cannot simply increase wages for a section of their workers without triggering off competitive wage increases in the local or national labour market, so that they are obliged to make higher wage positions contingent upon employee stability. Hence the tendency to build a promotional structure to attract and retain the stable workers.[9]

Piore (1972) has suggested that the growth of the division of labour can be related to the growth of the product market, borrowing from an argument advanced by Adam Smith. But growth in the product market merely facilitates occupational differentiation — it does not necessarily result in labour market *dualism*. A dual labour market is a special case of a highly differentiated one, and the reasons for its emergence are those outlined by Gordon — retention of scarce labour resources and reduction of employee solidarity. This last point does not depend upon any conspiracy theory of class interests, although of course employers can and do act collectively to protect their interest in the labour market.[10] Rather it rests upon the need for particular employers or groups of employers to buy off the most militant and best organized sections of the labour force. These workers are usually the most highly skilled workers who are able to exert their power more quickly and who have the resources to endure a confrontation with the employer. The segmentation of the labour force into more privileged and less privileged sections reduces the threat of a total strike, while reducing the impact on profits of particular wage demands — albeit on a temporary basis.

There may be limitations on the extent to which segmentation can develop. For example, some firms and industries may not be able to afford the necessary investment (this is linked to Piore's point about the growth

R. D. Barron and G. M. Norris

of the product market). Secondly, as Mackay *et al.* (1971) have shown for the engineering industry, there can be short run constraints on the process imposed by technology. Their study found that job ladders were relatively short in engineering because experience and skills acquired in one job did not always equip the worker to deal with the next job up in the skill hierarchy.

The growth of the primary sector as the result of the various strategies adopted by firms to reduce the level of voluntary and involuntary turnover amongst certain groups of employees; and as a response to the demands of certain sections of the labour force, has several important consequences for the structure of jobs in the secondary sector. The development of a primary sector is limited by the extent to which employers can offer their key workers the employment stability and higher earnings levels needed to reduce overall labour turnover among these workers in the ways outlined above. Instability occurs in the market economy not only at the level of overall effective demand, but, in a world of changing consumer tastes, at the level of the product demand for individual firms and industries. For the individual firm the problem is to minimize the impact of such unstable fluctuations upon its key workers.

In a situation of periodic fluctuations in product demand, a firm can control its output either by trying to stabilize the demand for its own products and thereby forcing the instability in the product market on to other firms, or by organizing its production system and job structure in such a way that fluctuations in its overall level of product demand can be accommodated by adjustments in the numbers of people employed on those jobs where employee instability is less costly to the firm. Firms which want to retain their key workers by raising their earnings levels, or at least by offering them the future prospect of raised earnings levels, may have a limited capacity to raise wages and will therefore try to keep them low in other areas of their job structures. *Levels of job security and earnings in the two sectors are therefore crucially interdependent and the growth or decline of one sector is bound to affect conditions in the other sector.* If it is in the interest of employers to maintain and expand the primary sector, it may also be in their interest to ensure that instability and low earnings are retained in the secondary sector. Of course, this strategy is necessarily related to the availability of a supply of workers willing to accept the poor pay, insecurity, low status and poor working conditions of secondary jobs.

Women as a secondary labour force

If the dual labour market model is a valid one, it follows that employers will look for, or at least tolerate, in a secondary workforce characteristics

Sexual divisions and the dual labour market

which are different from those that they would expect in a primary workforce. For example, they may make lower demands upon the stability of secondary employees, since high voluntary turnover rates make it easier for firms to adjust their labour supply in a painless fashion. This is not to say that employers are always happy about jobs with high turnover rates and low pay; very often they resent the higher recruitment costs which this situation produces. But the very fact that they tolerate these problems, rather than raising wages and improving conditions, or capitalizing and reducing their work force, demonstrates either their inability to finance higher paid jobs or their reluctance to relinquish the other advantages of the secondary sector.

Given the limited information about potential job applicants normally available to recruiters, it may often be difficult for an employer to obtain direct evidence about the likely reliability and stability of a potential employee. Therefore use is frequently made of relatively visible individual characteristics which are thought to correlate highly with these qualities. For purely operational reasons employers rely upon formal educational and training qualifications and other easily identifiable, personal criteria, such as sex, age, colour and possibly certified disability. The use of these broad categories as a basis for job allocation has two important consequences. When ascriptive characteristics, like sex, are used as selection criteria, it has the effect of confining the groups so delineated to the secondary sector over the whole of their working lives. The second is that the actual confinement of particular groups to the secondary sector will result in their having higher rates of labour turnover and job mobility. Thus a 'vicious circle' is created which reinforces the discriminating power of the trait which was made the basis of the selection criterion, and the labelling process becomes self-fulfilling.

There seem to be five main attributes that may make a particular social group or category a likely source of secondary workers: dispensability, clearly visible social difference, little interest in acquiring training, low economism and lack of solidarity. These attributes are the *product* of the social relationship between employer and worker, and not something which an individual possesses independently of that relationship. At the same time, they are qualities which are to some extent shaped elsewhere in the social structure and brought *to* the employment market. Thus they are not characteristics which an individual possesses solely by virtue of his market situation, but they help to determine an individual's market situation in conjunction with the interests and requirements of employers. They should be seen as *general* characteristics of a secondary workforce which may be used to examine the reasons for the preponderance of women in the secondary sector. But the test of their generality is their ability to account for the sorts of *men* workers who are

54

R. D. Barron and G. M. Norris

also found in the secondary sector, and in the following outline reference is made to these comparable groups of male workers

Dispensability The first of these five attributes is *dispensability*, defined as the ease with which an employee can be removed from a redundant job. Dispensability has two aspects — voluntary turnover and relative ease of involuntary separation.

1. The importance of voluntary turnover as a means of regulating the size of the workforce without painful redundancies and dismissals has already been discussed. Women, as a group, change jobs more frequently than men, although *some* of this difference, at least, must be explained by the position they occupy in the job structure. But, even if we were to remove the influence of their occupational position, their turnover rates would still be higher because of their relationship to the family — their tendency to leave jobs for childbirth or for other family reasons (Hunt, 1968). *Single* women may well have lower voluntary turnover rates than married women if age is controlled for, but marital status is so clearly age-related that turnover rates for married and single women tend to converge: single women having relatively high rates because of their youth and married women having relatively high rates because of their position in the family.

Differences between the sexes also manifest themselves in the *nature* of voluntary turnover. Men's job changing is more likely to be for careerist reasons — promotion or moving to a better-paid job — while much of women's turnover involves movement into and out of the labour force (Harris and Clausen, 1966; Hunt, 1968). The importance of job advancement as a reason for voluntary job changing among men, then, emphasizes their attachment to the primary sector where job changing for career purposes is accepted or even encouraged. The significance of non-work-related reasons for job changing among married women is that it makes women the only numerically important group in our society who can be fairly easily used as a variable work force.

The only male minority groups which share this characteristic are 'mavericks'[11] and youths. Young men change jobs frequently, partly to test out a variety of work situations and partly because of the low pay and tedium of many 'youth' jobs. Their turnover, unlike that of women, is highly work-related. Mavericks, too, change jobs frequently for work and personality reasons.

2. The second aspect of dispensability — relative ease of involuntary separation — is related to the following aspects of the social category's position:

   (a) The existence of social values which define the group as having a weaker claim on scarce job opportunities than other groups. In times of full employment, some groups are welcomed into the workforce, but when unemployment rises they are expected to make way for workers with a higher claim on jobs.

(b) The degree of acceptance of these values by the group in question.

(c) The possibility of alternative sources of economic support for the redundant group.

(d) The level of organization possessed by the redundant group.

(i)   The first of these points refers to the likely strength of support for dismissed workers in the wider community. Where there are strong beliefs that particular groups should have work opportunities, then local trade union and political pressures in defence of their lost jobs may be considerable. But when the consensus view is that the group in question is less 'deserving' of jobs, then these pressures are not so likely to be forthcoming; in fact, the consensus ideology may support the dismissal of these workers. Women are commonly held to be more dispensable than men in this respect because of the strength of family values — and even when a woman's income may be vital to family living standards (see Land in the companion volume), it is often said that her 'real' place is in the home with her family and that her husband is, or should be, the main source of income.

There are some groups of male workers who, according to fairly widespread values, have a weaker entitlement to scarce jobs. Older men, for example, are sometimes expected to make way for younger men with families to support, and this belief is enshrined in employer and trade union redundancy practices. Youths, too, are granted lower claims on jobs than older men with families. Employers can treat young people, particularly those who have not managed to gain a foothold in the primary sector, with a greater degree of casualness than they could treat adult workers. Immigrants and Blacks, according to some subterranean chauvinist and racialist values, ought not to occupy jobs that locally born and/or white workers could otherwise take, but this view has usually obtained little official support in Britain.[12] More important — as a factor in confining immigrant workers to the secondary labour market — is racial discrimination from primary employers and workers. Finally, the disabled *might* suffer to some extent from the belief that they should not

R. D. Barron and G. M. Norris

take jobs which an unemployed but able-bodied man could fill — but this is much less certain as public feelings on the subject are more confused.

(ii) The second important factor affecting ease of involuntary separation is the degree of acquiescence in the situation by the redundant group.[13] Women appear to fluctuate numerically more within the labour market than do men, but because much of the variation in their numbers can be accounted for by voluntary separations it is difficult to say whether women are also more malleable in terms of involuntary separation.[14] Although there is no evidence that formal redundancies are experienced more often by male workers, most redundancy studies tell us about men rather than women. We might expect women to accept redundancies more readily than men because of a lower degree of attachment to work as a career, and because of financial support from husbands (where this is substantial), but it would be difficult in practice to disentangle this possibility from the equally plausible hypothesis that women are less resistant to the loss of their jobs because many alternative jobs of a roughly equivalent nature are available to them.[15] The picture is complicated by the fact that the organization of women at the workplace is likely to be weak anyway (see on and Brown's paper, Ch. 2), so the appearance of acquiescence in job loss may be an indicator of passive resignation rather than a sign of the acceptance of any kind of principle of 'less eligibility'. To our knowledge, there is no detailed comparative study of men's and women's attitudes towards redundancy which would help to clear up this point. Older men are another group who may accept the inevitability of redundancy because of shared values concerning the place of the elderly in society.

(iii) The third factor which could affect a group's resistance to redundancy is the extent to which alternative sources of income are available. There are several complications to be considered, however. The first is that probably what matters most to a redundant worker is the *relative* fall in his income. For a very highly paid worker the fall in income that follows a redundancy may be considerable, though, of course, he may also have savings or compensatory lump sum payments available as a buffer against loss of earnings. For a lower paid worker the relative loss of income may be smaller because of his proximity, when in work, to the state poverty line. Married women are likely to experience more or less complete loss of individual income because they are often not entitled either to unemployment benefit or social security, but this total loss may be seen as minimized if their husbands have a good income. A further complication is that an individual's perception of income loss is probably related to the ready availability of other equivalent jobs.

(iv)   Women commonly lack the sort of organization needed to fight the loss of their jobs. Although they may be represented in trade unions, sometimes in considerable numerical strength, there is little or no recognition by the trade unions of their special interests, which all too easily leads to a tendency to ignore the impact of industrial changes on women as a group. Thus action by women activists is often 'unofficial'. The same pattern is noticeable among immigrant workers (Castles and Kosack, 1973). Other male minorities, older workers and youths, are usually too numerically insignificant to warrant special treatment either from the employers or from the unions of which they are members. Their numerical weakness means that their sectional interests are not only ignored by the unions but that they are also less able to unite in some sectional action. On the other hand, as union members they may receive a degree of protection against loss of jobs – but whether or not they do so is often determined by the union, not by the older workers themselves. When an employer can persuade a union that some redundancies are inevitable, the union will often agree to the 'early retirement' of its senior members.

In summary, of all the groups we have considered the representation of women in the workforce is probably most easily manipulated by employers – not only because of their relatively high turnover rates but because women can be involuntarily removed with less resistance and cost than most groups of male workers.

Social differences   It is likely that an employer will prefer as a candidate for a secondary sector job a worker who can be sharply differentiated from primary sector employees by some conventional *social difference*, preferably one which emphasizes the relative inferiority of the secondary group. This is because the existence of a primary–secondary jobs division can be both obscured and justified by the fact that it coincides with this social division. The division reduces the probability of an identity of interests developing between primary and secondary workers – a point

R. D. Barron and G. M. Norris

which was argued in Gordon's version of the dual labour market theory. It is not necessary that the employer consciously recognize the usefulness of the social division; on the contrary, he may be oblivious to its importance because it is a part of his own conventional world view. But this will not stop an employer from becoming aware of its usefulness when the need arises; if the boundary between primary and secondary workers is threatened, he can use the ideology that maintains it as one weapon in the struggle. Conflict is minimized if secondary sector workers share the values that define their inferior role in the economic system. Such a consensus over the status of secondary workers will at least limit demands by these workers themselves, or by other groups in the society, for improvements in the secondary sector.

Social differences are rarely used *by themselves* to support and legitimate economic differences. Normally it is claimed that they indicate differences in 'productivity', a more acceptable legitimation for differentiation in capitalist societies. Thus the reason given for the confinement of blacks to the lowest paid sector of the South African economy is not their race as such, but the alleged 'fact' that blacks are less productive workers than whites. 'Productivity', or a related concept, such as 'aptitude', therefore become important underpinning ideological supports for various kinds of social division when these are important in the labour market.

Sometimes appeal is made to productivity differences between men and women to justify sexual segmentation in the British labour market. More often, however, it is simply taken for granted that women will be confined to lower paid jobs than men — partly because of fairly widespread feelings that it is not right for women to earn as much as or more than their husbands or that women should not be in positions of authority over men at the workplace, and partly because the sexual categorization of jobs into men's and women's work enables the question to be avoided: women are lower paid as a group because their sort of work is low paid.[16] The suggestion that women are somehow peculiarly suited to repetitive tasks — a common argument among employers — is probably a more useful ideological ploy than a straightforward appeal to productivity differences between men and women, and it works in precisely this sort of circular way: because women *are* confined to these tasks they must have a special aptitude for them.

Sex, as a criterion for employment market segregation, is more useful than other social differences not only because sexual differences are highly visible, but because social divisions between men and women are deep seated, without, however, arousing the sort of ambivalent feelings that are associated with divisions between other groups, e.g racial or ethnic groups. Exclusion of women from male social activities is either taken for granted, or perhaps treated as a subject for humour. Few women are prepared to question their separate treatment in the social sphere, possibly because its existence is obscured by the fact that men and women clearly do get together in other, well-defined contexts.

The general acceptance of these social differences enables the division between primary and secondary workers at the micro-level, in the workplace, to be maintained with a relatively low degree of friction. The separate nature of men's and women's social lives outside the workplace facilitates the maintenance of similar divisions within it. A lack of identity of interest between male and female workers may be assumed, and employers can often deal with the demands for higher pay or better conditions for male workers without needing to fear a revolt from their female staff.[17] Moreover, male workers are much less likely to accept claims that there is an identity of interest when they come from lower paid female workers than from lower paid male workers.

The social division based upon sex is the most important one in our society from the point of view of enabling a secondary sector of workers to be clearly differentiated from a primary sector, but there are other (male) groups which share this property of social separation to some extent and which are therefore candidates for the secondary sector. Age cohorts are probably the most important of these, because the same kind of appeal can be made to productivity as a legitimating factor (young workers are only learning the trade and therefore do not have a very high output, while older workers have suffered a decline in their powers); and because age groups form the basis of social associations outside the workplace the possibility of a common identity developing between them is reduced. On the other hand, age groups are much less clearly defined. *Rites de passage*, such as the termination of an apprenticeship or formal retirement, do help to define boundaries for older and younger workers, but the fact that there is a continual progression across these boundaries means that they are less important as a basis for the formation of specialized interest groupings than sexual divisions.

Racial or ethnic differences can be used as social divisions, since as characteristics they share with sex the properties of visibility and stability over time. Indeed, there are many examples of firms which have used racial differences to create a primary–secondary division in the workplace. More often than not, however, the primary–secondary boundary is *also* defined by sexual differences – Asian *women*, for example, are a useful secondary·labour force. But any attempt to create a stable secondary workforce based upon racial divisions alone is fraught with dangers for the employer, as recent eruptions in the textile industry have shown (Sayle, 1973). With the important exception of the use of work permits to maintain a transient workforce in the hotel and catering industry, there is

R. D. Barron and G. M. Norris

no official policy of encouraging permanent divisions between primary and secondary workers based upon racial or ethnic differences.

Although social divisions can and do exist between the disabled and the non-disabled members of our society, it is difficult for most employers to exploit this division in maintaining a secondary workforce. For one thing, the disabled do present special problems at the workplace, problems which can confine them to secondary jobs anyway. For another, they are numerically too small a group and often require special provisions at work which restricts the numbers that an employer can take on still further. The social division between the disabled as a group and ordinary workers is confused, and — like racial differences — frequently a source of guilt or embarrassment because of social values which stress the need to integrate fully disabled people into the community. Nevertheless there are some instances where disability is used to define a secondary workforce, and employers are able to trade upon the gratitude which some disabled people have for any kind of paid work and their consciousness of the difficulties that confront them in breaking out of the secondary jobs sector. Once again, we can find instances of productivity differences having an ideological use for secondary employers.

Training The third desirable attribute of secondary workers is a relatively low interest in acquiring valuable training and experience. Secondary sector jobs are, above all, jobs in which there is a low investment in human capital. They do not offer training, and because there is little or no effort made by the employer to improve the quality of the worker, he is not particularly concerned about retaining his employees' services. It suits the secondary employer, therefore, to take on workers who are less concerned about the amount of training they receive and who have low expectations about moving up a job ladder. This does not mean, of course, that candidates for secondary jobs do not need to be skilful or intelligent; many secondary employers depend upon being able to obtain workers who are highly adaptable — the sort of workers who could be trained to do more highly rewarded jobs but who are prepared to accept that this training will not be forthcoming.

People have varied reasons for not interesting themselves in vocational training. First, an individual may believe that he or she is inherently incapable of undergoing the learning process which leads on to higher jobs. This belief may be acquired from a very early age or it may be acquired during the process of secondary socialization. More often than not it is acquired early on, and reinforced by later experiences. People can be made to feel inferior because they are slow to learn or less intelligent; but they can also be made to feel inferior through social processes which

Sexual divisions and the dual labour market

emphasize their membership of a social group which is itself held to be less talented or intelligent than other, dominant groups. Both processes can operate simultaneously and be mutually reinforcing. Research on race and intellectual achievement has demonstrated the operation of this process very well, and similar research has explored the conditioning of males and females in our society.

For whatever reason, there is a pronounced tendency for women to be under-represented in areas of higher education and in occupational training schemes. Part of the reason is certainly the sort of socialization in the home and the school which emphasizes the social definition of 'women's work' — i.e. pre-eminently work where training is either limited or irrelevant. Some of the explanation may be *general* feelings of intellectual inadequacy related to their sex, or to the belief that certain *sorts* of work and skill are peculiarly suited to 'male' aptitudes. These feelings are supported by the belief shared by many women that careerism does not accord with their place in the family after marriage. This is a complex problem, and cannot be dealt with properly here. But it is obvious that the attitudes of women are often bound up with expectations about their husbands' work (many do not want to be more skilled or educated than their marriage partners, and would encounter difficulties from their husbands if they were). Their attitudes are also bound up with their view of the employment market; in the case of women manual workers, there have been plenty of less skilled factory and white collar jobs available since the war which are relatively easy to get, whereas the prejudices and other obstacles that lie in the way of obtaining more skilled work are not — for many women — worth the effort that would be required to overcome them, given that they have to assume the additional responsibility of looking after home and family. Any willingness of women to subordinate themselves and to accept full domestic responsibility inside the family therefore supports their subordination in the labour market.

While women constitute the major group of employees who are relatively less interested in training, there are several categories of men who are also, for one reason or another, prepared to accept jobs with few or no prospects. First among these are, of course, older men — especially those who are close to or have arrived at the age of retirement. As in the case of women, older men are confined by a widely held social ideology which holds that opportunities should be provided for younger men because they have to bring up families. Employers, of course, favour younger men as training prospects, not only for these reasons, but because young men are easier to train and will provide a lengthier return on the training investment. Government and other training institutions normally have rules which restrict training opportunities to young and middle-aged men. In addition, many older men have fears and doubts about their abilities, particularly if training means learning entirely new tasks (Belbin and Belbin, 1972).

Although many disabled people are both keen to acquire training and feel that they are able to do so, a significant number are resigned to the fact that their handicap precludes them from obtaining jobs which involve the acquisition of complex skills.

Thirdly, there are men who lack or feel they lack the necessary ability. Like the disabled they have resigned themselves to their position and do not query an employer's classification of them as untrainable.

Fourthly, there are men who reject the settled way of life that training may require, and prefer a mobile life-style for ideological or personal reasons. Sometimes they have been conditioned to this existence by the absence of available opportunities in their youth, but some at least rejected the confinement of 'careerism' at the outset.

Finally, youths — particularly in areas of high unemployment — may come to accept that there are only dead-end jobs available and reconcile themselves to a degree of confinement to the secondary sector. Unlike the other groups mentioned, however, their situation is complicated by the fact that their exclusion from training opportunities runs counter to prevailing social values — i.e. beliefs that young people should be trained to the limit of their capacities. Thus they may have a passive attitude to the absence of training in a job in the face of a generally high level of unemployment in the local or national labour market, because of a widespread feeling that they are fortunate to be in work at all. It seems to be the case that in such circumstances the 'career' jobs should be kept for the slightly older people or for the most highly qualified school leavers. Both of the last two groups — mavericks and youths — are, however, much less well defined and stable as minority groups than the first three.

Economism   Much of what has been said about orientation to training can also be applied to what, for want of a better term, has been called 'economism'.[18] A worker who places a high value on monetary rewards is a possible threat to the stability of the secondary reward system. Direct comparisons of sexual differences in work orientations are both meagre and unsophisticated but comparative data from the National Board for Prices and Incomes Survey of low paid workers (N.B.P.I., 1971) suggest that women are somewhat less concerned with economic rewards in their work than men.[19] This is not very surprising given that many women are secondary earners and therefore are *perceived* as having less *need* to seek monetary rewards than men.

There are possibly some groups of male workers who are also rather less concerned with pay in their jobs. Pensioners who are limited by earnings rules and who do not in any case have families to support, are one example. Young people with access to parental resources are another possible category, but this claim is conjectural only. Fox suggests that life-cycle factors are important determinants of orientations to work, along with 'sanctions of family, group, community, new leaders, the mass media' (Fox, 1971). In fact, as Richard Brown suggests elsewhere in this volume, the determinants of orientations to work are interwoven through the mediation of the life cycle *and* the realities of the choices which individuals face in their work.

The fact that most women appear to be less economistic in their orientation to work than most men does not mean that women have more limited financial needs in any objective sense, nor can this aspect of women's approach to work be dissassociated from the fact that expectations held by women may be limited by the relatively low pay of the jobs available to them.

Solidarism   The question of collective organization and action among women workers and among the other categories which have been hitherto compared to women is too complex to dwell on at any length in this section, save to point out that women have been notably less successful than men in organizing themselves industrially and to suggest some of the reasons for this difference. It has been argued that a relatively low level of trade union or collective strength among a secondary workforce reduces the possibility of secondary workers driving their wages and conditions up to the level of the primary sector, and that an employer will, therefore, prefer a secondary workforce which is difficult to organize in this way, or which is *believed* to be difficult to organize.[20]

Lack of organization among women workers is not, unlike the other four characteristics that have been considered, a characteristic which is determined to any extent by forces outside the labour market itself. Indeed, to a very considerable degree it reflects aspects of the work and market situation of women — low pay (which makes union dues expensive), scattered workplaces which make communications difficult, high turnover and a high incidence of temporary and part time jobs. An additional problem for women trade unionists has been the necessary numerical dominance by men in the trade union movement. This dominance has in some ways hindered the development of a strong women's movement because the resources available to fight strikes on an official basis and to manage union affairs generally have remained in the hands of men, who often do not share the interests or outlook of their fellow women unionists. Even in industries where female representation is

R. D. Barron and G. M. Norris

very high (e.g. textiles, potteries, the retail trade) men retain a paternalistic control over their largely female membership.

Social differentiation based upon sexual divisions and women's acceptance of these help to maintain barriers within union organizations. A low level of interest by many women in either careerism (work as a lifetime prospect) or high pay reduces the need, in the eyes of many women, for solidaristic activity. Solidarism, therefore, is highly affected by the structure of the secondary labour market and by the sorts of factors that have already been discussed.

This is not to say, however, that women have never been successful in organizing their trades. From the famous 'matchgirls' ' strike of 1888 to the growth of unionism in contract cleaning today, there are many instances of successful industrial actions taken by women. But these efforts have either been absorbed into largely male-dominated union activity or have, in the words of a woman trade unionist, 'winked out' after short bursts of enthusiasm and activity.

Conclusions

This paper has sought to demonstrate the confinement of women to a sector of relatively low paid, less secure, less skilled and less rewarding jobs, and to suggest some of the reasons for this state of affairs.[21] It seems to us that women are the main secondary workforce in Britain, and that the fact that the primary-secondary division coincides with sexual divisions in the labour market has obscured the existence of dualism in the British labour market. Many researchers have ignored the dualistic aspects of the market because they have been concentrating upon the jobs held by men, and have therefore noticed inequalities rather than major structural barriers. This is not to say that there are not secondary 'dualisms' or divisions *within* particular occupational labour markets, but the existence of these should not be allowed to blind us to the larger divisions between men and women at work and between primary and secondary jobs.

Of course, as we have noted, some men may fall into the secondary category, and we have suggested some of the features which male members of the secondary workforce may share with their female counterparts.

The origins of the dual labour market lie with the forces of supply and demand in capitalist economics, though this paper has placed most emphasis upon the demand side. Our conclusion must be the perhaps gloomy, perhaps optimistic one that any attempt to alter the overall position of women within the economy cannot be achieved without either finding enough men to replace the large gap in the secondary sector that would be created by the upgrading required to create a more equal sexual balance in the labour market; or removing the pronounced division

Sexual divisions and the dual labour market

between primary and secondary jobs. It is clear that ending sexual discrimination in the employment system is therefore only one of the problems that has to be thought about if sexual differences in employment are to be abolished, and that sexual differences in the economy can only be ended through a massive attack on the inequality to which the dual labour market gives rise.

Notes

1. The combined mean for all men and women gives a figure of 71·4p per hour — Department of Employment (1972). Using gross *hourly* earnings, instead of weekly earnings, provides a partial control for variations in hours worked, but does not, for example, control for differences due to overtime rates, bonuses, etc. Fuller details may be found in our original B.S.A. Conference paper, of which this is a shortened version (Barron and Norris, 1974).

2. Two-thirds of the mean was 47·6p per hour in 1972. This has been used as a rough definition of 'low pay' for the purposes of this paper, on the grounds that a two-thirds measure accords with T.U.C. practice (in the case of male workers) and is quite closely related to the level at which gross pay becomes inadequate to maintain a small family. Low pay may be defined either in relativistic terms — as a measure of the degree of inequality in a pre-tax income distribution — or in 'absolute' terms in relation to the measured income *needs* of households. Variations in household size and composition and rent clearly affect needs when these are translated into monetary terms. Hence measures of 'low pay' which attempt to relate to some poverty standard are inevitably arbitrary (for a discussion of this point see, *inter alia*, Edmonds and Radice (1968) and Sinfield and Twine (1970). The two-thirds proportion has become something of a conventional wisdom in the field of social policy since it produces a monetary measure close to that derived from the needs approach while giving a useful standard by which any progress towards equality in pay might be measured. Usually, however, the two-thirds measure is applied to male earnings only.

3. Of course, it is often important to define 'low pay' differently for men in order to consider the situation of low paid male workers. But this procedure should not be allowed to conceal the fact that the vast majority of low paid workers are women.

4. 'Representation' in this context, is measured in relation to the proportion of women in the labour force. Thus a job in which

R. D. Barron and G. M. Norris

women are equally represented is one in which the ratio of women to men is roughly one to three. For a fuller discussion, see pages 6-10 of Barron and Norris (1974) and the accompanying tables.

5. Some authors (e.g. Bluestone, 1970) have suggested the usefulness of a tripartite division into primary, secondary, and irregular sectors. The last is the criminal or 'unofficial' economy which provides much unrecorded employment and whose workings are relatively unknown. A fuller discussion of the development of the dual labour market model is found in Barron and Norris (1974: 11-13).

6. Although there is not space within this paper to examine closely the detailed evidence which would be needed to confirm the existence of a dual labour market in the United Kingdom which coincides with sexual divisions, there is some evidence which can be briefly cited and which relates to the four conditions of segmentation outlined in the text.

1. *Division into high and low paying sectors.* The evidence of marked differences in earnings between men and women which accounts for the asymmetrical bimodal shape of the distribution of hourly earnings for all employees is cited in the text.

2. *Restricted mobility across the boundary.*

3. *The association between promotional ladders and higher paying jobs.* There are two main pieces of evidence here (for a fuller discussion, refer to our B.S.A. Conference paper). First, secondary analysis of information on occupational mobility over a 10-year period (taken from Harris and Clausen, 1966) indicates that men have higher rates of mobility —

   (a) from less skilled manual jobs to higher skilled manual jobs;
   (b) from all manual jobs to professional and managerial jobs;
   (c) from routine non-manual jobs to professional and managerial jobs.

   Secondly, data on the distribution of hourly earnings by age taken from the *New Earnings Survey* of 1968 suggest two important differences between male and female lifetime earnings profiles. The first is that for females the highest level of earnings is reached at an earlier age than for males, and the second is that the proportionate rise in earnings over a lifetime is much higher for men than it is for women.

4. *Higher paying jobs are relatively more stable.* Examination of the differences between the numbers of men and women

employed in manufacturing in all succeeding quarters between 1948 and 1971 taken from the Department of Employment *Gazette* indicates a clear tendency for women's employment to fluctuate proportionately more than male employment. Between 1948 and 1971 the numbers of women employed rose or fell proportionately more than male employment from one quarter to the next in 70 per cent of the periods. Moreover during that period whilst the index of male employment changed direction seventeen times the female index changed direction thirty-seven times.

7. This two-step procedure does oversimplify reality in one important respect. The characteristics of the workforce may be an important determinant of the way employers structure their job systems, so that supply factors can condition demand factors. In this paper we have given more weight to demand factors as determinants of labour market segmentation, but a fuller analysis would require a proper treatment of the reciprocal influence of supply upon demand.

8. Gordon, with his eye directed at the recent rapid increase, particularly in the United States, in the role of formal qualifications in obtaining jobs, overstates the newness of labour market dualism. The distinction between the 'aristocracy' of labour and the unskilled labourer has been with us since the beginning of the industrial revolution. Nor is the confinement of *women* to secondary jobs a new pattern, although, as Rowbotham (1973) observes, this confinement occurred *outside* the factory system in the early phase of the industrial revolution; that is, women were largely employed in secondary jobs away from the factory, yet economically dependent on the factory mode of production. Following the First World War, which had created a demand for women as *primary* sector workers, many women were forced back into secondary status. A full discussion of the development of the dual labour market and of women's place in the economy cannot be attempted here, but useful reference may be made to Rowbotham (1973) and Thompson (1963).

9. Promotional ladders need not be much more than increments for length of service. Special pay rates for longer serving workers are a feature of the Japanese market (Dore, 1973).

10. Gordon (1972) seems to subscribe to a version of the conspiracy theory, since he argues that employers as a class try to create internal subdivisions within the working class in order to resist the development of a broadly based class consciousness.

R. D. Barron and G. M. Norris

11. For the use of this term, which is preferable to a phrase like 'chronic job changer', see MacDonald (1973).

12. A notable exception is the European Voluntary Worker scheme introduced after the War (see Tannahill, 1958).

13. 'Acquiescence' is used, in this context, to mean a degree of normative acceptance of the redundancy situation; a group may of course 'accept' its redundancy in a *negative* sense because of points (c) and (d) in our original list of factors; i.e., because other sources of income are available or because the group lacks the organization required to fight the loss of jobs.

14. Under the terms of the Redundancy Payments Act (1965) workers with less than 2 years' service are not entitled to a redundancy payment, and the value of the redundancy payment is related to length of service. Thus high turnover among women employees reduces the costliness of involuntary job separation from the employer's point of view.

15. W. W. Daniel (1972) showed that women seemed just as concerned with the prospect of redundancy as men. The only evidence for a greater degree of compliance among women was the somewhat jejune finding that women were more in doubt than the men about the necessity for the closures, while more men were convinced that the closures were unnecessary. This might be read as a sign of weaker resistance among women workers and a readier acceptance of the official management line. Job loss may not be as serious for women because of a general buoyancy in the market for women's jobs (in semi- and unskilled work). Daniel found that fewer women reported difficulty in finding another job after the closures in Woolwich.

16. It should be noted that although the trade union movement in Britain has given formal recognition to the importance of obtaining 'equal pay' for men and women since the last century, the concept of equality of pay is a weak one in the context of a labour market which is sharply differentiated into male and female sectors. In fact the intentions of equal pay legislation may be circumvented by decreasing the area of overlap between men's and women's work and thus *increasing* the existing sexual divisions in the labour market.

17. Further discussion of this point may be found in Richard Brown's paper (Ch. 2).

18. Ingham (1970) contains a discussion of the concept of 'economism'.

19. For further discussion and references, see Brown's paper.

20. Brown's paper contains a fuller discussion of the arguments about women as trade unionists and makes the point that whether they are more difficult to organize or whether they merely appear to be less union conscious because their work situations have hitherto

constrained their opportunities for collective action, women nevertheless are *felt* to be less willing participants in union affairs than men, and that this is in itself a significant factor in shaping their participation.

21. In assembling the data upon which our arguments are based we have avoided, because of space limitations, discussion of the *part-time* job sector. This important but neglected part of the economy strengthens the case for the dual labour market model, since its jobs are usually even less well paid and are certainly an important source of work for many women.

4 Roger Smith

Sex and occupational role on Fleet Street

A plethora of recent research has indicated that considerable job-differentiation within occupations takes place on the basis of sex, both with regard to the attainment of hierarchical position and also areas of specialization within the occupation. In all fields so far studied, female participation has been found to decline as the upper echelons of power and prestige are approached (Mattfeld and Van Aken, 1965; White, 1967; Harris, 1970; Rossi, 1970; Epstein, 1971; Fogarty *et al.*, 1971a). Closely linked with this hierarchical differentiation in occupations is the delineation and maintenance of 'female' areas of specialization, which are almost exclusively the least prestigious insofar as the total occupation is concerned (Phelps, 1968; Brager and Michael, 1969; Epstein, 1971; Fogarty *et al.*, 1971a; Smith, 1971).

The conceptual framework within which most recent British research programmes on career women have been designed is that exemplified by Fogarty *et al.* (1971b) and the Rapoports (1971a, b). The guiding theme of such research is the linkage of work, and its demands, with the female life-cycle (i.e. domestic commitments at various phases) in order to explain female participation and success in the occupational sphere. Such an approach tends neatly to take attention away from the professions and other 'career' occupations and the role which *they* play in *structuring* female opportunity. The 'life-cycle' is taken quite unjustifiably as the independent variable, with 'work' the dependent variable, when it is clear that occupational experiences and expectations can easily affect decisions relating to the reified 'life-cycle' of women. The outcome of this theoretical orientation is that responsibility is laid on the family as the prime determiner of participation and success and the assumption that those women who do not work are in this position because their family organization is an inefficient agent in the 'enabling process'. Apart from the fact, already mentioned, that this ignores feedback from work experience to domestic decision-making, there is a good deal of evidence from other quarters that women suffer discrimination *regardless* of marital status or domestic obligations, both in rates of remuneration and chances for advancement (Bernard, 1964; Rossi, 1965). It would thus appear more fruitful to concentrate on the examination of the structures and ideologies of occupations themselves.

Research in the United States has tended to follow Hughes's (1952) conceptualization of 'dirty work' in investigations of the connected phenomena of low female attainment, and confinement to particular areas. All occupations are seen to have jobs, or specialisms, which are necessary to the continuation and efficient functioning of that occupation, but which are low in prestige. To ensure that they are filled, they are opened to those for whom such jobs would represent status. Women are obvious candidates. Becker and Strauss (1965) suggest that such groups will develop an ideology to make sense of and rationalize a situation they come to recognize as inferior and exploited. It would seem, however, that such explanations take an extremely static and ahistorical view of the development of occupations, and of individual careers, and tend to assume that exploitation will lead automatically to a rationalizing ideology, rather than consciousness of exploitation resulting in militancy and change. Within such a framework all that is explained is the original entry of women into prestigious occupations — the mechanics of the maintenance of sexual differentiation and stratification are not accounted for in any systematic way. Given that the incidence of sex-typing in occupations is as wide now as it was 60 years ago (Gross, 1968), it is vital that such maintenance patterns become a major focus of attention.

Women journalists on Fleet Street

The data used for this paper are taken from a larger research project which I am engaged in concerned with the social and educational backgrounds, occupational experience, behaviour and imagery of women in two fields — journalism and biological science. Women were chosen who had reached a high structural position within their occupation: operationally defined as Fleet Street and university faculty level, respectively.

The selection of journalists as one of the groups for investigation was prompted by the heavy concentration of much previous research on women *graduates*. Such research seems to assume that graduates are the only pool of potential high achievers, and ignores the fact that many career-oriented women may not have had the opportunity to go to university, indeed may have chosen not to — and they have entered a 'career' occupation immediately after school. Since a degree is not a prerequisite for entry to, or success in, journalism, and in fact is widely seen as either irrelevant or a positive disadvantage,[1] it was believed that this occupation, with its emphasis on informal training, would provide valuable contrasts with occupations where formal education to an advanced level is demanded.

Roger Smith

Samples of writing journalists[2] were selected from lists of by-lines[3] compiled from several weeks' copies of all the national papers, and the two London evening papers, and of editorial personnel from lists of names provided by the writing journalists. The information was gathered by open-ended interviews, tape-recorded in the majority of cases (in some instances taping was impossible and 'shorthand' notes were taken). Interviews lasted an average of 2 hours for the women, 1½ for the men.[4] In addition, opportunities for observation were presented in newsrooms, in the various newspaper pubs, and in the Press Club.

The system of sexual differentiation as it exists in journalism at Fleet Street level is complex and there are no adequate statistics available dealing with journalists on Fleet Street papers. Nor have I had Tunstall's (1971) good fortune in gaining access to any staff lists.[5] Thus whilst accurate statistics concerning the proportion and position of women on Fleet Street are being worked towards, and I have them for one newspaper, at the moment I am having to rely on the piecing together of information from respondents.

Estimates from respondents regarding the overall percentage of women on Fleet Street have varied between 5 per cent and 15 per cent, though, when pressed, individuals giving the latter figure have had much difficulty justifying it. Most, however, have chosen in the region of 10 per cent.[6] The overall percentage of women who are full members of the National Union of Journalists is 17 per cent, and of probationers 34 per cent.[7] Boyd-Barrett (1970) found that amongst those registered on National Council for the Training of Journalists' schemes, girls constituted a third of those on block release from newspapers, and a half of the pre-entry trainees (i.e. those who have been chosen by the N.C.T.J. straight from school to do a year's full-time course, and who are not actually employed by a newspaper).

Thus there is a gradual diminution of women as they rise through the ranks of journalism. Quite obviously some of this is self-chosen wastage as the result of marriage and child-raising. Such wastage is, however, unlikely to be the only, or even major, contributing factor to low Fleet Street membership, especially since we have seen that 17 per cent of full-time journalists are women. Other factors, relating to recruitment patterns and policies, would seem to have an important part to play, and these will be discussed in some detail later.

The very low proportion of women at the pinnacle of newspaper journalism having been established, the task is now to document what occupational roles and areas of specialism these women tend to gravitate towards. As might be expected from data collected on other occupations, journalism is characterized by extremely low female participation at executive and editorial levels. Insofar as senior women do exist, they tend to be women's page editors, not directly in the power hierarchy and well away from wider policy formation. Importantly, female news-editors or deputy news-editors are almost non-existent, and another point which seems crucial, and which I shall have more to say about later, is that there are *very* few women news sub-editors on any of the national papers.[8]

Insofar as specialist journalists are concerned, again women tend to be concentrated in fashion, and other areas with low prestige, like design, and welfare. The jobs which have most to offer in terms of prestige and financial remuneration — lobby, foreign, industrial and financial specialisms — are almost totally the province of males.

At a lower hierarchical level, amongst the non-specialist news and feature writers, further differentiation exists, although it is at this level that most women are concentrated. First, their representation on the news desk (10 per cent for the paper for which I have a breakdown) appears to be an aspect of exploitation rather than a recognition of merit. Women news reporters are kept on the desk for very specific purposes: because it is seen that the use of a female can be helpful in softening up some sources (e.g. crooks). More generally they are used for 'human interest' stories and to deal with news items which will affect women, such as price rises, etc. Insofar as 'general features' is concerned, women tend to make up a fairly high proportion of total staff. Again, this would seem to be part of a deliberate policy of using women for specific kinds of jobs — they are widely believed by men to have talents which fit them more for doing the in-depth interviews and social concern features which have recently become popular on papers, than for any other journalistic role. Finally, of the small number of women who actually make it to Fleet Street, the general consensus of respondents is that about 80 per cent of them work directly in the women's department, an area totally despised by almost every other working journalist, and feared by many of the women as a ghetto into which they may be pushed, typically described by both male and female respondents as 'a cosy corner totally irrelevant to the general run of the paper'.

Thus there is a very small overall proportion of women on Fleet Street, and those who do exist tend to be concentrated on fairly specific areas, well away from the mainstream of the paper and the most prestigious jobs. Two influences seem to have a good deal of power in explaining this situation — first, the typical patterns of recruitment into Fleet Street papers; and secondly , the highly informal training and passing on of relevant occupational knowledge which is characteristic of journalism.

Recruitment into Fleet Street   Channels of recruitment into Fleet Street tend to be extremely informal, since vacancies are very seldom advertised.

Roger Smith

Thus access to grapevines and informal contacts is of great importance. At provincial level, women are very rarely 'stringers' — people who act informally as local agents and sell material to the nationals — who are most likely to be in contact with the nationals, and thus know more about vacancies. A major channel of advance to the Street is by 'getting oneself known' to the paper by doing night-shifts and weekend work, and papers appear very unwilling to give women such opportunities. So far as night-work is concerned it is dismissed, on the face of it rather paternalistically, as totally unsuitable — 'you just could not send a woman out at night; she might get raped or murdered' was one male reporter's response, and fairly typical of other men's attitude. Weekend shifts are regarded as overtime and widely reserved for men because of the greater financial pressures they are seen to be under.

Working as holiday relief for the 2- or 3-month summer period puts the aspiring journalist in another potential recruitment pool. However, this is a more insecure mode of entry, as the established job will have to be given up in the gamble for Fleet Street acceptance. The already low proportion of women at this level will tend to have a self-reinforcing effect — girls on non-national papers will be painfully aware that their chances of success are slim. Moreover, experiences such as the following, reported by a woman who had finally made it through sheer determination, must also become part of female journalists' folk-knowledge:

> For three summers I gave up my jobs on locals and came to Fleet Street as holiday relief. Considering how difficult it is to get a permanent job, I was surprised at how easy it was to get in. But after the summer, the story was always the same — 'no vacancies' — when I knew bloody well that there were, but they were going to the boys. It took a long time to penetrate my pride that I was being taken on and used as cheap labour whilst they needed me, and then being discarded when I was of no further use.

Apart from doing marginal work for the nationals in one way or another, the other major recruitment channel is a rather fortuitous one. Local journalists will write in to papers, giving work experience and cuttings, etc., more or less asking for a job. It is widely testified that appointment via this channel depends very much on the luck of the draw — writing in at the right time. Unfortunately it has not been possible to get any details as to how many women apply in this way, and what proportion are taken on, but it is a method of selection which is widely believed by female journalists, and some men, to militate against women.[9]

In order to restore the balance somewhat, it is necessary to point out that there is an entry-route to Fleet Street for women that does not exist for men — that is, via women's magazines. It is also possible to enter without any journalistic training at all 'if you happen to be a high-born lady who's well-connected'. But these side entrances lead only to the women's pages and, as has been said, this area is widely despised by other journalists — partly precisely because of the lack of experience in basic journalism that the women who fill the jobs often have, but partly also because it is seen merely as a device for pulling advertising. Apart from being despised, it is also effectively a dead end — 'nobody is going to give you wider chances if they think the only thing you can scribble about is Yves St Laurent', commented one woman who had escaped from the women's pages. The easiest area for women to get into on Fleet Street, is also the hardest to get out of.

The internal channels of recruitment characteristic of national newspapers can thus be seen as contributing to low female participation at this level. What seems of crucial importance in explaining where women get to once they are on Fleet Street, is the totally informal nature of training and occupational socialization in journalism.

Training and occupational socialization in journalism The major explanation of most male journalists (and some women) as to why females are concentrated in particular areas or have certain specialized work-roles within areas, is that this is basically the result of their incapacity to do most other jobs. The expressions they use most commonly are 'lack of ability to use power'; 'domestic responsibilities'; 'wrong emotions'; and 'not tough enough'. There does indeed seem to be considerable truth in the assertion that most women would find it extremely difficult to do many of the jobs in the news organization, not for the reasons given above, but because many women *lack the relevant occupational knowledge.* Despite all the attempts of the N.C.T.J., formal training in journalism is generally despised by journalists because it is widely believed that the skills and knowledge necessary for becoming a good journalist can only be learned by actually doing journalism, and working in close proximity with other journalists. It is my contention that women are cut off from many key learning situations and contact with important occupational roles, and that the resultant differential distribution of knowledge is the major mechanism whereby sex differentiation and stratification are maintained.

The *knowledge* required of a journalist can be broadly defined as being of three types: technical, normative and folk-knowledge; and those journalists who have fullest command of these areas are likely to be those whose progress to prestigious jobs is most facilitated. The *key learning situations* seem to be: wide experience in hard news; some knowledge of sub-editing, or at least close contact with 'subs'; night shift working; the informal pub and club-culture. I shall now attempt to show how one or

Roger Smith

more of these key situations affect the learning process in each of the areas of knowledge, and how women as a group are generally disadvantaged.

Technical knowledge

The technical knowledge needed by a journalist is, despite the fact that there is no body of theory to master (Boyd-Barrett, 1970), relatively wide. At a very basic level it means knowing how to write a story that is : (a) acceptable to the sub-editors as newsworthy and reasonably written, so that 'subbing', by people under considerable pressure, is cut to a minimum; (b) legally acceptable — again to make the lawyer's job easier; and (c) consistent with the house-style.

Insofar as the first two points are concerned, there is rarely any direct teaching given to journalists. Wainwright (1972: 179), in a description of the newsroom, says that very little of what he calls the 'mental shorthand' used by the people there is ever put into words — thus the trainee has to learn very much by intuition. One way that learning is done is via the subs and the lawyer — a good sub will say *why* he has done a certain thing to copy, and a lawyer will explain *why* certain details or statements cannot be published. However, such aid is given on a very informal basis. As mentioned before, there are very few female sub-editors around — subbing tends to be a very masculine and self-protecting specialism, possibly because of its close links with printing. There is a traditional antagonism in the newsroom between writing journalists and subs, who are often seen as the uncreative destroyers of the journalists' purple prose. This antagonism is much stronger between subs and women journalists and tends to be *personal* as well as professional. My female respondents rarely knew any of the subs by name (even when they had been working on the same paper for years), and had no contact with them outside work. Male journalists — even the newest and youngest — tended to have far closer relations, both at work and socially, and though there might be sporadic disagreements about treatment of copy, this appeared not to extend into personal relations and the pub. Moreover, male journalists tended to have much greater understanding of the nature and constraints of the sub-editors' job, and were much more sympathetic. This is obviously the result of informal relations, and in turn reinforces them.

The picking up of legal information and other tips as to how to write an acceptable story would also seem to depend very much on the breadth of experience on different kinds of stories, and I have already argued that women in junior positions tend to be put to very specific uses. Gerbner (1969) has said that on many American papers women are assigned to what the newsdesk refers to as the 'junk'. The situation on many British papers would appear to be the same. I was fortunate enough to witness

Sex and occupational role on Fleet Street

this at fairly close range. During September 1973, three women reporters were interviewed on the day of, and the day following, an Oxford Street bomb explosion. In each case the story was the same — within thirty seconds of the noise being heard, the newsdesks were empty. Empty, that is, except for the three girls, who were kept back in the office to do the 'phoning. However, in one case much of the front page splash was made up from copy taken over the 'phone by one of the girls. But the four men who were out on the street got by-lines; she did not.

With regard to house-style, Wainwright (1972: 184) suggests that 'some papers rely on subs to hand down the house-style generation to generation like folk-legend'. For reasons given above, this would tend to militate against women. However, not all papers follow this practice — many have a house-style book, from which trainees are expected to work. The following experience, from a girl graduate taken on to a national, is illuminating:

> I was never given the style book because the great thing was to get me out as fast as they could. There was another university recruit — a man — and I saw him looking at this book and asked him what it was. He shoved it into his desk in a very angry manner and said 'You're not supposed to see this'. When he'd been given it he'd been told on no account to give it to me, 'so that she can't learn how to do things'.

Knowledge of subbing, the techniques and complex professional argot used, would not on the surface appear to be of any immediate relevance for most journalists. However, it was put to me by one male journalist that 'If you want to argue with a sub about what he's done to your copy, it does help if you know what you're talking about, and can use their language.' Another suggested that it was important to know what their job entailed, so that one could 'write to sub' — that is, have less important background or fringe information in separate and self-contained paragraphs, so that they can easily be cut out if the length does not fit, rather than give the sub more work to do, and the possible opportunity of ruining a story. Of the women I have so far interviewed, very few expressed any knowledge at all of what subbing involved, and only two had actually subbed (both of them, incidentally, are now in senior jobs). Aside from the fact that a reasonable knowledge of subbing can assist in negotiation of treatment of copy, experience of subbing is an almost mandatory qualification for advance to editorial positions.

The importance of various areas of technical knowledge, and the difficulty that many women experience, is probably best summed up by a male assistant editor, who said:

Roger Smith

> Getting to know all the little things about how to write, how a paper works, what different people's jobs involve, technical terms etc., they're all *vital* if you want, firstly, to get accepted, and secondly, to get on. You'll never believe this, but we had this girl in the office — been here for nearly two years and she still thought that 'going on the stone'[10] meant going out for a piss.

Another area which can perhaps be broadly defined as 'technical' is knowledge of where to go to for information. This kind of knowledge is obviously affected by the kind of assignments women get, and it has previously been argued that these tend to be rather narrow. Not only are they rather narrow, but one of the normative patterns of interviewing on Fleet Street — in the pub — appears again to be a learning situation from which women do not derive as much as they could. Most felt uncomfortable in this situation, and were conscious of exclusion. Consequently, there was often very little *learning* from colleagues, or from news sources.

The night-shift is an area that I have previously described as a 'key learning situation' — that this is so is clear from the responses of men, who described this as an area where they had picked up not just technical, but other kinds of knowledge as well. Often on dailies it is during the evening shift that the subs are most in evidence and do a great deal of their work. One girl who had managed to break through the informal prohibition on night work said:

> I've learnt more here in six weeks than I did in two years of working days. It's at night when most of the subs are around, and so you have a chance to get to know them, and exactly what it is that they do. Also, this is the time when the power hierarchy begins to manifest itself, and you see how and why decisions are made. It's an exciting and interesting situation to be in.

It is obviously not being argued that women do not pick up any technical knowledge of journalism — if they did not, then they would never make it to Fleet Street at all, except perhaps as women's page writers. What is being suggested is that they pick it up far more slowly, and less completely, than men, because the major area in which this information is picked up is in experience of hard news, which they seldom get. As a consequence of less complete knowledge (both technical and the other kinds to be discussed), their chances of becoming a news-specialist or roving reporter — the ambition of most men — are far less. They are more likely to be directed towards either a job on the women's pages, or in features. In this latter department, although their work situation is better, and their status situation generally acknowledged as being a little higher than news, it can also effectively be a dead-end. There are few editorial jobs available, and these are unlikely to go to women, and there is very little chance of a change-over to becoming a news specialist. Most of the men there have aspirations to go into the broadcasting media, and many do so. But these are notoriously difficult fields for women to enter (Fogarty et al., 1971a).

Normative knowledge

Besides formal technical qualifications being demanded for occupational statuses within journalism, auxiliary qualifications also develop in the expectations of colleagues and superiors. As Hughes (1958: 106) has put it: 'They become, in fact, the basis of the colleague-group's definition of its common interests, of its informal code, and of selection of those who become the inner fraternity.' Insofar as journalism is concerned, one of the major auxiliary qualifications would seem to be a knowledge of, and adherence to certain informal norms of behaviour and attitude. These attitudes and behaviour patterns are not necessarily those which would endear them to a public which already regards their trustworthiness as rather low.

That journalism has for some time been attempting to improve its image is testified to by the relatively recent formation of the N.C.T.J. and the Press Council. Leaflets and career information produced by the N.U.J. strive to project an image of the occupation in very professional terms — a picture of integrity and public service — and the journalist's code of professional conduct contains some basic attempts at an ethical code. All these policies and practices of the union would, however, appear to be more of a front designed to project a desirable 'public relations' image of journalism to the community and would-be neophytes, rather than any serious, or even possible, attempt to 'professionalize' the occupation.

The N.U.J. 'code of professional conduct', already referred to, contains a number of directions concerning what practices are permissible for getting information; how one should behave towards fellow practitioners in a variety of situations; and how the public interest can best be protected by journalists. With the belief that these elements were included because the areas under consideration were seen by those who are striving to make journalism more professional as in need of some reform, I wondered whether there were 'normative' practices which were in direct contravention to the code of conduct, and, if this were so, whether women as a whole were party to these normative practices. Consequently a number of statements from the code of conduct were extracted and male and female journalists were asked to describe their *own* behaviour in these

Roger Smith

areas, and also their perception of the behaviour of journalists as a whole, and to discuss the points generally.

A sketch of the responses of men and women to a selection of the statements used follows:

(A) 'News, pictures and documents should be acquired by honest methods only.' The immediate response of men to this varied between a wry grin and falling about all over the news-room. Most were quick to point out that 'it all depends what you mean by honest'. Women did not, in the main, recognise the gross ambiguity of the language, and believed that honest methods were widely used.

The reported behaviour of most of the men can be summed up in one word — trickery. A senior man said: 'Many men journalists tend to act as if each assignment were an episode of Z cars — it's all very raffish — makes good chat in the pub later.'

And from a woman:

> Most newsmen will never do things straight. One story I had to do was on a woman in hospital who'd been involved in a very nasty assault case. The gang (i.e. the male journalists) all turned up in a variety of what they thought were ingenious disguises, and were promptly thrown out on their ear. I went to the Hospital Secretary, and politely asked for an interview. He was so taken aback that he gave his permission and so I got an exclusive. When I got back to the office the newseditor asked me how I'd got the story, and was furious when I told him. The fact that I'd got an exclusive didn't seem to impress him at all, because he thought that I'd not played the game in the normal tricky way. But I haven't been trained in trickery, so I have to do things straight.

On the whole, male journalists were far more worldly in their interpretation of this point, and assured me that varying degrees of 'dishonesty' were normal practice. The women were far less certain that this was at all desirable, and with the exception of those who had had extensive newsdesk experience, less aware of it. Even when they *were* aware of it, as the above quote tends to indicate, they were not sophisticated to the techniques.

(B) 'Whether for publication or suppression, the acceptance of a bribe is one of the gravest professional offences.' Hardly surprisingly, no one has so far admitted to accepting a monetary bribe. But many of the men were aware of other journalists who they knew had accepted bribes, or who they strongly suspected of having done so.

Only two of the women could quote such a case.

Again, the wording of the statement is rather ambiguous — a facility

Sex and occupational role on Fleet Street

trip or even a meal could perhaps be interpreted as a bribe, and practically *all* respondents, regardless of sex, would accept these. The atypical respondent was a woman.

(C) 'It is unprofessional conduct to exploit the labour of another journalist by plagiarism.' Here again there appeared to be a difference in the responses of men and women. Men were more prone to plagiarise, although they did not 'like the practice referred to by this name. An assistant editor said:

> We *all* do it, all the time — although of course we wouldn't like it to be called plagiarism. If you haven't got all the facts on a story and one of your competitors has, then by the time the next edition comes out, you'll have 'borrowed' it. Perfectly standard practice.

Women tended to be far less prone to 'borrowing', mainly because they were afraid of being found out. The fact that it is 'perfectly standard practice' does not appear to have filtered through to the majority of them, although again the women with an extensive background in hard news were a little more worldly and less worried about being caught — presumably because they knew that the sanctions would be minimal.

(D) 'A spirit of willingness to help other members should be encouraged at all times.' Both groups saw their own behaviour as consonant with this, and the men saw it as characteristic of journalists as a whole. The women, as might be expected from material that has already been dealt with, had their reservations. What appears to be the more likely informal norm is that there is a spirit of willingness to help those who already subscribe to the other informal patterns of behaviour. Women as a whole said that they had had some difficulty in gaining membership to informal groups, the degree of difficulty depending largely on the nature of the group. It was the most difficult in the male-dominated specialisms. One woman, the first in a highly prestigious specialism, reported that she was totally ignored by every other specialist in the field, except for senior men from her own paper, for the first vital weeks when she was desperately trying to find her feet and prove that a woman was capable of the job she was doing. Moreover, 'colleagues' and news-sources between them managed to reduce her to public tears by her third day. Another, in a less prestigious specialism, explained that she did not collaborate with anyone 'because I am the only woman in my field' — a remark which would indicate how salient her mere sex was to her work-role even in her own eyes.

Even when women seem to be accepted into informal information-sharing groups, a number of instances of 'ratting' were evident:

> Last year when I was over in X covering the Y story, I had been working with this group of guys for about four days, and had given

> them every bit of information I got. Then they went and gave me — quite deliberately — the wrong time for an interview that had been fixed up, so I missed it.

This kind of story was never told by a man — indeed, many gave instances of where they had actually sent copy through for a (male) colleague who was in some way indisposed.

Such male clannishness is reported also by Fogarty *et al.* (1971a: 195) in their study of the BBC. A senior male is quoted as saying:

> I think we were a very male society. We all worked very closely with one another. We had an unspoken sense of male cameradarie — a kind of *lingua franca* — a television shorthand if you like. There was a high-powered woman there, but she didn't have it. She didn't speak our language.

The authors believe that not only do women, because of this strong male subculture, find it difficult to handle formal situations, but also difficult to break into informal groups (Fogarty *et al.*, 1971a: 196). As a result of this, their chances of advancement are much hindered. I would not typify the whole of Fleet Street as a male subculture, but the *key learning areas* remain strong male preserves, where the development of such subcultures is most facilitated, and this is the reason masculine supremacy is maintained.

Responses to the first three of the four statements I have used for this paper would appear to validate the idea that there is a differential distribution of normative knowledge of the practice of journalism; responses to the fourth to emphasise how that knowledge is acquired, and to whom it is given.

It must be stressed that whilst broad sex differences existed in the knowledge of what is approved, or at least permissible, behaviour, there are differences in the responses of women. Those whose replies were closer to the men's, were those who had been in one or more of the crucial learning situations. The most primary of these tends to be extensive hard news experience, which appears to give easier access to bar-room chat as 'one of the boys', but subbing also seems to contribute to exposure to normative behaviour and knowledge. However, those women interviewed who have experience in these highly masculine areas tend to have got this experience for very idiosyncratic reasons — a common one being that they began in journalism at the end of, or just after, the war, when there was a great manpower shortage, and thus they were given jobs which would normally have been the province of males.

Folk knowledge

Anyone who has ever read a book about Fleet Street by a journalist must have been immediately struck by the wealth of anecdotes about the Street that are included. Journalists would seem to revel in stories about drunks and eccentrics who used to inhabit the place. For the most part such characters are gone — it was put to me, rather wistfully, by an assistant editor, that newspapers can no longer afford to indulge themselves in employing amusing alcoholics. Since this folk-history seemed to be an elemental part of the mystique of national journalism, an attempt was made to discover whether such knowledge is differentially distributed, how it is passed on and what its importance and functions are.

Quite obviously, personal knowledge of Swaffer and the rest of the most famous characters is confined to only a few of the oldest men still left on the Street. However, each paper tends to have its own office folklore, of a little more recent origin, but still, I am assured by many people, beyond the personal recollection of anyone under 35. This folklore does, however, appear to be passed down like legend within the pub-culture. The younger men had considerably more knowledge of the exploits of all the great characters. To the women they were merely names, or completely unheard of.

Insofar as the independent importance of this knowledge is concerned, this is difficult to assess. But since this tends to be one of the common topics of conversation in after-work gatherings, it would tend to *consolidate* informal groups, membership of which has been shown as important in gathering other kinds of requisite knowledge. Moreover, since anecdotes are generally related by the older members of staff, who are also likely to be more senior, a common ground for casual conversation will exist between them and the junior men. And in fact men did have far more outside work contact with senior members of staff than women did, and reported easier relations with them. Importantly, the telling of tales of con-men, villains and drunks by someone of greater age or seniority would tend to give reinforcement, and perhaps the impression of tacit approval, of specific patterns of behaviour.

Apart from folk-history knowledge, current folk-knowledge — in the form of shop-talk and gossip - is understandably a major topic of pub conversation. It was generally believed that men were given far more opportunity for indulging in internal politicking as a result of the socializing, the drinking in the right pubs and clubs and the easy social contact they tend to have with one another. This again will militate against the advancement of women. A good knowledge of internal politics, the rise and fall of various individuals and their 'empires', and the existence, or possible existence, of vacancies, is of extreme importance in an occupation

Roger Smith

like journalism, with its uncertain career structure, and especially with the insecurity produced by the current parlous financial state of the national newspapers. The traditional maleness of Fleet Street pubs has served to keep women on the periphery of an important area of learning.

Conclusions

Several issues arise from this research which point to possible changes in the structure and practice of journalism which could be seen as contributing towards greater sexual equality in that occupation. The situation of women on Fleet Street has probably improved in recent years, but not enough to satisfy the majority of women who are now there. The growth of the 'Women in Media' group, which contains a large number of journalists, and the formation of the N.U.J. Committee on Equality, testify to the general unrest. It has been argued in this paper that sexual differentiation is maintained by the relative exclusion of women from certain key learning areas. Thus, if the position of women is to be improved, these areas must be forced open. It is accepted that employers cannot force informal groups to admit women, but they *can* ensure that they are allowed experience in hard news, sub-editing, and on the night-shift; and the N.U.J. *can* exert such pressure as it has to encourage employers to take on women in the first place.

Training could no doubt be improved if the N.C.T.J. was able to work much more closely with employing papers. Perhaps a particular individual on each paper employing trainees could be given official responsibility for ensuring that *all* trainees are given full opportunity for using and developing the knowledge and techniques which are imparted to them on block-release courses.

The mandatory advertisement of all vacancies may be seen to improve the opportunities of women, who are often cut off from informal grapevines. If such advertisements contain no reference to the desired sex of applicants, then perhaps more women will be persuaded to apply for jobs that at present they dismiss as male preserves.

In addition to the above points, which refer explicitly to journalism, a number of more general issues relating to the equalisation of occupational opportunity for women should be mentioned. Most sets of recommendations as to how to improve the occupational position of women are 'catch-all' suggestions, exhaustively detailing all those areas of social experience which contribute towards the impairment of female potential (early socialization, school, vocational advice, occupational socialization and training, marriage and child-raising, etc.), and concluding that change is needed in all (Fogarty *et al.*, 1971b; Griffin, 1973). To say that massive social change is necessary is a truism, and not especially helpful in that the particular points at which consciously directed social change might be most fruitful are not pinpointed. This is a reflection not on the technical expertise of the authors, but on the unwillingness of professional sociologists to commit themselves to longitudinal research programmes, which would seem more likely than cross-sectional studies to identify the most crucial variables in the complex process of female educational and vocational development. But, even given our present state of ignorance about the key variables in the developmental process, it would seem desirable to put sociologically-informed stress upon particular areas where the lever of change might be most effective. To this author the prime concern lies with the occupational structure. Women who enter occupations hitherto defined as masculine, and women who attain prestigious positions in any occupation, can serve a number of important functions: as highly significant role models for younger females; as potential sponsors and informal teachers for entrants to the occupation; and as agents for modifying the consciousness of male practitioners in particular and the wider population in general. Moreover, I do not share the optimism of those researchers (Fogarty *et al.*, 1971b; Epstein, 1971) who see technological change and the increased division of labour as in themselves leading to an improvement of women's occupational position, because of the new specialisms which will be thrown up and which will have no history of sex-typing. Historical evidence demonstrates that hierarchical positions of power and prestige within newly-developed specialisms will rapidly become the province of men (Gross, 1968; Simpson and Simpson, 1969; Brager and Michael, 1969; Sathyamurthy, 1974), and women may well be relegated once again to the 'dirty work', low prestige areas.

In addition to the need for more longitudinal research already advocated, there are more specific sociological concerns which can be taken up once a number of conceptual issues are clarified. The recent development of the 'sociology of women' as a sub-discipline has suffered a theoretical drawback which stems largely from the personnel who have entered the field. Many of them have tended to be 'family' sociologists with a predisposition to see the woman first and foremost as a 'member of a family'. Whilst nobody could argue that the effects of such a group membership are irrelevant, there is a danger that all explanations of female occupational disadvantage and under-achievement will be posed entirely in terms of the effects either of the family of origin ('parental influence') or of procreation ('domestic responsibilities'). Hence the tradition of the 'women's two roles' approach which dominates the literature on the sociology of women's work, and the concentration on the latent, rather than manifest, roles of women in the workplace. This leads us away from the examination of *specific and investigable* power structures which

Roger Smith

women have to contend with in the sphere of work, to intellectual panaceas like 'patriarchal society'.

What is required is an approach more informed by organization theory and the sociology of occupations. Given such a fusion, we may begin a more valid investigation of the interrelationships between female participation and organizational form. Existing research has seen the former as determinant of the latter — bureaucratization and rigid hierarchy being the results of female entry into an occupation (Simpson and Simpson, 1969) — rather than examining the ways in which the form itself affects modes of participation and orientations to work. Linked with this, we need to know *what kinds* of organization and career structures influence the formation of male subcultures and occupational communities, and thus affect the career chances of women. We must not assume that women who have dropped out of particular occupations have done so for 'family' reasons; such women constitute a pool of extremely important potential informants who have been almost totally neglected in research. Finally, studies aimed at locating the major 'gate-keepers' in particular occupations — those in positions where they can most effectively block the entry or progress of women — may, with information derived from studies of the kind advocated above, help to remove some of the barriers still preventing women's occupational equality.

Notes

1. There is considerable antagonism towards graduates among the overwhelmingly non-graduate newspaper staffs, and of those respondents interviewed who did possess a degree, practically all of them reported experiencing hostility directed towards them.
2. I have used this term to denote *newsgathering* journalists — those members of a news organization whose task it is to go out and find the news, contact news sources and then write up the story. The material they provide is then fed back to the editorial staff, or *news-processors*, who determine which stories warrant publication, in what form and where in the paper they should be placed. They may also reconstruct stories completely if this is seen as necessary.
3. If a story provided by a general reporter is judged to be meritorious, a by-line is given as a reward — the author's name appears in print with the story. For feature writers and news specialists a by-line is almost automatic.
4. Certain sections of the interview schedule did not apply to the men.
5. The current sensitivity of males to possible accusations of sex

discrimination in journalism has led to varying degrees of suspicion and hostility directed towards me when it was discovered that I was interviewing female, as well as male, respondents. Similar suspicion was expressed by a high-ranking N.U.J. official, who greeted my enquiry as to whether any sex-split statistics were available with preliminary manoeuvres to have me removed from his office, amid cries that 'a journalist is a journalist is a journalist.'

6. The paper for which I have a breakdown has only 11 women out of a total staff of just over 200.

7. Calculated from figures given on page 32 of the N.U.J. *Annual Report for 1973-4*.

8. There are a far higher number of female sub-editors on the women's pages, but they do not wield anything approaching the power that news subs have.

9. One story may be illuminating. A senior woman on one paper told me that she was fed up with getting letters from a feminist organization telling her that her newspaper discriminated against women reporters, so she went to the man responsible for hiring to ask him about it. He said the explanation was simple — no women ever applied. Sure enough, when they went through two years of files, there was not a single application from a woman. If pushed, no doubt one could come up with one or two banal explanations for this social phenomenon. Fortunately, however, this is not necessary, since it is not true. Some weeks previously I had interviewed a woman reporter on the same paper, who said: 'There was a vacancy in the news-room recently, and a very efficient woman I know from another national applied for it, but of course a man got the job.' So where was her application in the files?

10. Common trade argot which refers to the practice of one of the editorial staff going to the printing department to check that there are no mistakes in the layout and content of the printing plates.

5 Emily Hope, Mary Kennedy and Anne de Winter

Homeworkers in North London

Many thousands of women in Britain today are in paid employment as homeworkers, but very little is known about them. This paper reports the findings of a study of some women homeworkers in North London which was carried out in 1972 and briefly reviews some of the information available about homeworking generally.

This study represents the work and interests of a group of women who came together as a Women's Liberation group and concentrated on an investigation into the conditions and situations of women doing paid work at home.[1] The group was based in an area of North London where there is a conspicuous market for homeworkers, mainly in the garment industry. The subject was of special interest to the group because it was thought that homework exploited and reinforced particular aspects of the woman's situation in our society, which are indicative of her oppression, namely: isolation and the tie to the home while looking after young children, and low expectations and lack of opportunity in relation to the job market.

Apart from the Liberal Party's study of homeworkers in the lace industry in Nottingham (1972) and a few Government reports (N.P.B.I., 1969; C.I.R., 1973; C.I.R., 1974)[2] we found very little information about the present situation of homeworkers. We decided to carry out some empirical research to add to the literature on homeworking, to find out to what extent our own assumptions about women homeworkers were borne out by facts and to draw the attention of researchers and policy makers alike to this almost totally ignored section of the work force, comprised predominantly of women.

Very broadly defined, *a homeworker is a person who is employed directly by a firm or by an intermediary or agent of a firm to carry out work in his or her own home, not directly under the control or management of that employer.*

While the term 'outworker' is sometimes used to refer to a person who does paid work at home, the term has not been used in this study because its usage is open to misinterpretation. Employers appear to use the term 'outworker' to refer to an employee who does not work within his factories or offices and for whom, by implication, he is not responsible. Trade unions normally use the term 'outworker' to refer to the middle men or women who act often as subcontractors to the employers and who themselves might contact, employ and pay the homeworkers. In these circumstances the outworkers, as sub-contractors, would be paid by the employer for each garment or item completed by the homeworker. In some cases the outworkers may occupy the same premises as the firm giving out the work but remain completely independent of that firm.

The homeworkers we discuss in this paper are involved in manufacturing of one sort or another and are paid on a piece-rate basis. The women we interviewed were doing paid work at home for small local factories and employers, with the majority machining clothing for the chain stores or making other things connected with the clothing industry — such as hats, belts, ties and button holes. Although our sample, due to the locality, revealed this predominant connection with the garment trade, the type of homeworker whose situation we were interested in would characteristically be working at one or another of a variety of different kinds of piecework production; for example, packing crackers, stuffing toys, pasting jewellery, knitting, crocheting, making hooks and eyes, carding buttons and thread, wiring batteries or making and mending netting. Equally, a homeworker might do work such as copy-typing, addressing or stuffing envelopes.

The work situation of a childminder, who in one sense is certainly a homeworker, would not satisfy our definition in that the employers are individuals rather than industrial or commercial firms. We would expect to find, however, that childminders are in many ways like the homeworkers we discuss and indeed for many women childminding may be selected as an alternative to homeworking.

We also exclude from our category of homeworkers men and women who are free-lance[3] operatives who choose to work at home — architects, artists, writers or business consultants, for example. However those working in professional or semi-professional occupations who *must* work at home because they are 'housebound' (predominantly married women) will suffer many of the disabilities of homeworkers. They may, to some extent, be able to get more varied and more remunerative work than our less mobile, less educated and less confident homeworkers. It should not be forgotten, though, that many homeworkers are skilled and experienced in their different trades.

Homeworkers in North London

In this section we discuss the methods and findings of our study of

Emily Hope, Mary Kennedy and Anne de Winter

homeworkers. We have included some case material about one of the homeworkers we interviewed, whom we came to know, in order to illustrate the kind of woman and the kind of domestic and working situation we found in the course of our investigations.

Our findings are based on information gathered from interviews with 21 women. Initially, contacts with homeworkers were made through play groups, neighbours and friends known to the women who carried out the study. Ten interviews were obtained through these personal contacts. In the text we refer to these homeworkers as *Sample A*. A further eleven interviews were obtained from a systematic house-to-house survey which was carried out in a neighbourhood known to the interviewers and where it was thought that many women would be doing homework for the small local firms and factories dotted in and around the immediate area. We refer to these eleven interviews as *Sample B*.[4]

The house-to-house survey was carried out over a period of 2½ months from May to mid-August 1972. A total of 216 houses in two parallel roads were canvassed for homeworkers.[5] One of these houses was used as a cushion factory employing both indoor workers and homeworkers to do machine sewing and a number of the women who were interviewed had worked or were working for this firm.[6]

Houses were canvassed for homeworkers at times when husbands were likely to be out, either in the mid-morning or mid-afternoon. It was felt that the husband's presence would inhibit women from talking freely and would make it more difficult to establish rapport with them. The questions could also have been perceived as a threat to a man's image as provider. We told whoever answered the door that we were from a group of local women doing a survey on work done at home and that we wanted to find women doing homework who might be willing to talk to us. If asked what we would do with the information, we explained that we might write a pamphlet based on what women told us about homework. We anticipated fears that we were representatives of officialdom and at the outset made it clear that we were not from the Inland Revenue, Social Security or the local council. When there was no response at the time of the first call, a house was visited a second time.

The interviews were based on a list of twenty-three questions about what sort of work they did, the amount done each week, regularity of work, who provided equipment, experience needed and training given, feelings about their work, help from relatives, contacts with other homeworkers and details of how they were paid. The questions were studied in advance and a questionnaire was not used directly in the course of interviewing.

We received responses at 164 of the 216 houses canvassed but in fact made contact with many more households as so many of the houses were in multi-occupation. We know that there were many more homeworkers in the houses than were willing to talk with us. In addition to the eleven who agreed to be interviewed, we found another ten homeworkers who refused to be interviewed and suspected another eleven homeworkers[7]. We suggest that at least thirty-two of the women living in the 164 houses where contact was made were doing homework.

Three specific aspects of the homeworker's situation as we observed it might explain the refusal or reluctance to be interviewed or to admit to doing homework. First, we could have been seen as coming to investigate undeclared earnings (undeclared to the tax authorities, or to prevent loss of welfare benefits). Secondly, there is the issue of the illegal use of premises. Much of the accommodation was rented and rent contracts commonly contain clauses forbidding the use of the premises for business purposes. This was explicitly given as a reason for refusal by the son of one of the interviewees and another woman's husband would not allow his wife to be interviewed, hinting at the fact that it was illegal for the premises to be used for homeworking. Thirdly, the work situation of homeworkers is unstable and the demand for work greater than the supply. Given this situation, questions about the work could have been viewed as threatening to job security.[8] Finally, some refusals were from women who did not speak good English.

A case history of a homeworker

Jean works in her bedroom. She machines pillowticks while watching the clock. She is pleased because she can make twenty-one in 1 hour and soon she hopes to be quick enough to make twenty-four. She finds it difficult to build up speed, though, because she is always being interrupted by the demands of her family. Jean has four children of school age. Her husband, John, works in a shoe factory and with 5 hours overtime he brings home £27 a week, not enough to support a family.

They live on the first floor of a large old house, next to the underground station. There is one bedroom for the whole family. It is divided in two with a hardboard wall — the parents in one half and the four children in bunk beds in the other half. The sitting room has the curtains drawn, there is some furniture and a television set and the washing, hanging up to dry. The kitchen looks out over a short garden that Jean longs to use and over a steep bank is the railway line. There is no bathroom. The lavatory is next to the kitchen and is used by fifteen people and cleaned by Jean because no one else will do it.

Jean and her family are sitting tenants and do not yet qualify for a

Emily Hope, Mary Kennedy and Anne de Winter

Council flat. They are trying to manage to buy the house they are living in jointly with Jean's relatives. Otherwise they will have to leave the area.

When the landlord first offered them the house Jean thought she ought to earn some money to help with moving, repairs and eventually the mortgage. She bought an industrial sewing machine on hire purchase for £114 although she knew little about sewing. Her friend, who is an experienced machinist, showed her how to machine a cushion cover like the ones she was making for the local cushion factory. It took Jean 3 weeks to summon up the courage to go down the road to the factory:

> I was dead scared of knocking on that door. I mean it's only a factory and they can't hurt you. I told the man I'd got this industrial machine and I said I was very experienced and he didn't test me. He gave me five cushions with fringes.

When Jean returned the cushion covers 3 days later, he wasn't very pleased and said she would need to get a zip-foot attachment, but that would have cost her £1.

Jean then decided to go to local evening classes in dressmaking to improve her sewing. She went to a few classes and then stopped because she did not find them much help. Then she found a drycleaners which had a skirt factory at the back. She was told she could have as much work as she wanted. They did not seem to be very concerned about the standard of sewing. The work consisted of making a whole skirt except for finishing off the hem. At the first attempt she took a whole evening to make two skirts; the next day she made three skirts in 'one or two hours.' For each skirt she was paid 12½p.

A month later she saw an advertisement in the local paper for machining pillow-ticks at home. She went to the factory, was tested and given a dozen ticks to make on trial. She was paid for this and was then given more work. At first she could only make twelve ticks an hour. When she is working at speed she can make a pillow tick in 2½ minutes. She is paid 2p for each tick. In order to make a pack of three dozen she machines for a minimum of 1½ hours and is paid 72p. Often it takes her 2 hours to earn the 72p, if she slows down or is interrupted. She earns roughly between 36p and 54p an hour if only the machining time is taken into account.

After the ticks have been machined they have to be turned inside out, the corners poked out, then packed and labelled with Jean's name in case of any complaint. This work is always done by John in the evenings and takes a considerable amount of time.

Jean earns between £9 and £10 a week for which she does between 19½ and 28 hours machining, depending on how fast she is working. This does not take into account John's contribution to the work nor her overheads (electric fire, machine attachments and all the hidden overheads such as insurance, sick pay, lighting, rent, rates, etc.). In reality she might be earning less than half of what she appears to earn, which would amount to less than between 18p and 27p an hour. She had not realized how the factory was saving at her expense.

Jean has a long working day, which begins before 7 a.m. and ends usually after midnight. She does her sewing in whatever time she can manage during the day between cooking, cleaning, collecting children, etc., and again in the evenings. Three afternoons a week she works at a local pre-school play group and earns £1.25 for a 3-hour session, but Jean believes she is earning more money making pillow-ticks.[9]

Findings

(a) **Characteristics of women homeworkers** In all we interviewed twenty-one women who were or had been homeworkers. Three of these were much older and had done homework some time ago so that tables 5.1 – 5.3 refer to eighteen women who were currently or had recently been homeworkers.

The sample was ethnically diverse and included women who were born in the West Indies, West Africa, Southern Europe and Cyprus as well as in England and Ireland. This was expected of course from our knowledge of the area. The remainder of the table brings out the striking similarities of our women's marriage and family position.

Most of the women were at the same stage of the family cycle. More women were aged below 40 (11 out of 18) than above and with two exceptions our women were all married and living with their husbands. One of the exceptions had an adult working son living at home. Only one woman did not have children living at home, while most had more children living at home than the national average. These children, however, were not by any means all under school age. Nine out of eighteen women did have children under school age, but this leaves several women whose children were all at school and therefore out of the home for at least part of the day.

We had not expected this degree of uniformity in the information about marriage and children. We were surprised to find no one-parent families. Many women in this position are of course already subject to prying by Social Security officers and they may well not have wished to speak to us. The absence of women without other full-time earners in the household probably reflects the low wages they get as homeworkers. The money to be earned from homeworking does not constitute any kind of living wage. In general, the uniform family position strongly suggests that

Emily Hope, Mary Kennedy and Anne de Winter

Table 5.1 Characteristics of the sample

Ethnic origin		Women's age		Marital status	
English	7	Under 20	0	Unmarried	0
West Indian	2	20–29	3	Married	15
Nigerian	2	30–39	8	Divorced/	
Irish	2	40–49	2	Separated	1
Cypriot	1	50–59	2	Widowed	1
Spanish	1	Over 60	1	Don't know	1
Italian	1	Don't know	2		
Guyanese	1			Total	18
Don't know	1	Total	18		
Total	18				

Total no. of children at home		Age range of children at home	
None	1	All under 5	1
One	1	Under 5 and under 16	8
Two	5	All over 5 but under 16	4
Three	4	All over 16	2
Four	2	Don't know	2
Five	3		
Don't know	2	Total	18
Total	18		

homework is not a chosen occupation for those who are relatively free of family responsibilities, but is instead a form of work which is temporary and occurs at a particular stage in the family cycle.

(b) **Income and rates of pay** A primary object of our study was to gain information about the 'economics' of homework from the women homeworkers' point of view. In particular we were interested in the rates of pay and the contribution homework makes to the family income. The information we gained about the income of homeworkers in the case of fourteen out of eighteen of the women we interviewed is summarized in Table 2. In general our figures are roughly comparable with figures given for homeworkers' incomes elsewhere.[10]

Table 5.2   Weekly earnings[11]

Weekly earnings	Sample A	Sample B	Total
Less than 2.50	1	1	2
£2.50–£4.99	3	2	5
£5.00–£7.49	2	2	4
£7.50–£9.99	2	–	2
£10 or over	–	1	1
No data	2	2	4
Total	10	8	18

Out of the fourteen women for whom we have data, eleven had weekly incomes from homeworking below £7.50, with seven of these having incomes below £5.00. The lowest weekly income was £1 and the highest was £11.50. These figures are obviously very low, even for women's work which is badly paid everywhere.

The demand for homework in the area we studied seemed high. Several women whom we met who were not employed as homeworkers asked us if we could get them work.[12] At least half the homeworkers mentioned difficulty in getting enough work or regular work. One woman said:

You just do as much as you can; [there's] no minimum, but if you aren't quick enough you might lose your job. They return badly sewn stuff.

Because she had been unable to get enough cushions, this woman had been forced to plunge into much more skilled work, making dresses and blazers, which she was finding difficult to cope with. The women who appeared to be able to get enough work and are therefore at the top range of our earnings scale were women who had had previous experience in factories.

The homeworkers were not trained by their employers. Most of the work was sewing or machining in connection with the clothing industry. Of the twelve women in our sample who did this kind of work, five had worked in factories as machinists before, where they had had some kind of on-the-job training. Only one woman, however, mentioned a proper training course. Of the remaining seven, three mentioned that they had learned machine sewing skills at home, either as part of growing up or when they had had children. Even the highly skilled workers were prevented from doing the more skilled work at home because the very

Emily Hope, Mary Kennedy and Anne de Winter

complexity of the work would have demanded more space than could be found.

The absence of training for women without previous experience and the restrictions on the amount of work they can obtain, help to explain why weekly earnings are low. We were most interested, however, in the amount of time that was needed to make these small sums. It proved very difficult to work out an hourly rate for homeworkers. The calculations we were able to make are shown in Table 5.3, but even here some of the figures are approximate.

In order to calculate an hourly rate one needs to know the piece-rate and the length of time needed to produce each item. This would appear to be simple enough information to gather, but very few homeworkers discussed their work in these terms. Where an hourly rate was calculated, more often than not it had to be derived. Typically, a woman could state how much she earned per week and how much she received per item, i.e. the piece-rate, but homeworkers were often decidedly vague about how much time they worked each day or each week. A woman might say she spent a morning or an evening on homework, but exactly how many hours this meant more often than not had to be assumed.[13]

Where it was possible, an hourly rate was calculated using the weekly earning figures, which were considered the most reliable, together with the number of items made, the total time worked and the piece-rate. In some cases, where all the relevant data were available it was found that two totally different rates per hour could be calculated: the hourly rate based on the piece-rate and time taken to make each item, and the hourly rate based on the total number of hours worked and the weekly income figures.[14]

Table 5.3 Estimated hourly rate for seven homeworkers

	Weekly rate	Hourly rate	Average number of hours worked per week
Sample A	£9.50	82p	12
	£7.90	45p	17½
	£3.00	13p	23
Sample B	£6.50	30p	16½
	£4.50	24p	18
	£3.50	20p	17½
	£11.50	£1	10

The difficulty of calculating an hourly rate for the homework in itself suggested some peculiarities of the homeworkers' attitudes to their work and earnings. These observations are perhaps a more significant outcome of our research than the collection of factual data about homeworkers' rates of pay.

The homeworkers did not appear to consider their income in relation to the time it took them to do the work nor in terms of the market value of their skills.[15] The motivation to do homework is primarily and perhaps only to earn money. Homeworking offers no fringe benefits such as social contact with fellow workers or a change of environment. Most of the homeworkers commented on the monotony of the work they were doing. Yet they evaluated their earnings in terms of the total amount earned each week with apparently little or no consideration for the number of hours worked to earn it.

Of the women we interviewed, most expressed dissatisfaction with the rates of pay. There was a general awareness that the rates of pay were low and that factory rates were better, but only some women saw themselves as being exploited. Others wanted to do yet more homework to increase their earnings and others looked ahead to a time when they would be able to go out to work and obtain better pay. None of the women saw any alternative to accepting the low rates of pay. As far as homework was concerned they accepted the *status quo*. The women competed for what employment opportunities there were for homeworkers, with no prospect or expectation of increased rates of pay. One woman we talked to, who pasted up belts, had stopped the work in 1962 and started again in 1971 at exactly the same rate of pay (8½p per dozen).[16]

Our findings indicate that the earnings of homeworkers are vital to their family incomes. In one case the homeworker's income was used to pay off a mortgage and in another case to redecorate the house. But most of the homeworkers used their earnings to make ends meet, mainly to buy food and children's clothing. Women with four or more children were under particular pressure to supplement the husband's income. In no instance did homeworkers indicate that their money was spent on luxuries or on themselves.[17]

While the homeworker's earnings might be vital to the family income, they can never provide more than a supplementary income whether the primary income is from the husband's employment, social security benefits or an old age pension. The rates of pay are too low to allow these women to make a 'living wage'.[18]

The homeworkers we interviewed did not receive sickness benefits, accident insurance, pension schemes or paid holidays. As far as we know this is generally true of all homeworkers. Furthermore, the homeworkers we surveyed who did machine sewing supplied their own machines and

Emily Hope, Mary Kennedy and Anne de Winter

needles and were not compensated for machine repairs nor for their expenses incurred while doing the homework; for example, the cost of electricity. Some homeworkers mentioned the fact that they did not pay National Insurance stamps as a positive aspect of homework.[19] At the same time they seemed unaware of their overheads when thinking about their earnings.

The advised calculation of overheads for a professional freelance graphic designer, who is one of the authors, provides a striking contrast to the situation of the homeworkers. She bases her fees on an hourly rate which includes the cost of overheads (heating, lighting, rent, rates, insurance, telephone, postage, materials, and unsaleable time: public holidays, sick leave, time spent in administration and looking for work). Just over two-thirds of her hourly rate is costed for such items (see Goslett, 1971). A homeworker might not have quite such high overheads as some professional freelancers, but she could well spend a considerable amount of time collecting and delivering work and looking for it; and homeworkers are often left idle for weeks at a time by firms which expect them to take on a heavy load regularly during the rest of the year. Also some firms close for several weeks' holiday during the year, leaving the homeworkers without work or holiday pay. It would be reasonable to say that homeworkers should be paid at least twice as much as factory workers to cover their overheads.

In employing homeworkers the manufacturer avoids paying rent, rates and insurance for industrial premises, as well as insurance against accidents to the workers themselves. He does not have to provide all the facilities required by law in factories, such as heating, lighting, power, toilets, canteen, subsidized meals and industrial clothing. He does not pay for holiday leave or sickness leave or public holidays. All these items are hidden expenses to the homeworker.

Even if we excluded the whole issue of overheads, a skilled machinist who can work fast enough to earn a good hourly rate could never keep up the intense pace at which the work has to be done at home to make a reasonable weekly income. Few concentrated and uninterrupted work hours are available to a woman working at home.

(c) **Family roles** Any explanation of why it is mainly women who do homework and why they have the attitudes they do towards their work and income cannot ignore the family roles of these women. We suggest that homeworkers cannot calculate with accuracy the time spent doing homework because it is done in the home where it is likely to be interrupted by family and household responsibilities.

Homework is done in whatever odd time is available during the day between housework, shopping, cooking and looking after children, or late in the evening.[20] It is not concentrated work and the homeworker, in isolation, has no standard of productivity other than her own output, which is totally dependent on personal factors. The family and domestic routines of a homeworker's life do not appear to be organized to accommodate homework, as they would almost certainly have to be if the woman went out to work during the day. Homework is fitted around domestic duties *and not vice versa*. While it is an economic necessity for these women to work, it would seem that homeworkers are homeworkers precisely because they regard the family and domestic chores as their primary work: they are unwilling to curtail their services for their husband and children.

All the women in our sample considered housework and child-care to be their responsibility and regarded help from their husbands as a generous concession and it seemed to be a rare one. Only four of the twenty-one women we interviewed said that their husbands might help them with the housework or do the cooking or washing up so that they could carry on uninterrupted. The woman's responsibility for child-care appeared to be the single most important factor affecting their work situation.[21] The majority of the women interviewed had worked outside the home and homework was done only when the birth of children made other work impossible from their point of view. Some homeworkers, however, had not gone out to work even when their children were of school age, and two of the women we interviewed continued to do homework when their children were grown up but still living at home.[22]

In two cases women had given up doing homework for the sake of the children: one because she could not manage it with five children to look after and the other because she believed it was necessary to devote herself completely to her baby until he was at least six months old. Both of these women made their decisions in the face of financial difficulties.

Some of the homeworkers specifically commented on the disruptive effect children had on their ability to do homework. In some cases this made them take on less skilled and therefore less well-paid work than they might have done. One of the skilled machinists we interviewed said she would have derived greater satisfaction and better pay from making dresses rather than cushion covers, but that she could not take on dress-making because the children would have 'spoilt' the garments. In connection with this, it should be noted that many of these women and their families live in accommodation that is inadequate and cramped even without the trappings of homework.

Homework does enable the earning of money while at the same time permitting the care of the home and children and this is seen as a positive aspect of homework by almost all of the women in our sample. However,

Emily Hope, Mary Kennedy and Anne de Winter

the exhaustion produced by the difficulties, frustrations and sheer hard work is great.

Comments on the history and present conditions of homework.

The tradition of homework in this country, both before and since the Industrial Revolution, is a long one. For the purposes of this study the main developments can be indicated briefly within four periods.

With the emergence of the household economy in the sixteenth and seventeenth centuries and the growth of the cottage industrial system, work and family life tended to be closely interwoven. Husband, wife and children generally worked together in and around the home using some human-powered machinery to manufacture the products of pre-industrial society, such as cotton and woollen cloth, hosiery, clothing, lace, boots and shoes, rope and netting, and chains and nails. As the family was the economic unit, the members contributed to the common work process, and had a restricted, albeit a precarious, economic freedom for themselves as a group, controlled by the head of the household.

The coming of industrialization in the latter half of the eighteenth century led to the concentration of capital, men and machines in factories and the major part of the economic process moved out of the home. Homework was now beginning to be done in isolation and homeworkers became dependent on the factory employer having a surplus of work to be done when the market demand was high. This meant that homeworkers, the majority of whom were women, worked even longer hours than nineteenth century factory workers, for starvation wages, outside the existing inadequate factory legislation. Homeworkers were considered as *casual workers* or as *supplementary wage earners* who could be and were paid low wages.

Between 1885 and 1908 there was public agitation over 'sweated labour', and several reports on the sordid and unhealthy working conditions and inadequate pay of homeworkers in particular were published (Irwin, 1907; Black, 1907).[23] This, combined with pressure on Parliament, led to the establishment of the first four Trade Boards (later Wages Councils) in 1909 to watch over the chain-, lace-, and box-making trades, and sections of the clothing industry. Government inspectors were to be appointed to see that rates of pay were not below the statutory minimum. In addition, since 1911, all firms employing homeworkers have been statutorily obliged to submit lists of these workers to their local authorities to protect both the health of the homeworker and the health of those who receive their products.

But by the 1920s, although there were thirty-five Trade Boards covering half a million workers, official and public interest in the homeworkers' conditions was fading away. In 1925 a report by the Chief Inspectorate of Factories and Workshops remarked that: 'There is a consensus of opinion that homework is on the decline.' The report also considered that there is 'not much room for casual work in modern industry . . .' Since 1926 there have been no official reports in the *Ministry of Labour Gazette* (1920–1939 and 1946–1967), nor in its successor, *The Employment and Productivity Gazette* (1968–1972), dealing with homework as a separate category of industrial employment. But evidence of the continuance of homeworking within individual industries does exist, though buried, particularly in the regions where traditional types of homework have always continued — for example, the hat trade in Luton (Dony, 1942; Freeman, 1953), lace-making in Nottingham (Liberal Party 1972), chain-making at Cradley Heath and the clothing industry in the East End of London. Homework is still more prevalent than people wish to believe.

Today work done at home for a manufacturer is predominantly done by women. Because it is based on the home and therefore isolated, and done by women, the situation of the homeworker is largely unknown and ignored. It is extremely difficult to find out about homework since there are no national statistics. There is a complex and ineffective system of minimum wages, few homeworkers belong to a trade union, employers are reticent and homeworkers themselves are nervous about discussing their conditions of work publicly.

The Department of Employment (1973) maintain that there are no overall figures of the numbers actually working as homeworkers, as homeworkers do not have their own insurance cards.[24] The National Insurance officials at the Department of Social Security consider that it would be extremely unlikely that many homeworkers could or would register as self-employed as this would be an expensive matter on a regular weekly basis and one they could hardly afford out of their low earnings.

Audrey Hunt in *A Survey of Women's Employment* (1968) with a sample of 10,000 households, estimates that in 1965 3·7 per cent of women were working in their own homes. It is probable that many of these women would be doing homework as we have defined it in this study. More specifically, a report on the clothing manufacturing industries (N.B.P.I., 1969: 64) estimates that in November 1968:

> There were then some 14,000 female homeworkers and probably under a thousand male homeworkers directly employed by firms and appearing on their payrolls. We did not attempt to estimate the number of homeworkers employed by agents or intermediaries of the firms.

This figure is quite helpful since the majority of women we

Emily Hope, Mary Kennedy and Anne de Winter

interviewed were involved in working for the clothing industry. It should also be kept in mind that the position of homeworkers is individually varied as well as unexplored and, as mentioned, often still attached to specifically regional industries or traditional local trades.

In principle all homeworkers should be covered and protected by the Wages Councils appropriate to their type of work or under the care of the Wages Inspectorate. There are fifty-three Wages Councils covering some 3 million workers in this country, mainly operating where there is no other adequate machinery for the regulation of pay and conditions of work. These are statutory autonomous bodies continued or established under the Wages Council Acts of 1945 and 1959. Each Council consists of not more than three independent members and equal numbers of employers and workers in the trade or branch of the trade concerned. We found no evidence that homeworkers ever sat on their appropriate Wages Council because they were unknown to the trade union representatives and probably because they would be unwilling to lose valuable working time for which they would not be recompensed.

The Wages Council's main functions are to fix a statutory minimum wage which applies to all workers at that level in the particular trade or industry, including the homeworkers. In practice the minimum wage is normally set at a low level and is slow to react to changes in the wage structures in the rest of industry. Most homeworkers we interviewed did not know what their minimum rate of pay should be.

In addition, it is laid down that the employer should allow for any necessary expenditure by the homeworker in doing the work in the clothing industry and should keep lists of their homeworkers which should be deposited with the Public Health Department of the local District Council. The latter ruling derives from 1911 and the Factories Act of 1961 to prevent the spread of contagious diseases and to control working conditions in certain occupations. In practice we found that the homeworkers we interviewed either did not know of the regulations or were afraid to ask questions in case they might lose their jobs. The weakness of the local authorities' Public Health lists of homeworkers, if they are kept, is that they are not open to inspection by the public or by trade union officials (N.B.P.I. 1969: 64).

Generally, homeworkers are not entitled to holidays or holidays with pay from their employers with the exception of the Retail Bespoke Tailoring Industry. Homeworkers are not covered by any superannuation pension schemes operated by employers for their indoor workers. There appear to be no regulations about compensation for the homeworker in the case of accidents or sickness arising from the work situation.

None of the homeworkers interviewed belonged to a trade union, although in the clothing industry there is no bar to their membership as long as they work for a clothing firm. The trade unions see the problem as deriving from their own staff shortage and the difficulty they have in covering the factories and the indoor workers' conditions. In principle, however, they would like to see homework abolished, and either men paid higher wages so that wives do not have to work, or women working in factories. One official of the Tailors and Garment Workers' Union said, 'Homeworkers, because of the isolated and individual nature of their work, are usually unknown, uncharted and unprotected.'

Certainly at present the interests of the homeworkers are poorly represented. It ought not to be too difficult for the unions to arrange for homeworkers to be paid for their time while they sit on Wages Councils — which would then enable some women to attend such meetings. And these meetings need to be much more frequent. Currently the homeworkers are represented by male union workers who do not know and/or are not unreservedly sympathetic to their problems.

Conclusions

The information we gathered about homeworkers' attitudes to their work, together with their attitudes towards their rates of pay, contribute to building up a picture of the homeworker as a woman who sees her primary role as a mother, who has little contact with the world outside her home and neighbourhood, who has little confidence in her skill, and a low opinion of the value of her skills in relation to the market. She is a woman who works alone under the pressure of domestic responsibilities and out of financial necessity. The homeworker is a casual labourer exploited on the basis of her ascribed role as a woman/wife.

The women we discuss in this paper want and need to earn. Most of them would prefer to be working outside the home. They have chosen to do homework largely because they have accepted that their primary role is in the domestic sphere and they see no alternative form of work available to them, given the constraints imposed on them, particularly at the stage in the life-cycle when they are caring for dependent children. For these women home is an acceptable solution to an immediate and relatively temporary situation. Their acceptance of this type of work is insured by the socialization process, their lack of training and their continuous low level of expectation in relation to the job market and, very possibly, economic restraints within the household. While these homeworkers are likely to take up employment outside the home at a later stage in their life-cycle and thus at least marginally to improve their conditions of work and rates of pay, they will inevitably remain part of the secondary sector work force.

The economic and social situation of the homeworker is in effect an

Emily Hope, Mary Kennedy and Anne de Winter

extreme instance of the situation of women in general. Factories use homeworkers whenever increased production or a quick turnover is necessary. And generally, in certain sectors of the economy women comprise a reserve labour force (Gardiner, 1974). Currently the percentage of women in the workforce is high but the persistent and dominant image of women in our society is of domestic creatures. The image and the ideology emphasize women's reproductive and consumer roles and women as productive workers and wage earners remain socially invisible.

The situation of the homeworker embodies this contradiction. She is *in* the home yet she is a worker and thinks of herself as such. Homeworkers are mothers, wives and wage earners in the same place and often at the same time. This situation contributes to a low level of consciousness among homeworkers about their rights as workers in terms of pay, conditions of work and benefits. This low level of consciousness is exacerbated by the isolated nature of their work situation.

The homeworker does not have what are accepted as the basic rights and protection of workers in our society. Their low wages, lack of social insurance and protective legislation and long hours of work are in many ways typical of an earlier industrial situation. The whole problem of homeworking is compounded by the nineteenth-century character of many of the small, dispersed and labour intensive industries they tend to work in, particularly evident in the clothing industry. Employers of homeworkers cope with competition, fluctuations in product demand and the general uncertainties of their businesses by using, on a temporary basis, an available pool of skilled or semi-skilled labour. This keeps their costs down and avoids their taking risks by investing in buildings, machinery and a regular work force.

From our observations it also seems that many industries using homeworkers are operated by small employers who may often be from the same ethnic groups or have a personal or even family relationship with their outdoor employees such as is unusual or totally absent in more highly industrialized firms. This further complicates the possibilities for change (see Maher in the companion volume).

Homeworking may thus be regarded as a marginal occupation in relation to the wider economy and is often all that is available for people in a marginal position in the labour market. The homeworker is likely to be someone with a handicap; age in the case of a pensioner, a physical handicap, or (curious though it is to see it as a 'handicap') motherhood or domesticity which are disabilities for women as workers, given the lack of child care facilities and the assignment of women (and not men) to the domestic role.[25]

Notes

1. In addition to the authors, other members of the group who contributed to this collective study are: Alice de P. Abreu, Carol James, Vanessa Maher, Juliet Mitchell, Jean Radford and Ann Whitehead.

2. This last report was published after this paper was written. Its findings corroborate our own conclusions (C.I.R., 1974: 466-8).

3. Although homeworkers do not have a contract with an employer, a high degree of loyalty is expected by the factory. Unlike the freelancer who works for several firms at once, the homeworker usually stays with one factory until the work runs out. If there is a heavy load, she is expected to work harder (see also Maher's paper in the companion volume).

4. Other methods of gaining information about homeworkers were tried, namely: following up advertisements in local papers; a questionnaire to firms employing homeworkers; contacts with trade unions. These yielded little or no information. As we did not want to be identified with employers in any way, no attempt was made to contact homeworkers through employers and it is doubtful that this would have been a successful approach in in any case.

   Previous Government Reports on the clothing industry have had very small samples of homeworkers, drawn from the manufacturers' or local authority lists. Thus, the N.B.P.I. (1969) Report had sixty women (twenty in each of three areas), though the authors estimate that there were 'some 14,000 female homeworkers'; the C.I.R. (1973) Report had a sample of thirty; and the C.I.R. (1974) Report, thirty-eight – though they estimate there are over 19,300 homeworkers in this one trade (clothing) alone.

5. The area in which the house-to-house survey was carried out is mainly residential but segmented by major roads and near a business and industrial area with many small factories. The houses are large, late Victorian terraces given over to multi-occupation with many families living in overcrowded conditions. The population is predominantly working class and ethnically diverse. Just over half the inhabitants were English with less than an eighth Irish, the rest being West Indian, Cypriot, Maltese and other nationalities.

6. The factory premises of small firms typical of the area, clothing manufacturers among them, are often found above and at the back of shops or local social clubs or in terraced houses.

7. It was quite common for a woman or man to claim that no one did homework when the interviewer could see a row of identical dresses

Emily Hope, Mary Kennedy and Anne de Winter

hanging in the background or had noticed that vans came and went from the house to deliver and collect work.

8. One woman told us that the Greek women of the area thought our project was aimed at taking work from them to give it to English women. Clearly our research touched on aspects of community relations.

9. We visited Jean 15 months later. It was 4 p.m. and we met her coming down the road with a friend. 'We've got jobs in a multiple grocers', she said. 'I couldn't do enough homework and now that the youngest one's at school I've stopped doing it. I can do what hours I want so I go after they've gone in the morning and come back at 4. And the pay's good − I get £13 a week, more than I got for the pillow ticks, *and* I have the evenings free, so it's all right really.'

10. A survey of homeworkers in Basildon, Central London and Luton in 1968 indicated average weekly earnings of homeworkers to be £5 9s 6d (£5.48) (N.P.B.I., 1969: 65).

    Another survey carried out in 1972-73 into the Pin, Hook and Eye, and Snap Fastener Wages Councils (C.I.R., 1973) indicated that the rate of pay of these homeworkers had recently risen from 18½p an hour to 20½p an hour (£8.20 for a 40 hour week). In practice such homeworkers would probably work much longer hours.

11. These weekly earnings figures represent the amount the homeworkers said they earned in an average week. They are not an average earnings figure, which would have been based on more data and would have considered weeks when earnings were low or nil.

12. Our impression is that black women are more thwarted than white women in attempts to find employment. Seven women (Africans and West Indians) told us they wanted to do homework but had been unable to get any. In our sample the black women who were doing homework appear to be working for very low rates and in worse conditions than the white women.

13. Similar findings are contained in the two C.I.R. Reports (1973: 14; 1974: 47). Thus it

> proved extremely difficult to obtain earnings data either from companies or from the homeworkers. None of the homeworkers were paid by the hour. Jobs were usually priced per gross and there was never any indication of an hourly rate or of how many hours the worker should take to pack or sort a gross. Employers were therefore able only to provide an earnings figure for each homeworker without any indication of the hours worked or the amount of work done.
>
> The majority of individual homeworkers did not accurately

know their hourly earnings. However, most were able to say how long it took them to do a certain amount of work and the price they were paid for this and from our own observations of the job being done we were able to estimate approximate hourly earnings figures.

Enquiries have shown the difficulty of measuring their hourly rates, arising from the timing problems that occur in the domestic situation.

14. For example, one informant said she worked each day from 10.30 a.m. to 4 or 5 p.m.; and that she made about twenty-four dresses a week. Her piece-rates were as follows:

> 15p for a simple dress.
> 35p – 40p for a more elaborate dress with collar.
> 25p for hot pants and dress.
> 20p for hot pants with bib and straps.

She said she was a slow worker and estimated a dress took her about 50 minutes to make up. She makes about four or five per day. She reckoned to earn £4.50 a week. The discrepancies in the figures are obvious.

15. Certainly, as far as the women machinists are concerned, a low evaluation of skills is not confined to the homeworking situation. An official of the National Union of Tailors and Garment Workers told us that in her view women did not realise that machining is skilled work and that as such their rate of pay should be much higher.
It appears also that when men do 'women's work' like cooking or sewing it is classified as skilled work but when women do this same work, it is classified as unskilled or semi-skilled work. Industry exploits this situation where, for example, in some recent recommendations for the shirt-making trade, wage differentials appeared to be based on gender and not on skills (Shirtmaking Wages Council, 1971).

16. This belt paster is a very quick and expert worker. However, since the process of making the belt occurs in two stages she could not estimate how long it took her to make a dozen.
Other examples of low piece-work rates we encountered were:
Winding hosiery thread on to cards – 60p per 1,000.
Making up dresses ('incomplete', i.e. no zip or hem) – 8½p per dress (taking 30-45 minutes to do; earning the woman approximately £3 a week).

17. Hunt (1968) reports that the wages of 53·6 per cent of married working women are mostly used as a supplement to housekeeping,

Emily Hope, Mary Kennedy and Anne de Winter

especially among wives of the less highly skilled men. A N.B.P.I. report (1969: 18) notes that 'The majority of homeworkers are married women whose aim is to supplement the family income'.

18. In order to do a more thorough analysis, it would be essential to know both the husband's occupation and any family income exclusive of homeworker's earnings, but we did not obtain this information in the course of our interviews.

19. It could be suggested that homeworkers save money (as compared with those who go out to work) on childminders and fares. In fact, some do spend money on bus fares collecting and delivering work. They do save on childminding, though our observation indicates that homeworkers do not take this saving into consideration when evaluating their situation.

20. Some of the women we interviewed felt that factory work would be less monotonous than homework and mentioned the regular tea breaks of the factory situation as something they miss at home where work is continuous.

21. With the exception of the Southern European women in the sample, we observed that the homeworkers were not particularly houseproud or overly conscientious about housework.

22. Several women we spoke to (English, Irish, West Indian and Nigerian) indicated that they would have worked outside the home if there were adequate child care facilities. The Southern European women, however, appeared to keep their children in a highly dependent relationship. This was one area in which we felt that cultural differences affected the choice of work and the attitudes towards it.

23. In 1906 there was a famous Sweating Exhibition organized by the *Daily News* and the formation of the Anti-Sweating League. In the following two years Parliamentary Select Committees on homework investigated the situation and recommended statutory minimum wages.

24. Part I of the 1911 Insurance Act made specific provision that an outworker should be insurable for health insurance. This seems to have covered only those employed full time at home (Report of Committee, 1923).

25. Again, information in the C.I.R. report on homeworkers (1973) supports our observations. It says: 'Homeworkers in the industry (pin, hook and eye and snap fastener) are primarily female, either mothers with young children or old age pensioners, doing homework to supplement their income'. See also the C.I.R. report (1974).

Political economy of domestic labour in capitalist society

The main concern of this paper is an examination of the political economic role of unpaid housework and childcare performed within the family. Because currently in our society this work is performed predominantly by women, as mothers and wives, even where these women also work outside the home (see Hunt, 1968), and because domestic labour did not even exist as a theoretical category before the current feminist movement made it into an area of theoretical and political debate, the paper is predominantly concerned with women's domestic labour. The reasons why women's domestic labour requires a specific analysis apart from the analysis of domestic labour in general is discussed in the final section of the paper.

The existing analysis of women's domestic labour derives from two major sources: first, Marxist analysis of class societies and of the capitalist mode of production (CMP); and, secondly, feminist analysis generated since 1969 by the current women's movement and itself based in part on reinterpretations of Marxist theory.

In the earliest contributions from the women's movement to a political economic analysis of women's role in the family (for example, Benston, 1969), emphasis was placed on viewing the family as a mode of production in which women were bound by personal dependence to individual men and thus analogous to slave labour. Reference was made in vague terms within this discussion to the benefits derived by capital from housework, but the relations between the family and capitalism were not elaborated theoretically. The family was viewed as an area of production of use values separate from the production of surplus value.

Since that time the focus of the debate has shifted towards an emphasis on the role of female labour in the family in maintaining and reproducing labour power, since this provides a theoretical link between the family and the CMP in which labour power is bought and sold (Morton, 1970; Dalla Costa, 1972; Larguin and Dumoulin, 1973). Out of this literature have come a number of questions.

1.   Is housework productive?

Jean Gardiner

2. What is the nature of the benefit housework represents for capitalists?
3. Does housework contribute to the production of surplus value and/or profit?
4. In what sense does the wage of the man pay for the labour of his wife?
5. Can housewives be treated as a class?

Before attempting to work out answers to these questions it is necessary to elucidate certain Marxist concepts around which they are framed since these are surrounded by considerable confusion and controversy. For example, the concept of productive labour has been interpreted in different ways by different writers on the question of female labour. This is due in part to Marx's own contradictory treatment of the problem and in part to people's misinterpretations of the intended scope of Marx's study of *Capital*. Both of these points will be taken up in the next section. Despite these problems, Marxist theory, specifically as developed in *Capital*, provides the most appropriate basis for analysis of female domestic labour, since it is the only political economic framework which enables us to look behind market relations and superficial money flows at the real social relations of production; that is, to see which groups contribute by their labour to social production and which groups are in a position to appropriate the labour of others. For example, Marx does not regard only work which receives a money payment as economically significant. Whether or not labour receives a money payment depends on the relations of production in which it is engaged. Slave labour, like female domestic labour, receives payment in kind for the subsistence of the labourer rather than a wage payment. The pre-occupation of non-Marxist economists with labour which involves a money transaction (and hence their total neglect of housework) obscures the true nature of productive relations. See Marx (1961 : 539):

> In slave labour, even that part of the working day in which the slave is only replacing the value of his own means of existence . . . appears as labour for his master. All the slave's labour appears as unpaid labour. In wage labour, on the contrary, even surplus labour, or unpaid labour, appears as paid.

Clarification of some Marxist concepts

It is often not understood that the concepts developed by Marx in *Capital* and *Theories of Surplus Value* were defined in a way to help elucidate the laws of motion of the CMP in its *pure* form. The economy he is analysing thus consists of two classes: on the one hand the capitalists who own the means of production, on the other the proletariat who own nothing but their labour power. For the most part all labour power under consideration falls into the category of either wage labour employed by capital or the reserve army of unemployed from whose ranks wage labour is recruited by capital. Thus in this model all useful labour performed is translated into exchange value; that is, it is embodied in commodities which are the property of capitalists.

In all modes of production based on class divisions, for example feudalism and capitalism, exploitation takes place. In other words the subordinate class perform surplus labour: that is they receive the equivalent of less than they produce, the surplus being appropriated by the dominant class. In the pure CMP surplus labour takes the specific form of surplus value: that is, the excess of commodities produced by workers employed by capital over the commodities entering those workers' consumption. Because Marx is concerned with the pure CMP he states (1961 : 218) that: 'The rate of surplus value is therefore an exact expression for the degree of exploitation of labour power by capital'. But once one allows for other modes of production subordinate to the CMP within capitalist society and for productive relations other than those of wage labour working for capital, such as domestic labour or peasant production, forms of surplus labour other than surplus value have to be taken into account. Since in any actual capitalist society neither the production nor the consumption of labour power is confined to commodities produced under capitalist relations of production, the rate of exploitation of labour power will not be synonymous with the rate of surplus value but will include other forms of surplus labour. This point will be taken up again in the next section.

Turning now to productive labour, Marx distinguished between labour that is productive in general and labour that is productive from the point of view of capital. Productive labour in the general sense is any labour that produces use values; that is, goods or services that are socially useful. Productive labour for capital is labour which produces surplus value. It is with this latter sense of productive labour that Marx was concerned. It will be obvious from what has been said above that the two are by no means synonymous in a capitalist society, given that all production of use values is not organized within the CMP (defined in the pure sense described above) although it is dominated by it.

Some writers on the question of women's labour have departed from Marx's approach whilst adopting his terminology. Thus for example Dalla Costa (1972: 31 and 52 fn. 12) writes:

> It is often asserted that, within the definition of wage labour, women in domestic labour are not productive. In fact precisely the

opposite is true if one thinks of the enormous quantity of social services which capitalist organization transforms into privatized activity, putting them on the backs of housewives. . . .

What we meant precisely is that housework is productive in the Marxian sense, that is, is producing surplus value.

She is here using the term productive to denote socially useful labour, that is productive in the general sense rather than in Marx's sense, and is also implying a different definition of surplus value.

There is considerable confusion about the meaning Marx attached to productive labour for capital. This originates in part from Marx's rather contradictory treatment of the concept in different contexts and in part from the quite distinct alternative definitions which have been adopted by subsequent Marxists. What follows is a brief summary of my own interpretation of Marx's usage.[1]

Marx had two distinct approaches to the concept of productive labour. In *Capital*, where he is concerned with the CMP pure and simple, the distinction between productive and unproductive labour applies to wage labour working for capital. All labour working for capital is productive whose labour is *technically* indispensable for the production and distribution of commodities (including both goods and services). Unproductive labour working for capital is that labour which is required only because the production takes place under capitalist relations (for example, management in its coercive as opposed to technical role and workers in commerce).

This usage can be rejected on the grounds that it is not possible to separate out what is technically necessary in capitalist production from what is socially conditioned. This definition of productive labour also conflicts with the second one discussed below, according to which the productiveness of labour is in no way dependent on the use values produced.

The second approach which Marx adopts is outlined in *Theories of Surplus Value*, (1969). Here the distinction between productive and unproductive labour hinges on whether the labour is paid out of capital or out of revenue (consisting of profits and rent spent on consumption, and wages). Thus productive workers are those employed within the CMP — whatever useful form their labour takes — whilst unproductive workers are those whose labour power is bought by capitalists or workers for personal consumption. This distinction appears more meaningful than that adopted in *Capital*. All workers employed by capital produce surplus value and are defined as productive from the point of view of capital. All labour not employed by capital is unproductive in that sense. The problem here is more that of the relevance of this distinction, and especially its relevance to female domestic labour. It was a useful device for analysing a society in which capitalists employed large numbers of domestic servants in their homes as well as employing labour in their factories, since it pinpointed the distinctive contributions to capitalist accumulation of the two groups of workers. However, it cannot be applied in the same way to payment of housewives out of wages. In fact I would argue that it is misleading to place wages and profits spent on consumption in the same category of revenue when the aim is to develop an analysis of the contribution different workers make to the total pool of capital available for accumulation. This takes us on to the problem of the determination of the worker's wage and its relationship to female labour.

The wage and female labour

The question of wages seems to be one of the least adequately treated areas in Marx's analysis. There is a tension in *Capital* between, on the one hand, an exclusive concern with the CMP, and on the other a recognition that the maintenance and reproduction of labour power itself is organized within workers' own families. Marx (1961 : 572) says:

> The maintenance and reproduction of the working class is, and must ever be, a condition of the reproduction of capital. But the capitalist may safely leave its fulfilment to the labourers' instincts of self preservation and propagation.

It seems that the level of the wage or the value of labour power (the two always tend to equal each other in Volume 1 of *Capital*, at least where the wage is a value not a price concept) is determined according to Marx by the value of the *commodities* entering into the historically determined subsistence level of the workers. In fact Marx (1961: 170) does not explicitly state that but instead:

> The value of labour power is determined, as in the case of every other commodity, by the labour time necessary for the production and consequently also the reproduction of this special article.

Certain writers have interpreted this to mean that the wage includes payment for the labour time of housewives who bear and rear children and look after their husbands. But Marx does not appear to have taken into consideration female labour in the home. When he goes on to argue that the wage will vary with the value of the means of subsistence, he is clearly thinking of the workers' consumption as consumption of commodities. For whilst the labour embodied in commodities consumed by the worker will clearly be directly related to the value of the wage, the labour time spent by the housewife in caring for husband and children will normally vary inversely with the wage, as she will be forced to substitute her own labour for commodities which the wage is insufficient to buy.

Jean Gardiner

It was Marx's implicit assumption that the workers' means of subsistence consisted of commodities only, which exchanged at their values, that enabled him to state that the wage in value terms would have to be equal on average to the labour time required to maintain and reproduce labour power. In fact wages do not include payment for the full costs of reproducing the labour force but only for the costs of the commodities purchased and consumed by workers' families. Put another way, housewives perform surplus labour on the assumption that the average labour time spent by them in caring for their families exceeds the labour embodied in commodities consumed by them out of their husband's wage packet (assuming the housewives do not also work for wages). Because the latter is usually kept to a minimum since housewives do not receive payment in their own right, it seems plausible that very great savings in labour time arising from socialization of housework and childcare would be necessary in order for it to be more profitable for capital or the State to take over the functions currently performed by women in the family. On the other hand, if demand for women as wage workers is sufficiently high it becomes more likely that it will be profitable for some socialization to take place and for more housewives to become wage labourers.

The family in its role of producer of labour power has clearly undergone significant changes with the historical development of capitalism — for example the development of State education — and there is no reason to suppose that the form it currently takes is any more definitive from the point of view of capital than previous ones. The important point is that female domestic labour within the family is a source of surplus labour for capital as well as wage labour and that the relative contributions of the different spheres of labour to capitalist profits will depend on the conditions of capitalist accumulation ruling at a particular time.

An illustration of the relationship between female domestic labour and the CMP

What I have argued is that female domestic labour is not engaged in the production of surplus value and is therefore not productive in Marx's sense because housewives are not employed directly by capital, but that female domestic labour none the less contributes to profits which incorporate forms of surplus labour other than surplus value. This can be elucidated further.

Except in three special cases, profits (including for the sake of simplicity rent and interest) will be a much wider category in capitalist society than surplus value, which is here taken to mean the surplus labour performed by all wage labour employed by capital. The three special cases where surplus value will be equal to profits (in value terms) are as follows:

1. The case where the only mode of production is the pure CMP (or, more precisely, the CMP together with possibly wage labour paid out of profits for the purpose only of the personal consumption of capitalists).

2. The case where other modes of production besides the pure CMP exist but no exchange takes place between those and the CMP, i.e. they do not produce commodities for sale within the CMP. This would imply the survival of other modes of production independently of the CMP, for example, self-sufficient primitive societies — if any exist.

3. The case where other modes of production exist and trade with the CMP but are not dominated by the CMP and thus have power to establish equal exchange relations (for example, the socialist mode of production?).

Where, on the other hand, other modes of production coexist with the CMP and have exchange relations with it which are not based on equal power, a material basis is established for the appropriation by capital of surplus labour performed outside the CMP. To take an illustrative example other than the relationship of the family to the CMP, consider peasant production of raw materials purchased by capitalists at less than their value. Here the surplus labour of the peasant producers would contribute to the total profits of capitalists.[2]

A scheme for analysing female domestic labour along these lines can be developed by use of a numerical example in which both production and consumption is measured by the number of hours' labour time embodied in each. It would seem most appropriate to take the case of a married couple with dependent children as an illustration, since in Britain the proportion of women working full time at home is currently highest in this group.

Let us look at an example (Table 6.1) of a family with two children in which the husband performs 12 hours' wage labour and gets paid 6 in his wage and the wife does 12 hours' housework. The labour required to reproduce both husband and wife includes the consumption of their children, who represent their replacements in the next generation.

In this example, because equal amounts of labour performed and consumed have been assumed for the man and the woman, the resulting profits derive half from surplus value created by the man and half from surplus labour performed by the wife. In fact the assumption that the wife consumes as much as the husband is unlikely to hold, in part because the wife's unpaid status will tend to keep her own consumption down to a

Jean Gardiner

Table 6.1

	Commodities consumed by	Housework required for	Labour performed by	Labour required to reproduce	Surplus labour
Husband	2	2	12(W)	3(W) 6(D) 9	3
Wife	2	2	12(D)	3(W) 6(D) 9	3
Boy	1	4			
Girl	1	4			
Wages	6	12	Necessary Labour	18	Profit 6

W: Wage labour
D: Domestic labour

minimum. Certainly in families experiencing poverty it has been found by many studies that women are consistently the most deprived.[3]

It is also assumed in this example that either the use values produced by the wife domestically are not produced in the capitalist sector or if they are that productivity is equal in the two sectors.

It must be emphasized that the use of the above numerical example is not intended to serve the purpose of estimating how much surplus labour is actually performed by housewives in a particular society or how much profit going to capitalists results from that source. Nor is it intended as an analysis of why the family has survived in a particular form in capitalist society and why reproduction of labour power has remained in the main a task carried out by women within the family. This discussion by no means exhausts the economic arguments which need to be developed in order to find answers to these questions (for instance the whole question of female wage labour has been ignored). Moreover it leaves out of account analysis of the role of ideology which is of crucial importance.

What I have tried to do is to provide one possible approach to the questions the paper began with. I have argued that housework is not productive labour in the Marxian sense since it is not directly engaged in the pure CMP. But labour which is not productive in that sense may none the less contribute to profits when other modes of production, like the domestic one, coexist alongside and are dominated by the CMP. Thus it is possible to see female domestic labour engaged in the maintenance and reproduction of labour power as a source of surplus labour in capitalist society. In these circumstances surplus value is not the only source of profit, since other forms of surplus labour also contribute to profit. The male worker's wage does not include payment for all the labour performed by his wife, but only for that part needed to maintain her. Whilst female domestic labour thus contributes to profits by keeping down the costs of maintenance and reproduction of labour power, it will not always be more profitable for it to be organized in this way. This will depend on factors such as labour requirements in the CMP and the relative costs of socializing child care.

The particular characteristics of female domestic labour

Before looking briefly at the political implications of this analysis it seems necessary to work out the relationship of female domestic labour to domestic labour in general. The domestic labour analysed in the paper has the following characteristics:

1. Being performed by women as mothers and wives, it is concerned with caring for other members of the women's families as well as themselves and therefore has a strong personal service element.
2. Because it is unpaid work — the women merely receiving their maintenance from husbands — it is associated with economic dependence.
3. Because domestic labour in each family is performed by women who:

    (a) take major responsibility for domestic tasks; and
    (b) perform the bulk of labour required by those tasks,

    it severely restricts the opportunity for the women to take paid employment and/or it affects the kind of paid employment the women will take. Domestic labour thus contributes to worsening, for wives and mothers, a labour market position which is already inferior because of other aspects of sexual inequality.

The other kinds of domestic labour which exists currently in our society can be summarized as follows:

1. Domestic labour performed by single people of either sex caring for themselves only.
2. Domestic labour performed by men as fathers and husbands, taking major responsibility for care of home and family.
3. Domestic labour performed by men as fathers and husbands which has minor significance in relation to both the men's total labour and the total domestic labour requirements of the family.

Jean Gardiner

4.   Domestic labour shared equally and co-operatively by all members of a household and not a source of relative economic dependence for any member.

The first category differs from the form of domestic labour which has been analysed in this paper because it is not associated with either economic dependence or personal service. In addition it is not a viable way of organizing domestic labour for the society as a whole since it does not provide for the reproduction of the labour force in the next generation.

The second case is feasible in principle but very rare, not least because the earnings a family forgoes if the father stays at home or works only part-time are likely to be much greater than those of the mother. A man in this situation will be in an analogous position to a housewife except that he does not start from the already inferior labour market situation experienced by women.

The third case is the most common form of married men's contribution to domestic labour. Because it does not entail either a major assumption of responsibility or a major commitment of time it is different in nature from the domestic labour of wives and mothers both quantitatively and qualitatively.

The fourth case is a pattern of domestic labour which is not feasible for the population as a whole, given the structure of working hours and wages and the lack of requisite State services, although it is attainable for a minority of relatively privileged economic groups.

For all these reasons an analysis of domestic labour in general which failed to focus specifically on the domestic labour of wives and mothers would obscure some of the key points in the kind of analysis attempted here.

Conclusion: Political implications of women's domestic labour

Finally let us turn to the last of the questions the paper began with and look briefly at the political implications of this approach to female domestic labour. If classes are, in the words of Lenin (1969: 486), distinguished from each other by

> the place they occupy in a historically determined system of social production, by their relation ... to the means of production, by their role in the social organization of labour and, consequently, by the dimensions of the social wealth of which they dispose and the mode of acquiring it,

what are the implications for class analysis of recognizing the distinctive role of domestic labour?

There do not seem to be any grounds for viewing *women* as a class since they are distinguished as half the population by their sex and not by their relationship to social production. A much more serious argument is the one that *those engaged in unpaid domestic labour* share a common class position.

Domestic labour to maintain and reproduce labour power within the family is the only form of labour in capitalist society which has remained at the stage of the simplest social division of labour, that within the family unit. Female domestic labour performs surplus labour as does wage labour, but the mode of appropriation is quite different in the two cases, as is therefore the place of the two groups in the struggle between classes. This can be seen by separating out the different levels of the class struggle in the following way:

1. The labour extracted from workers in the capitalist production process.
2. The money wage bargain between wage labour and capital.
3. Prices set by capitalists.
4. Taxation and social benefits set by the State.
5. Domestic labour to organize the family budget and supplement the wage.

It is only at the first two levels, in which wage labour is engaged, that the collective nature of production has enabled a high degree of organization to develop in the form of trade unionism.

At the other three levels, workers in their individual families, and especially women as housewives, face the capitalist class as a whole either through the price mechanism or via the State. The wage labourer sells his labour power to the capitalist for a given number of hours during which time the capitalist has total control of that labour power and strives to make the maximum profit out of it. The housewife on the other hand is bound throughout her married life to caring for her husband and children, but the actual hours she works always appear to be her own to dispose of. Whilst in the case of wage labour, surplus labour is appropriated collectively and coercively, in the case of domestic labour it is appropriated individually and apparently voluntarily on the basis of personal, familial ties and commitments. It is interesting to note that the wage work done by women in the home occupies an intermediate position in this analysis between unpaid housework and childcare and wage work in socialized production (see Hope *et al.*, Ch. 5). Finally there is the question of economic dependence on the husband which again places female domestic labour in a distinctive class category.

None of this of course implies that housewives as a group will see themselves as a class or have the basis for organizing collectively to defend their interests. On the contrary, one of the features of their class position

Jean Gardiner

is the individual and isolated nature of their labour and economic dependence on, and thus identification with, the male breadwinner.

What I have argued is highly tentative but it would seem important to consider seriously the class position of housewives, although this contravenes traditional approaches to analysis of class, for the domestic labouring role overlaps for the majority of women for considerable periods of their lives with other class positions and is crucial in affecting questions of consciousness and organization. Moreover, the experience in socialist countries, where women have to a large extent retained their role as domestic labourers, highlights the importance of taking this question seriously.

Notes

1. For further elucidation see Gough (1972) and Harrison (1973).
2. For a similar approach to labour in the State education sector see Rowthorn (1974).
3. See Booth's study of London (1889), Rowntree's study of York (1901, 1941) and Syson and Young (1974).

The rationalization of housework

Do everything at the proper time
Keep everything in its proper place
Use everything for its proper purpose.

This paper is an attempt to put forward some very preliminary ideas about a subject which, until a few years ago was not only neglected but, on all levels, treated with contempt. The idea of asking serious questions about housework seemed unthinkable. Until about 1970, only the amusing and provocative American piece by Pat Mainardi, *The Politics of Housework*, circulated within the women's movement, even raised the issue.[1] She ends with her husband saying: 'Housework? Oh my God, how trivial can you get. A paper on housework!'

Housework, like housewife, is a catch phrase covering a multitude of activities and attitudes. In contemporary society both tend to be residual categories used to fall back on when an activity or person cannot be classified in any other way. Yet neither of these terms, nor their meaning to us, is universal or 'natural', rather they are culturally and historically specific. Housework can, for example, be looked at as *work*, including physical, psychological and social components, although for reasons, some of which are considered here, it is systematically left out of both popular and sociological discussions of work.[2] Housework can also be analysed as part of an overall economic system. (Gardiner, Ch. 6; Secombe, 1974). And as in this paper, it can be considered as part of the culture of the society. It is hoped that this general discussion can be illuminated by looking at a specific historical case — late eighteenth and nineteenth century England.

The focus of the following discussion will be on middle and upper class (i.e. servant-keeping) households. This is justified, first, because I believe that the sexual division of labour which developed throughout the nineteenth and twentieth centuries had elements which cut across all class lines, and that this similarity has increased in recent times. (Whether this was a result of deliberate ideological manipulation by dominant groups or because of economic and social developments in the total society is an

Leonore Davidoff

open question (Davidoff *et al.*, 1975). Thus what I have to say has relevance for all sections of society today. Secondly, the majority of recent economic analyses of housework have in the main been related to working-class households only (Secombe 1974; Harrison, 1973).

In studying the development of households in the nineteenth century, the most striking facts are the separation of the household from public concerns into an intensely private sphere and the elaboration of domestic life. In the twentieth century, both these patterns, but particularly the latter, have been reversed. Domestic life has become less rigid and less formal. Specialized activities in the home have been merged. Even architecturally we have moved to the 'open-plan' house where functions like cooking have been reincorporated into general family life. The problem is to account for this change as it developed at this particular historical time.

A clue to understanding the pattern of nineteenth century domestic life may be found in the fact that the same period was also the time of an intense emphasis on the purity of women and the idea of a double standard in moral affairs.[3] The evolution of these ideas was a slow process and can be traced back to the end of the seventeenth century. This was also the period when English society was faced with the disruptive effects of nascent capitalism, in agriculture as well as in commerce and manufacturing. The establishment of a free market and the attendant concept of individualism were making inroads into received notions of hierarchy. It was in the middle class that these developments were most marked and it was given to middle-class women to become the moral protectors of society. Women began to be seen as more moral, more pure (and more clean) than men. They had to be kept so, segregated in private homes free from the taint of market forces which would have weakened paternalistic authority (Davidoff, 1974). Eventually, the fear of market activity as an agent in undermining the purity of women extended to any work which included manual labour even within the home. Obviously, by this definition truly genteel and pure women could only be a relatively small proportion of the total female population. Those who must work, therefore, were ideally only to be engaged in work which protected the purity of others, i.e. as domestic servants, washerwomen, charwomen — or prostitutes. Women became the purest, most ethereal, most unworldly of all creatures, but they also, as protectors of the moral order, had constantly to wrestle with the impure.

Three questions must then be asked about the historical case under discussion. Why were women singled out for this special task? What part did the elaboration of housekeeping play in this pattern? Finally, how did these two factors intereact — how did the household become more 'rationalized' in order to serve as the moral centre of society, while at the same time this goal raised fundamental contradictions to the process of rationalization itself?

For an attempt to answer such questions we must first turn to a more abstract level of analysis.

Culture, domestic work and the sexual division of labour

Because the components of housework have existed since Biblical times (and before), it is often assumed that housework itself is a constant feature of all societies. But even though the activities may be timeless, the context and meaning are not. Who does it, where, when and for what reasons — both acknowledged and latent — are the important questions to be asked. Take, for example, sweeping a floor, an activity which has changed technologically very little over the years. Sweeping can be a form of ritual; making patterns in dirt, sand or gravel with magical and/or aesthetic meaning, periodic ritual cleansing as in spring cleaning, or even a kind of exorcism. But sweeping a floor can also symbolize a humble position, a special kind of relationship to the social order: As the well-known stanza runs:

> A servant with this clause
> Makes drudgery divine
> Who sweeps a room as for thy laws
> Makes that and action fine.

Such subordination can merge into sweeping, or scrubbing floors as a humiliation and punishment, as in the Army, prisons, orphanages and mental hospitals, where the most menial domestic work is also used as discipline to keep order. On the other hand, it can be seen as part of 'scientific' dirt control to combat diseases by removing places for them to breed. Or, most often, it can be all of these combined.

Significantly, too, such activities have not always and everywhere been carried out by women, particularly adult women; it is only our stereotypical thinking that equates domestic work completely as part of the adult feminine role. Indeeed the concept 'domestic work' itself is culturally dictated (Mead, 1970). Very often such tasks as fuel gathering, simple cookery, child minding and water carrying have been turned over to young children, and old or handicapped people of either sex, i.e. those too physically weak or socially marginal to be involved in productive tasks (Clark, 1968).[4] In colonial societies, it was very often native men who were used for most domestic work for the foreign dominant group (Mehta, 1950).

Note also the use of batmen in the armed services and the arrangement of domestic work in all-male situations, such as on board ship or in mining camps.

Leonore Davidoff

In the most basic sense, housework is concerned with creating and maintaining order in the immediate environment, making meaningful patterns of activities, people and materials. The most important part in the creation of such an order is the separating out of the basic constituents and making clear the boundaries between them. For example, cooking food is the transformation of raw ingredients into a new substance. This process makes the ingredients into an element which can then be used in family or social ritual. In this sense the raw food has now 'participated in the family — by cooking, food is made to pass from the natural to the human world' (Dumont, 1972: 183). More than this, however, when the cooked food is eaten, it penetrates the boundaries of the body, truly binding together those who 'break bread' around a common table.

A meal itself is made up of ritually prescribed patterns of cold and hot, sweet and savoury food. Unless it is patterned in this way it is felt that it is not proper food. Yet changes in the rigid daily meal pattern can signify changes in the season or a holiday release provided by the deliberate inversion of this formality.[5] Who partakes of the meal, when and where, helps to create the boundaries of the household, of friendship patterns, of kinship gradations. Only the family eat hot Sunday dinner together, lesser acquaintances are invited for drinks, not a full meal, etc. (Douglas, 1972). These eating patterns vary between and help to define the boundaries of classes, ethnic, religious, age and sexual groups.[6]

Cleaning (clearing, tidying and washing) is another operation of the same kind, which is very widespread although perhaps not as ubiquitous as cooking. In separating wanted from unwanted matter, defining what is to be saved and what is rubbish, we are imposing a pattern, defining boundaries. As Mary Douglas has said, 'dirt is essentially disorder . . . eliminating it is not a negative movement, but a positive effort to organize the environment . . . making it conform to an idea (Douglas, 1970: 12). But the idea must precede the efforts to maintain the boundaries and, therefore, the disorder must first be perceived. The perception of disorder is a cultural artifact which changes through time and place (see Douglas 1970: 48):

> Cleanliness or tidiness is a relative idea. Shoes are not dirty in themselves, but it is dirty to place them on the dining table; food is not dirty in itself, but it is dirty to leave cooking utensils in the bedroom or food bespattered on clothing; similarly bathroom equipment in the drawing room; clothing lying on chairs; out-door things in-doors; upstairs things downstairs; under-clothing appearing where overclothing should be; and so on. In short, our pollution behaviour is the reaction which condemns any object or idea likely to confuse or contradict cherished classifications.

The rationalization of housework

Freedom from the responsibility of maintaining these particular boundaries or of even perceiving them is one of the rewards of power positions. The enforcement of basic order can be ignored because it can be delegated to others. Although I have indicated many exceptions, by and large, everywhere and at all times, women have been more concerned with these 'core' boundary maintaining functions than men. Why?[7]

If we look more closely at the core activities of cooking and cleaning, we see that they are attempts to impose cultural patterns upon the natural world. Pollution and purity rituals often seem to be part of this relationship between nature and culture. They are an attempt 'to generate and sustain systems of meaningful forms (symbols, artifacts, etc.) by means of which humanity transcends the givens of natural existence, bends them to its purposes, controls them in its interests' (Ortner, 1974). Since women are for a longer period of time more involved with physiological processes (menstruation, childbirth, and lactation) they are seen as closer to nature than men. They also bring forth new unplaced individuals for the society to absorb. Because they are usually assigned to care for small children, they spend more of their lifetime with those who are unsocialized and thus 'uncivilized' forces. Men are seen as people, but women are ambiguous simply by the fact of being also conscious beings who are not men but who do take some part in the culture of the society. Yet women are active beings in their performance as a 'mediating agency' between nature and culture: the raw and the cooked (Ortner, 1974).

Thus women are a moral force of the utmost importance, the first line of defence against fundamental symbolic as well as physical disorder. Because of their marginality and ambiguity, however, they are in danger of being unclean or threatening themselves. 'Those nearer to the "non-structure", i.e. those who are more marginal, can unleash more dangerous powers, are more polluting' (Douglas, 1970: 118). As a result, even when they are engaged in maintaining the purity of others and of the environment, they are often segregated spatially into limited areas of action. This physical segregation becomes an integral part of the system, a feature long recognized by anthropologists but until recently ignored by many mainstream sociologists whose conceptions of social systems often seem to exist in free floating space. Physical invisibility is also social invisibility and this is one of the reasons why much of women's activity has been systematically left out of sociological and other analysis.

Housekeeping activities are not only concerned with segregating and maintaining categories, they are, as I have indicated, related to the ways in which these categories are ordered in terms of power.[8] Hierarchical boundaries are always some of the most salient in any society. This has two important implications for our discussion. First, those who deal with potentially polluting activities, such as transforming the raw into the

Leonore Davidoff

cooked, and dealing with the detritus of personal life, are very often those at the bottom of the hierarchy, indeed sometimes even outside it, i.e. 'outcasts' (Dumont, 1972). For example, body substances in many societies are regarded as *boundary overflows* and therefore particularly dangerous (Tambiah, 1973). Hence those who deal with such defiling material must be defilers themselves (Srinivas, 1965).

Secondly, societies which are exceptionally concerned with hierarchical ranks will be also usually concerned with maintaining distances between them and fearful of the confusion caused by the blurring of their boundaries. In every case, of course, these boundaries are ultimately enforced by power. But there is also a whole symbolic system used by the agencies of power to legitimate their rule. When the power base is shifting, the symbolic system becomes doubly important. A preoccupation with the *listing* of hierarchy and the forbidden contacts between groups seems to be a feature of such a situation when, *at the same time*, a great deal of actual mixing is going on (Tambiah, 1973).

Domestic work and hierarchy in the English historical context

In eighteenth- and nineteenth-century English society, hierarchical boundaries were under attack. There were no legal restrictions on entry into various social strata, and new sources of wealth were being used to build up what was potentially a new definition of legitimate rule outside landowning groups. The order based on the mixture of domestic industry and agriculture was increasing challenged by manufacturing interests (Perkin, 1969; Thompson, 1964). In this situation a rigid classification of hierarchical ranks was officially proclaimed.

> The rich man in his castle
> The poor man at the gate
> God made them high or lowly
> And ordered their estate

was sung in Sunday schools across the country, but social boundaries were, in fact, permeable. Although mobility was not easy to accomplish it was quite possible if limited in degree. The response to this situation seems to have been, indeed, a preoccupation with classifying and segregating various strata of the society (by *sex*, *age*, and *'usefulness'* or moral worth, in addition to class), as well as great pressure to build up the moral force of the society to take part in the task of keeping disorder at bay. The rise of Methodism, the Evangelical movement within the Church and the beginnings of the Temperance Movement (whose rhetoric with its emphasis on purity, e.g. 'My Drink is Water bright' is interesting in this context) can all be seen as part of this process.

The rationalization of housework

Another separating and ranking device emerging at this period and given into the keeping of women was the idea of 'Society' — the category of being *in* as opposed to *out* of 'the World' (Davidoff, 1973). Within this concept of a clearly demarcated Society, the older ideals of gentility, based on honour were recast in the new and more flexible definition of *lady* and *gentleman* as understood in the nineteenth century (Newby, 1975). According to the aristocratic code of honour, work itself, any work, implied a drop in status whether it was in trade, manufacture or in the professions. The manual, physical side of work was beneath contempt while, at the same time, manual *skills*, in sport, in swordsmanship and other arts of war or in intricate embroidery or music-making had high esteem. In middle class culture, on the other hand, work activity was highly valued for itself and it was only the actual physical or literally manual work which came to be particularly despised as ungenteel. Following on from this, it is not accidental that *hands*, their whiteness, smoothness, smallness, their encasing in gloves, or conversely largeness, filthiness, roughness, redness, bareness, should become a preoccupation of this period.[9]

The symbolism of hands was only a part of the division between dirt and cleanliness which increased as the nineteenth century progressed. The striving for order and control by keeping dirt away, by washing and brushing, polishing and sweeping, had been associated with various groups in earlier periods (e.g. many Protestant sects and even medieval burgher households) but these tended to be small minorities easily ridiculed for their finicky ways. On the whole, up to the middle of the eighteenth century, the distinct life styles of the rich and the poor had depended on the amount and type of food, of gold or silver ornaments and plate and sumptuousness of clothing. Most people in all classes had lice and diseases associated with dirt.[10] The concern with personal and domestic cleanliness, with the stricter ordering of things and people in the house came later. And it emerged as an important way of marking the middle classes off from those below them, well before the germ theory of disease was discovered much less understood by the general public. It is true that by the second quarter of the nineteenth century there was a growing feeling that somehow a connection between dirt and disease existed. For example it was acknowledged that drinking water, so polluted that it was brown and stank, had something to do with the scourge of cholera. But the connections were dimly appreciated and often based on explanations such as "myasmic contagion"; a vagueness that caused many problems for real control through bacterial destruction. (Rosen, 1974). Historical explanations of sanitary improvements solely in terms of what William James has dubbed "medical materialism" (Douglas, 1970: 44) have too glibly overlooked this question of the timing of the reforms.

Leonore Davidoff

Part of the preoccupation with cleanliness was due to the obtrusiveness of new kinds of dirt, e.g. the increased use of coal in large cities and manufacturing areas which produced unusable by-products of cinders, smuts and dust. Also in large cities garbage and sewage which would have been useful as fertilizer in the country became sheer waste as it festered on the curbs and in muck heaps by the doorsteps. (Housewives still often refer to garden soil as "clean dirt".) New definitions of what was and was not waste were part of a new definition of the relationship of human beings to nature which was taking place at the same time, in for example, the Romantic movement in the arts.

The point to be stressed, however, is that nineteenth-century cleanliness really had more to do with tidying and polishing — sparkling glasses, gleaming silver, brass, copper and polished wood — than our notions of dirt control. Tidiness was seen to be as much a moral as a physical attribute. (A Place for Everything and Everything in its Place.) Indeed, furnishing, equipment and clothing were all so elaborated, embossed carved and trimmed that they inevitably harboured and even created dirt.

Women's place in this control system was clearly stated in the tracts, manuals, advice books and fiction of the period. Women were purer than men, they were by nature more moral and should be cleaner. "There can be no love of long duration, sincere and ardent love in any man towards a *filthy* mate", wrote Cobbett in 1829 and he went on to urge the prospective suitor to look between his intended bride's fingers and behind her ears for traces of grime (Cobbett, 1968: 170).

> Lords of Creation are neither in practice nor is it their province to be as domestically clean and orderly as ladies. . . . Even those men who have some degree of satisfaction in seeing that things *are* clean, are apt to be unreasonable and impatient if obliged to witness the operations that must make them so; whilst the implements of domestic purification are their confessed abhorrence (Anon, 1852: 75).

It was assumed then and is to an extent to this day, that boys are by nature dirtier than girls. It was women and girls who spent so much of their lives carrying, heating, and steeping their hands while washing things, clothes and people in *water* — that fluid element which dissolves matter and is so often used in rituals of purification: 'water symbolizes the primal substance from which all forms come and to which they will return' (Eliade, 1958: 188). The middle and upper class house, within its walls and continuing down its front steps and path (ideally maids were supposed to wash both back and front paths as well as steps every day) was the clean tidy haven in the midst of public squalor and disorder

(Davidoff, L'Esperance and Newby, 1975). It was the housemistress's responsibility to make it so.

Even more important than the equation of femininity with cleanliness, was, of course, the equation of cleanliness with class position, part of the parcel of behaviour and attitudes bundled together in that imprecise but vital concept *respectability.* Whatever the other strands in respectability — church going or temperance — cleanliness was supposed to be its hallmark. In the nineteenth century the labouring classes, the poor, the proletariat were, in middle-class minds 'The Great Unwashed'; they *smelled* uncontrolled and disordered (Schoenwald, 1974). This view persisted well into the twentieth century, and George Orwell is one of the very few writers to discuss openly the implications of this fact. He was in no doubt as to its effect on efforts at social equality. 'That was what we were taught — *the lower classes smell.* And here obviously you are at an impassable barrier' (his italics) (Orwell, 1959: 129) — a barrier created in childhood and so doubly difficult to break down.

Smell and sound as well as sight of dirt and disorder were more obtrusive in crowded cities than in the countryside, and the idealization of Nature as pure compared to towns as impure may be connected to this fact. 'The great unwashed were socially unclean, too, the typical attitudes first expressed to this emergent group by those above them were [also] stereotyped — a blend of contempt, fear, hate and physical revulsion' (Dyos and Wolf, 1973). Himmelfarb notes a disturbing habit of Victorian observers of using the same word to describe both the sanitary condition (Chadwick) and the human condition (Mayhew) of the poor; i.e. 'residum' was the offal, excrement or other waste that constituted the sanitary problem; and was also the name applied to the lowest layer of society (Himmelfarb, 1971).

Conversely, manual work and hence dirt, or the absence of cleanliness became associated with ideas of masculinity (Lockwood, 1958: 122-5). Personal habits associated with dirt and mess, e.g. spitting, chewing tobacco and smoking, became strictly masculine from the end of the eighteenth century onwards. Similar attitudes were part of an aggressively proletarian identification, and held by the type of radical who was 'goaded to fury by the sight of a clean shirt' (Shipley, n.d.).

A second element used in the separation of classes was fresh air. Again, the recognition of the value of fresh air undoubtedly had much to do with new forms of physical pollution — smog was already a feature of London life in the eighteenth century. But the metaphorical use of the term 'fresh air' to blow away and cleanse social problems was also a constant theme. Newman in his *Apologia* wrote: 'Virtue is the child of knowledge, vice of Ignorance. Therefore education, periodical literature, railroad travel and ventilation seem to make a population moral and happy

Leonore Davidoff

(Young, 1966: 7). 'Morality was intimately connected with the free circulation of air — exposure to public gaze' (Stedman Jones, 1971: 180). Middle-class children were told that servants' bedrooms were inevitably fuggy and stale smelling because they did not understand the benefits of fresh air. Charity workers and others brought the message home to their working class (largely female) audience with tracts such as those put out by the Ladies' Sanitary Association 'A Word About Fresh Air', 'The Black Hole in our own Bedrooms', etc. (c.1850). And until very recently, the 'airing' of rooms, bedding and clothing was seen as one of the English housewife's indispensable daily tasks.[11]

I have indicated that one of the rewards of a superior position within a hierarchical structure is the protection of the superordinate from potentially polluting activities. The ultimate nineteenth-century ideal became the creation of a perfectly orderly setting of punctually served and elaborate meals, clean and tidy and warmed rooms, clean pressed and aired clothes and bed linen. Children were to be kept in nurserys with nursemaids; animals and gardens cared for by outdoor servants; callers and strangers dealt with by indoor servants. In other words there was to be a complete absence of all disturbing or threatening interruptions to orderly existence which could be caused either by the intractability, and ultimate disintegration, of things or by the emotional disturbance of people (Davidoff, 1973). In the nineteenth century this ideal of perfect order could only be approximated by that small group of wealthy and powerful individuals who could command the attendance of numerous domestic servants. Below this small group, *men*, middle class and to a certain extent the best paid, most regularly employed of the working class, were provided with an intensely personal form of ego-protection and enhancement by their wives (or daughters, nieces and unmarried sisters), aided by female general servants.

This process must be recognized as a relational aspect of social stratification. It should not be substituted for an analysis of the distributive aspects of inequality. Drawing attention to the part such interaction plays in the maintenance of stratification, however, emphasizes the way the system was divided along *both* class and sex lines.

Budgetary separation of the enterprise and household economy

The attitudes and behaviour relevant to nineteenth-century middle-class housekeeping — cleanliness, order, the segregation of activities in time and place, careful overall planning, diligence and hard work — had all existed and been commended for a very long time. Not only do they appear in Puritan and other Nonconformist precepts, but they go back as far as the moralists of Roman husbandry. They are echoed in fourteenth- and fifteenth-century Florence by such writers as Alberti and continued in various places where trade and commerce flourished as far apart as sixteenth-century Holland, Defoe's London, and eighteenth-century Pennsylvania. There the rubric reached its fullest expression in the writings of Benjamin Franklin, 'the perfect bourgeois', particularly in his *Autobiography* and *The Way to Wealth* (Sombart, 1967). The purpose of all these guides to conduct was, in every sphere, to make life more calculable, to balance expenditure with income in an effort to save. Thrift in regard to both time and money was the cardinal virtue. The goals of saving might vary (a dowry for a daughter, an extra piece of land), but the primary drive, for continued saving, for saving as a way of life, was to create capital for commercial expansion. And it was the growth of capitalist commercial enterprise which was responsible for the critical organizational change: the separation of the business 'house' and the domestic household. Even more important than physical separation was the budgetary division of these units (Weber, 1968). Strangers began to be admitted as partners into what had been an organization of kinsmen, brotherhoods or guilds. This process reached a critical point in the adoption of detailed accounting and eventually the introduction of double-entry book-keeping into business practice (an invention of seventeenth century Holland).[12] With this development, business and commercial activity were finally cut loose from other goals of family life, allowing the systematic accumulation of capital. Such expansion of the enterprise is not possible without the use of rational accounting, which in turn must use an all purpose medium of exchange — money. Only then can any true calculation of input and output, of profit or loss be made.

It is also true that the rational ordering of life is quite possible whatever the chosen ends, even if they are 'unworldly' ones. This is a point worth remembering in the context of the present discussion. For example, European monasticism was just such a system of living, for the glory of God, with its minutely calibrated daily activities rigidly prescribed by the constant ringing of bells. Yet even under monasticism, such attitudes seem to mesh most easily with the rationalization of economic life, for the monasteries were also very often large farming and productive enterprises. As Weber noted, 'the Reformation took rational Christian asceticism and its methodical habits out of the monasteries and placed them in the service of active life in the world' (Weber, 1971: 235). In this way, the stage was set for economic expansion, in enterprises which had 'no boundaries to this process of addition' (Sombart, 1953: 35), and it is this type of enterprise and its descendants which have been the concern of social commentators from the seventeenth century onwards.

Few have asked, however, about what happens to the household which has been thus disengaged from production. Before trying to answer

Leonore Davidoff

that question it should be remembered that this separation was a very slow process starting with a few mercantile and tradesmen's households which were exceptions to the general case of more or less self-sufficient units which drew their sustenance directly from the land; which ranged in scale from great landowners to cottagers. A high proportion of the income of such households remained in kind, not cash. The large numbers of rural households which were partially dependent on outwork (e.g. textiles, straw-plaiting, lace-making) further complicates the total picture. Nevertheless, the trend was for more and more household relationships to involve a cash nexus, whether in the form of proletarian wage earner, salaried or professional occupation, tradesman, rentier, capitalist or a mixture of these. This shift was associated with a higher proportion of families living in towns, and, although this was an important aspect of the change, it is not possible to discuss it here. The final and complete break, however, was not reached in England until full extension of limited liability with the passing of the Company Acts of 1856–62, which once and for all freed business activity from any restraints imposed by kinship obligations.

The very slow pace of the separation of household and enterprise and the persistence of home production of a great many commodities did not prevent attempts to rationalize activity in bourgeois homes as well as commercial enterprises. In particular there seems to have been a transfer of the values of business into the home. But these attempts were, and are to this day, unsuccessful for two fundamental and interrelated reasons. The first, and probably the more obvious, concerns the limited size of the household. Neither vertical nor horizontal extension is really possible and this means that economies of scale and the benefits of specialization are not practicable for a household. While the goal of economic rationality is always the expansion of the enterprise, there are inherent and quite narrow limits to household expansion.

Of course it is possible to point to examples of really large establishments, but these are very exceptional. While one of the biggest in the nineteenth century, Woburn Abbey, had fifty to sixty indoor servants and could house several dozen guests, the mean household size in social class I in York in 1851 was 6·02 (Bedford, 1959; Armstrong, 1974: 189). As far as growth through devices such as mergers or take-overs is concerned, there was a certain amount of transfer of income and/or services between households across generations or between siblings, but the whole tendency has been for each family unit to act independently.[13] In addition, because of other effects of nineteenth- and twentieth-century capitalist developments, households have tended to grow smaller as measured by house size and numbers of inhabitants (Government Statistical Office, 1973: 12–13).

The second point concerns the goals of family and household (it should be noted that although the two terms are now almost synonymous this has not always been the case). The problem here is not that non-pecuniary ends cannot be reached by rational means, but that the goals themselves — the maintenance of hierarchical boundaries and ego-servicing of superiors — *deny* the use of rational calculation.

The struggle to keep unlimited calculation — 'the need to see the world in terms of figures'[14] — from creeping into every sphere of life was a long drawn out and even bloody one (Thompson, 1964). Nowhere was it more visibly demonstrated than in the segregation of women and of the home from market forces. The use of money means that there are no longer 'mysterious incalculable forces that can come into play, but rather that in principle all things can be mastered by calculation'. Money is the most rational and formal means of orientation because it makes possible calculation *within* a unit and *between* units. It is the demystifying instrument *par excellence.* The resistance to the application of rational calculation to the family, and hence women, is of utmost importance; and because it reflects a primordial concern for order, for protection from pollution, it has a deeper basis in collective life than social theorists have so far acknowledged. In this sense, housework has remained not a residuum left over from a previous mode of production, but is seen as a positive purposive activity in capitalist and non-capitalist societies alike.

The analysis of housework by contemporary Marxist economists is quite correct in showing that the real productive labour power of women in domestic tasks is obscured; and that this particular obscuration is superimposed on the general obfuscation (and thus legitimation) of extraction of surplus value within the capitalist mode of production. The labour of the housewife in preparing and sustaining the husband for his labour, as well as in producing new workers in the form of children, is mediated through the labour (and thus the wage) of the husband. It is true that for this kind of analysis 'it matters not at all that the concrete conditions of domestic labour are privatized' (Secombe, 1974: 9); but sociologically, and for the women themselves, this is crucial.[15]

Simply exposing this double obscurity, and the double oppression it implies, does not show why the oppression takes the *form* which it does. Indeed, if we look at the early period of industrial capitalism in England the overwhelming need for workers, together with a reluctance to use adult male labour, led to a factory system based mainly on female and child labour, which was more tractable, and cheaper, than the former. But this practice was met with storms of protest from all sections of the society and it is just at this period that the ideology of women's domestic place was being most intensely propagated. Capitalists, as public men, were supporting the cult of domesticity, while at the same time, as rational

Leonore Davidoff

entrepreneurs, they were recruiting women workers into their mills and mines through the back door. However, the whole history of this period has yet to be systematically studied (John, 1973).

The movement towards rationalization of housework in eighteenth and nineteenth century England

I turn now to look in more detail at the move towards rationalization of housework in a more specific historical setting. A useful way of proceeding is to consider the physical artifacts left by those groups who were most subject to the appeal of rational calculation. The whole development of middle-class housing and furnishings from the sixteenth century onwards is one of increased separation and specialization of function. The hall or large living place gradually gave way to separate smaller rooms for cooking, eating and, eventually, solely for sleeping. The massive central chimney provided flues for 'kitchen and parlour' instead of 'hall and service'. As time went on, beds were no longer found downstairs in sitting rooms or doubling as seats for receiving visitors. This evolution eventually affected all social classes, although obviously resources varied enormously and up until very recently working class families were still cooking in the 'house-place' or living room rather than in a separate kitchen. On the other hand, this arrangement was very often made in order to free another room, the parlour, for ceremonial or front stage purposes analogous to the middle-class drawing room where ceremonies of integration and exclusion could take place at ritually defined times, e.g. Sunday, Christmas, weddings and funerals. This is a prime example of rational segregation for non-worldly ends.

It is known that in the nineteenth century the level of consumption of food, furniture, china and decorations rose rapidly with increasing middle-class prosperity, but if we look closely at the way these resources were deployed — for example, separate cutlery and crockery not only for nursery, kitchen and dining room but for every day and holidays — the divisions represented by the allocation of these resources indicate which categories were most important to the participants in the rituals. In the period from about 1800 to 1840 meals changed in character (Henderson, 1795; Glasse, 1748). Dinner began to be eaten later in the evening. Instead of having one or two large courses, including a selection of as many as twenty-five different dishes, set on the table at once in a mixture of roasts, 'made-up' dishes, sweets, tarts and jellies, the meal began to be served sequentially, starting with soup and moving through a variety of tastes and textures to a sweet, a savoury and finally dessert. This order was accompanied by the proliferation of specialized utensils and dishes to prepare and present the extended meal and much more labour was needed to serve it. At the same time there was, at least for family meals, a move to make food predictable. Increased resources were not used to allow choice to run riot. Rather the sentiment was that 'it is an excellent plan to have certain things on certain days' (1827), and this laid the basis for the Victorian rigidity of joint on Sunday, cold on Monday, hash on Tuesday, etc., which dominated English cuisine for generations afterwards.

The spate of housekeeping books of the late eighteenth century and early nineteenth century, shows that this was a period of experimentation with various forms of rationalizing household affairs. It was during this period, for example, that the keeping of strict and detailed household accounts was continually advocated, and these accounts dealt with both income and expenditure within various time spans (A Lady, 1829: 15a):

> Those articles extracted from the Cook's and Footman's books, or paid for in ready money, are to be entered in the first column and transferred to the cash-book as weekly sundries. Those bills which are paid monthly or quarterly, to be in the second column as a register to the consumption, that the weeks may be compared with each other: and the mention of the number of persons in the family and what guests dine either accidentally or by regular invitation, will be found useful, as a standing explanation of any excess in the weekly bills.

> Make an exact estimate of your *Net* Income; reserve two-fifths of net income for emergency. To ensure this compare your *Weekly* Expenses with a computation which you may easily make of how much your *Annual* income will afford every *Week* (Kitchener, 1825: 7).

From the above quotations it can be sensed that there was coming into use a new time structure which was made up of shorter, controllable units, and which was freed from intimate dependence on the agricultural calendar of sowing and harvest. In prosperous households, instead of the quarterly orgies of washing of huge stocks of dirty linen, the span between launderings dropped first to every six weeks, then to three weeks, until by the mid-nineteenth century the weekly wash was the norm (Hole, 1953; Bayne-Powell, 1956).

Housework schedules began to be drawn up with regular daily, weekly, monthly and annual tasks to be followed; and the remnants of these survive in our rituals of spring cleaning. Early rising was the constant exhortion to mistress and maid alike. Artificial light was improved to even out the day and night throughout the year, and thereby to increase the time so carefully hoarded. An often quoted maxim from early in the century warns:

Leonore Davidoff

> Lost, yesterday, somewhere between sunrise and sunset;
> Two golden hours, each set with sixty diamond minutes.
> No reward is offered for they are gone forever.

Gongs and house bells were now used to mark times for rising, for prayers, for meals, for dressing for meals. The generally increased use of clocks and watches for timing household operations as well as accurate weights and measures in cooking are all indices of the same tendency.

> In a well regulated family all the clocks and watches should agree . . . the Dining room should be furnished with a good going clock; the space over the kitchen fire place with another, vibrating in unison with the former so placed that the cook may keep one eye on the clock and the other on the spit.

stated Kitchener (1823: 30) in one of the most influential early nineteenth century cook books.

In the critical sphere of social relations, middle- and upper-class house mistresses kept visitors' books, or calling books, into which they transferred the information from visiting cards left and received (Davidoff, 1973). A commonplace book of the 1830s belonging to a merchant's wife has dated double-headed columns for each month of each year to record visits received and visits paid, gifts received and gifts given, evenings spent at home and evenings spent out (Young, 1828-40) — a kind of commercial balance sheet of home and social life.

The most fundamental index of rationalization, however, was the vastly increased employment of specialized domestic servants and the concomitant withdrawal of the housemistress from actual household tasks to a supervisory position, even within quite small establishments. The early nineteenth century was the period when the concept of the 'domestic' as opposed to the farm servant became established in both popular and legal terminology. Of course nineteenth century servants were paid in cash as well as board and room, but the ideology of the home stressed the familial and service side of their attachment. Within the household a symbolic head/hands hierarchy was established either by the mistress herself directing one to three servants, or, where larger staffs were employed, by their separation into upper and lower staff.

Running the house was broken down into minutely specified spheres of action: cook cleans back passage and steps, housemaid cleans front steps, hall and landing only, parlour maid is responsible for dining room and drawing room. The records covering three generations of an upwardly mobile banking family show that in the 1830s two maids did every sort of job including gardening. In the 1870s the daughter-in-law had three maids, sub-divided as cook, housemaid and nursemaid, and the third generation added a gardener and under-housemaid in 1900. While it is true that the increase in numbers of servants in this family was related to its increasing wealth, the form of specialization, for instance as between indoor and outdoor, between kitchen and house side, is significant (Vernon, 1966).

In studying the housekeeping books of the nineteenth century culminating in that often cited monumental volume, Mrs Beaton's *Book of Household Management* (first published in book form in 1861), I have come to suspect that what they provide is more a legalistic model, a 'grammar of conduct . . . concerned more with what ought *not* to be done rather than what should be done' (Tambiah, 1973: 15), rather than an account of what *was* actually going on in many households. Interview material and careful reading between the lines of memoirs indicates that there was, in fact, a good deal of transfer of personnel as well as blurring of the job demarcations and that the mistress of the house did more manual work herself than was admitted publicly (even if it was with blinds drawn as in Mrs Gaskell's *Cranford!*).

Nevertheless, there is still no question that the final aim was a rigid division of front and back stage and a relegation of household work to special times and places. In England particularly there was an unusually strong effort to remove the housemistress, even in quite modest households, from her core function of cooking. By 1845 Mrs Loudon (an extremely practical and working gardener herself) could recommend that a charcoal stove be set up in the housekeeper's room so that the housemistress might be able 'to make any dishes in French cookery, or any cakes or preserves that you may take a fancy to do yourself, with the assistance of your maid, apart from the observation of the other servants' (Loudon, 1845). The segregation of activities became so important that it included an intense dislike and fear of cooking smells in front rooms or even the sounds of any domestic activity, such as clinking dishes or thumping of irons. An examination of house guides and architectural books shows that architects of the period clearly saw provision for the separation of facilities for domestic work as a major part of their brief.

Here is clearly a case of specialization for ritual ends. Fears about female purity had reached such a pitch that an introduction to a mid-century cookery book (Rundell, 1845: xi) says:

> In the higher ranks an idea is entertained that any consideration connected with eating is injurious to the delicacy of the feminine character; this notion being strengthened as it descends, by an indisposition to undertake the toils which attention to the table must necessarily involve. Eating is an unpoetical thing: Lord Byron disliked to see women eat . . .

This attitude was bemoaned by writers, preachers and housemistresses themselves, but by and large it was accepted and represented a very

Leonore Davidoff

real shift in norms from the eighteenth century where a young woman's diary could record: 'read a little Greek, then made custard and tarts — which was very notable, then set the codlin' bar in order, produced myself in the parlour and were mighty agreeable' (Grant, 1924).

Most of these attempts at rationalization were eventually abandoned; those that remained produced contradictions that are still with us. For middle class, much less working class, households neither are nor were rational economic organizations. On the contrary, as I have tried to show, their aims are principally concerned with boundary maintenance at various levels. As Dorothy Smith has written, 'in a capitalist society, the house constitutes a dead end. The surplus above subsistence which enters it does not pass beyond it into a productive activity with others' — rather it performs a display function which is used to mark off the household's position, and 'thus the household order enters a semiotic structure . . . money stops at the family, there is nowhere else for it to go' (Smith, 1973: 21-22).

Consequences of the contradiction between rationalization and the purposes of the household

The attempts at rationalization within a context of incommensurable ends had, and to a certain extent still have, several consequences for household management. When pre-industrial traditions of labour distribution within the home broke down, there was, theoretically, no rational check on labour input. Any deficiency was made up by more intensive labour on the part of the housewife and servants; it was not only 'in the abodes of the poor [that] every defect of spending power has to be made good by the toil of the woman's muscles'[16] (Black, 1915). In principle only the physical exhaustion of the wife (and/or children), or in the case of servants the availability of alternative opportunities (other jobs or marriage) which enabled them to quit, put a check on the length of the working day or the expenditure or energy in housework. Although the individual husband (or master) might have tried to ease his wife's burden by *giving* her help either in the form of better equipment or hired help when he could afford it (Davidoff, 1974), housework had to remain labour intensive because there was no way of genuinely calculating alternatives to the woman's labour in the form of capital investment or labour from the external market.[17] Conversely, middle- and upper-class women could be carried as completely unproductive members of the households because ideology refused to allow the 'costing' of womanly love and service. (The fact that such women were in fact constantly reminded of the cost of their support was a bitter portion of their dependence.) The other possible ways of limiting the work load and of estimating the efficiency of housework — i.e.

by governmental investigations or trade union pressure — were of course, completely absent. How many were maimed or even killed, and how many became ill through exhaustion and the close nature of their work we will never know. Drinking among cooks was considered a joke, not an occupational disease.

Secondly, because it can never be really accepted that women's efforts in housework and household management should be measured in monetary terms, the worth of all women's work is affected. The census classification itself over the nineteenth century reflects this ambivalence, making something of a mockery of refined attempts to analyze the female labour market in purely statistical terms. The Registrar-General warned in 1901 that the apparent 'remarkable decrease' of occupied women from 34·4 per cent in 1891 to 31·6 per cent was due to struggles with classification rather than empirical fact, because (Census, 1904: 76):

> In 1881 and earlier, daughters and other female relatives of the Head of a Family, who were described as assisting in household duties, were classified as unoccupied. In 1891, however, it was considered that, the nature of daily occupations of such persons being thus evident, they would be properly reckoned in Domestic Service. . . . In deciding on the rules of guidance of the clerks at the recent census (1901) however, we came to the conclusion that, on the whole, it would be better to revert to the method of 1881.

Domestic service as a position between paid work and family attachment is, therefore, the crucial example of this equivocal orientation and from about 1850 to 1950 it was *the single most important form of employment of women and girls* (over a million and a quarter in the last part of the nineteenth century and never less than a million until the mid-1930s).

What is wage work in the life of Mary H. (born 1876)? At 13 she went by the day as companion-guardian to a mentally ill neighbour after helping her mother at home morning and evening (as she had done before leaving school). From 14 to 16 she was a paid living-in nursemaid to a publican, then spent almost a year living with her married sister to help with a new baby, receiving board and room only. This was followed by another nursemaid's job at 3s 6d a week, then six months living at home helping in the house and another nine months with an aunt to help with the housework and young baby. Back to London as a house/parlour maid at 4s a week, promoted at age 22 to head housemaid at 7s 6d a week, she then married a tram conductor and, as his wife, kept house for him, receiving set 'housekeeping' and thus was no longer officially 'working' (Anonymous MS.).

Secombe may be correct in saying that the spurious attempt to

Leonore Davidoff

calculate the 'wage' value of housewives' work is 'an exercise in bourgeoise reasoning, i.e. wages as a measure of the value of work done rather than a monetary package paid to ensure the family subsistence' (Secombe 1974: 13). Nevertheless we now live in a fully wage oriented society where only cash can buy support. If women are, in this sense, as individuals, not fully and legitimately within the labour market — which in the nineteenth century they certainly were *not* — then they must find support in the only other way they can, through the marriage market and its corollary, prostitution.

For with the falling away of economically 'mixed' households depending on small-holding, craft-type workshops, and even the taking in of washing and/or lodgers, more and more households exist solely as consumption units.[18] A consumption unit cannot by itself either create or increase income; it can only save by cutting expenditure. Some saving can, of course, benefit the family in the form of house purchase, for example, but the amount of saving that is possible on most salaries let alone wages makes this a remote aim. The point is that household support really depends on cash currently coming into the household. If no 'housekeeping' is brought into the home by the husband for *whatever* reason, from personal spite to unemployment, there is no money for the housewife to live on or for the support of the dependent children. Because of this a goodly proportion of poverty, however measured, was, and to a certain extent is, female and child poverty. In 1910, the Webbs wrote (Webb, 1910: 103):

> The amount of destitution in the country, generally, caused by the death, absence or desertion, of the male head of the family . . . we should estimate to be 35% of the whole.

An example, among dozens, of the confusion caused by the failure to grasp this point is from Littlejohn's *Westrigg*, where he tries to show how the wife in the working-class family can maintain the status of the household (Littlejohn, 1963: 123)

> and can be responsible for its downfall into the non-respectable 'slum class' . . . the difference between 'rough' and 'respectable', bare boards versus cloth, china versus enamel, cooked meals, clean clothes, lack of debt to salesmen are all part of the household and therefore female economy.

Granted that there are variations in the ways in which money can be spent and in the energy and skill which women put into household management, yet no miracle of 'make do and mend' can create china or lino, or the fuel to cook meals, nor the soap to wash clothes.

It is almost impossible to tell what proportion of their husbands' income wives in various social classes received or how these levels were arrived at, or whether the housekeeping rose during inflation. It is notoriously difficult to gain this information now; Indeed 'women are woefully ignorant about family finances in general and their own families in particular' (Margaret Stone in *The Times,* Business News); so that trying to reconstruct the distribution of income within the family historically will be a daunting task (Oren, 1973). However, it is clear that our ignorance of these matters is not fortuitous and is due not so much to the husband's meanness about disclosing his total income but rather to the fact that it is thought to be *inappropriate* to apply cash reckoning to family life.

Another crucial area of calculation which can only be briefly mentioned here is the supplying of the household through buying-in goods; that is to say 'shopping', which is a peculiarly modern urban phenomenon in that no supplies are grown by the family or traded for at a local market. One of the acknowledged and lamented, but never questioned, penalties for the nineteenth century urban working class was the necessity to buy in minute quantities every day, or even several times a day, from the corner shop:[19] 'screws' of tea, ounces of sugar and dabs of jam. And even if the poorest sections of the population could have bought in larger quantities they had nowhere to store provisions.

However, given some margin of expenditure, what would be the most 'rational' way to buy in various kinds of provisions, both perishable and non-perishable? When a household no longer lives off its own produce, is it 'economy' to buy in bulk and store goods or is it a 'good general rule never to purchase anything until you absolutely need it'? (Anon, 1854). Both of these incompatible courses were (and still are) urged on housekeepers. The fear of wasting of time and materials, became a leitmotive of nineteenth-century writers on domestic life. But what is waste in this context when there is no standard to measure expenditure by? In the household there is a constant tension between the aims of hospitality, generosity, lavish display (or 'wilful waste') on the one hand and the aims of economy, rational planning and careful forethought (or meanness) on the other; in nineteenth-century idiom, the tightrope between 'Profligacy' and 'Parsimony'. These two orientations can be seen as the contrasting characteristics of upper-class and middle-class life-styles, an antagonism of outlook which goes back at least 300 years (Stone, 1967). The major problems of many nineteenth-century households were due to the fact that they tried to combine both.

Finally, the lack of calculability in the housewife's work has meant that the 'striving for perfection, the ingenious refinement of the conduct of life and attainment of increasing mastery over the external world', which is the *modus operandi* of rationalization (Freund, 1968), is

Leonore Davidoff

constantly being brought up short, being thwarted. Thus 'the physical disorder of the house is marked by the housewife's own psychological disorder' (Oakley, 1974b) and housework is seen as a battle, with the housewife waging war on dirt and chaos and the dirt and chaos constantly attacking her. This is basically a defensive operation, under ordinary circumstances: a struggle to stay out of debt while maintaining certain standards of living. It is brought out most clearly in times of war or economic crisis when the housewife is exhorted to save, and to 'contrive and consider' every action. It is a mentality of going from shop to shop looking for lower prices, turning cuffs and collars, saving string, making casseroles out of leftovers and unravelling old pullovers to knit into gloves.

The attitudes bred by this situation were fatalistic and passive. Only those with aims and resources to enter Society through elaborate entertainment could begin to direct their activity to a more positive goal, and even that had traditional limits. In constast, the capitalist entrepreneur's mentality was a product of the internal pressure to expand. He must 'conquer, organize, deal, speculate and calculate' into a 'boundless infinity' (Sombart, 1967).

The housewife's position, reinforced by isolation and subordination to her husband's authority, produced the feeling that it was right for her to adjust to the lack of calculability, indeed that this adjustment could be a moral virtue. Far from seeking efficiency, it was 'better' to prepare food by hand, to use a hair sieve rather than a moulé, and the use of tinned foods carried a moral stigma which lingers on to our day. (A separate issue from both taste and nutrition but often confused in discussions of this point.) Such attitudes of resignation and passivity are the antithesis of an entrepreneurial ethic; indeed they were positively viewed by both men and women as a *protection* of society from the full effects of that ethic.

Nowhere is this attitude more evident than in the lack of pressure to rationalize the physical plant of the house and in the reluctance to invest in basic equipment such as hot running water.[20] This fatalism is prominent in literature for housewives. A typical statement is by Fay Inchfawn ('the Poet Laureate of the Home') in a poem (Inchfawn, 1920):

Within My House

First, there's the entrance, narrow and so small,
The hat-stand seems to fill the tiny hall;
That staircase too, has such an awkward bend,
The carpet rucks, and rises up on end!
Then, all the rooms are cramped and close together;
And there's a musty smell in rainy weather.
Yes, and it makes the daily work go hard
To have the only tap across the yard.

These creaking doors, these draughts, this battered paint,
Would try, I think the temper of a saint.

However, while washing the breakfast dishes she stops grumbling and starts
to pray:

'Lord' (thus I prayed), 'it matters not at all
That my poor home is ill-arranged and small;
I, not the house, am straightened Lord, 'tis I!
Enlarge my foolish heart, that by-and-by
I may look up with such a radiant face
Thou shalt have glory even in this place;
And when I slip, or stumble unaware
In carrying water up this awkward stair
Then keep me sweet, and teach me day by day
To tread with patience Thy appointed way.
As for the house . . . Lord, let it be my part
To walk within it with a perfect heart.'

The application of science and technology

The ethos which I have been discussing was not only linked to rational
calculation in every sphere of life, but it also promoted a utilitarian
approach to most problems, an 'insistence on empiricism and
experimentation, the expenditure of physical energy, the equation of
contemplation with idleness, the handling of material objects with
industry' (Merton, 1970: 93); in short a set of characteristics congruent
with both a scientific outlook and good housewifery. The application of
science to production whether directly in textile manufacture or, for
example, in the improvements in coach construction and road surfacing at
the end of the eighteenth century, were characteristic of many spheres of
life. But household management, even though it was partially based on
many empirically proved dicta, never progressed very far beyond the 'cook
book' [sic] stage of scientific development. To this day housework
remains an art, making use of a mixture of traditional maxims, empirically
proved rules of thumb as well as more fully 'scientific' procedures (Ravetz,
1965); e.g. 'to take fruit stains out of table linen, boil 3 pints of water
with 4 tablespoons of lemon juice, steep for four hours, rinse and dry in
the open air' could equally well have come from an eighteenth-century
manual, a nineteenth-century cook book or a twentieth-century woman's
magazine.

Not only was the fundamental contradiction discussed in the last
section an important element in the limited application of science and
technology, but the predominant forms of household authority

Leonore Davidoff

relationships also blocked any such development. Within the private household, housework was done in accordance with the wishes and beliefs of the superior. In the case of servants, part of the definition of service was the legal requirement to do the work in the way that the superior prescribed.[21] Hierarchy had to be maintained as well as order in a material sense. For example, it must have been known by experience that soaking very dirty pans in water overnight made it both much easier and much quicker to clean them, but it was the rule that every single pan had to be scoured and polished and put away before the servants were allowed to go to bed, no matter how late the hour, and young scullery maids could be hauled out of bed to scrub the pans if they had neglected this duty (Rennie, 1955).

A scientifically based criterion of cleanliness (in the sense of destroying all bacteria as in a hospital) was not the standard of the family wash. What, then, is cleanliness in, for example, clothing: how is it to be defined; how clean is clean? In the nineteenth century the internal organization of a household on traditional lines came into conflict with the demands of the external economy and no objective scientific level of cleanliness was, or could be, invoked to settle the issue. Considerable strains were put on water supplies and tempers because:

> They that wash on Monday
> Have all the week to dry
> They that wash on Tuesday
> Are not so much awry
> They that wash on Wednesday
> Are not so much to blame
> They that wash on Thursday
> Wash for very shame;
> They that wash on Friday
> Wash in sorry need
> They that wash on Saturday
> Are lazy sluts indeed[22]

Contrast this ubiquitous rhyme with an excerpt from an investigation into laundries (Fabian Tract, 1902).

> The washing does not arrive at the laundry, as a rule till Monday afternoon, and must be returned on Friday. Hence the necessity of working young girls till 10, 11 or even 12 at night. This argument exalts a domestic custom to the dignity of a law of nature. There is nothing in the constitution of the universe which demands that dirty linen should be collected on Monday, washed on Tuesday, dried on Wednesday, ironed on Thursday and sent home clean on Friday.

The rationalization of housework

There is no reason in the nature of things why families with a normal supply of linen should not have their 'washing' called for on a certain day of the week and returned on the same day in the following week.

Again, is it scientific disease control that is the rationale for an affluent linen cupboard (*c.* 1890s) to be marked 'guests, adults, children, servants and sides-to-middle' (for illness) (Interview); or is this another instance of status and ceremonial segregation and the creation of categories which required a large investment in money and labour? The resistance to the installation of more efficient stoves and heating apparatus has been the despair of engineers from Count Rumford in the 1790s onwards, but until very recently the open coal fire remained one of the most potent symbols of the boundary between the private domain and the world, the focus of hearth and home (Ravetz, 1968; Teale, 1883).

Really fundamental changes in food preparation came from outside the private home, from, for example, people like Alexis Soyer, who significantly was a chef first in a club and then in the Army of the Crimea, where his innovations in Army cooking were as important as Nightingale's in medicine. What must be kept in mind is that technical improvements in equipment, such as those exemplified by the use of the small electric motor, are not of the same order as a fundamental change in the organization or aims of housework. A washing machine may be used, for example, to produce more efficiently a clean, white linen tablecloth for every meal. Yet the use of the cloth is still for ceremony and display, a purpose whose effectiveness can, in turn, by its nature never be subject to scientific tests of efficiency[23] (Weber, 1968).

How women were introduced to scientific ideas and how the latter were absorbed into the women's conception of her role in the nineteenth century have all to be explored. An organization such as the Ladies Sanitary Association has left records showing how closely ideas of physical cleanliness were related to ideas about social and moral purity. The assimilation of scientific ideas also involved reconciling the need to teach domestic skills to girls who, according to the ideology of the time, were domestic creatures by nature. The whole domestic economy movement which started as early as the 1870s was an attempt to deal with a situation produced by the primacy of social goals among the middle class and lack of domestic experience of working-class girls employed in factories. It was couched in terms of a return to the traditional skills, a girl's birthright, which had been somehow taken away from her by the over-civilizing effects of modern life. In fact, girls in neither class were necessarily 'by nature' fitted to carry out domestic tasks and needed to be equipped to cope with *new* demands created by higher standards of living on every

Leonore Davidoff

level of society. (If you don't sleep on beds, you don't have to know how to make beds.)

In its attempts to become more and more 'scientific', the growing unreality of the domestic economy movement culminated in the idea of the kitchen as a workshop, in the 1920s. The 'time and motion' study approach of Frederick Taylor was imported from the United States in an effort to maintain the standards of middle-class households faced with a drastic shortage of labour (Frederick, 1920).

The twentieth century: the importance of child care

In the middle- and even upper-class households some of these contradictions between rationalization and non-calculable ends began to be exposed in the decades just before and increasingly after the First World War, when domestic servants were harder to recruit and more difficult to control. Family and social life had to be simplified, tasks had to be combined, and ceremonial polish neglected. The mistress of the household now faced more directly the problems of food preparation, dirt and refuse control, as well as child care. Alternative investment in technical improvements or domestic service began to be more closely appraised, but the outcome remained uncertain until lack of servants forced a change of goals. In 1932, the upper-class journal *The Queen* solemnly ran an article to query whether it was worth the investment in gadgetry to continue entertaining on Sunday evening which the maid had acquired the right to take off (*Queen*, 1932):

> You can't entertain without a maid and look after your guests as you would like if you have not reduced catering to a fine art. The equipment needed includes a dumb waiter, dinner wagon, electric coffee percolator, electric toaster, table cooker and refrigerator.

Because of these threats, earlier generations had made more serious moves in several directions to change radically the pattern of middle-class life. One was the growth of service flats and residential hotels. (Some upper middle-class men had always been able to live, at least part of the time, in colleges, chambers, clubs and barracks, while middle- and some working-class men could live as lodgers and thus be 'serviced' without the complications of marriage.) On the fringe, there were people such as Edward Carpenter who tried to pare and simplify domestic life to a bare minimum by a Thoreauian retreat from the world (Carpenter, 1916). John Brett, a minor artist and architect, designed and built his own flat-roofed, centrally-heated, completely 'labour-saving' house in Putney in the 1870s (Brett, 1911). Many schemes for various forms of cooperative living and shared services were proposed in this period, although few were actually tried. Clementina Black, in 1919, urged municipal cleaning services which she called, even then, 'home help' (*Queen*, 1919). Yet none of these proved viable on a larger scale, and through the twentieth century middle-class housewives carried on trying at first tò maintain considerable ceremony, particularly in crucial boundary areas like answering the front door and meal time ritual. Working class wives were also caught up in the pattern: the hearth-stoning and black-leading may have faded in significance but other cleansing activities have taken their place: the shining sinks, polished floors and sparkling windows of the media image.

It is now a commonplace that child care has moved into the forefront of housekeeping as fewer children are born but more of them are expected to reach adulthood. Previously in all sections of society child care was, in a sense, subordinate to other household aims and activities. When the standard of living was high enough not to have to make use of child labour, children tended to be cordoned off into areas, times and activities which were separated from the main concerns of the household, and the whole philosophy of child care was one of containment. Middle class child training in the nineteenth century, in keeping with the other patterns I have discussed, placed great reliance on rigidity of routine, and segregation by time and place. Obviously this was only completely possible with specialized servants to give their whole attention to the children but it was the principle that applied to all child care. A nursemaid recalled in the 1950s (Streatfield, 1956: 17) that changes in discipline are the most striking of all:

> not that we were strict with the children, but they led such quiet lives, and had so little time to themselves. You see, with the two walks (morning and afternoon), meals regular as clockwork and the hour downstairs from which they were back in the nursery by six o'clock sharp . . . in a well-run nursery with everything to time outbreaks of naughtiness were rare and soon suppressed.

In the 1920s and '30s it took a scientifically based psychology and the institution of progressive schools to rediscover and reintroduce the idea that children's joy in unbound limbs — bare feet, ungloved hands and bared heads — was important for their health and development. A central part of this educational reform was play with dirt and water in the carefully provided sand pit and paddle pool.

The change in views of early childhood care, and the accompanying concern with imagination and language formation, have brought out conflicts *within* the basic constituents of housework, i.e. boundary maintenance through dirt control and tidiness, the latter often incompatible with the socializing of young children when given a new tolerance of their 'disruptive' behaviour (Newson and Newson, 1963). On

Leonore Davidoff

the surface, changes in children's clothes, particularly for girls — from starched white pinafores to blue jeans — illustrates this development. A closer look, however, shows that the more casual clothes still have to be kept 'Persil' clean, and while all housewives are torn between these aims there seem to be important class and educational differences in the tasks which housewives favour (Oakley, 1974a).

Conclusion

Despite some public shifts in attitudes, it is still women who are seen today as basically responsible for servicing members of the family, protecting them from the pollution of dirt, waste products and untidiness, for transforming the raw into the cooked; and for transforming 'little savages' into civilized adults. In the vast majority of cases it is women (particularly mothers, but also the women responsible for the elderly and chronic sick) who peel the potatoes, wash, sort and put away the socks, mop up the vomit, change the nappies and the sheets. These activities are still performed for love (and support). Mary Stott asked in a recent *Manchester Guardian* article ('Are You a Slave or a Slut?'):

> When you buy a new piece of equipment — washing machine, dishwasher, etc ... is it because it will save money, save time or because you rather fancy it? Do you cost your time in relation to the purchase — or for instance in relation to whether you take the washing to the launderette?

At the end of the article she gives no answer, because, I believe, there is no answer.[24]

How much longer will this continue? Are our concerns with pollution and boundary maintenance so fundamental that women will always remain within the cluster, housewife? I do not know, but it is significant that J. K. Galbraith, in his most recent book, gives a central place to women and their role in what he coyly calls 'the administration of consumption', i.e. housework (Galbraith, 1973). Such recognition is only the first step. A great deal more needs to be learnt about how such patterns evolved in the past in order to help understand how they operate now. One thing is certain, however. Historians, economists and, above all, sociologists, can no longer go on turning their attention to everything *but* the kitchen sink.

Notes

1. cf. however Goul (1968) and the recent work of Lopata (1971), Hall (1974) and Oakley (1974a,b).

2. For a recent example of the usual assumption that work can only be located in a 'workplace' see Wedderburn and Craig (1974).

3. These ideas on purity and its relation to women's work have developed in discussion with Jean L'Esperance.

4. In fourteenth and fifteenth century England upper-class boys began their apprenticeship by serving in aristocratic households, service which included laying out body linen, fetching water and emptying slops (Furnivall, 1888).

5. The Pic Nic Society dates from 1802 — the more formal middle and upper class dining etiquette became, the more attractive eating 'au naturel' seemed (Battiscombe, 1951).

6. One of the sharpest breaks between the 'respectable' and 'rough' elements in the nineteenth-century English working class was meal time behaviour (P. Thompson & T. Vigne, 'Work and Life Before 1918', S.S.R.C. Project, University of Essex).

7. The emphasis in this paper on women's role in boundary maintenance should not blind us to the sheer power of men over women, power partly derived from physical strength but mostly from the vulnerability of women with very young children which is in part at least the cause of their powerlessness. In this way they are locked into their subordinate position (Brown, 1970).

8. 'Both Durkheim and Marx have shown us that the structure of society's classifications and frames reveals both the distribution of power and the principles of social control' (Bernstein, 1973).

9. The first chapter in a little handbook (c. 1860) on *How to Behave — A pocket Manual of Etiquette* is completely taken up with care of the hands and 'a lady can always be known by her hands'. Hence the whole panoply of the Victorian 'language of gloves', e.g. a pair of white gloves for a maiden's funeral wreath, keeping one glove of a lover, etc. A. J. Munby is a case of this cultural preoccupation becoming a private obsession (Hudson, 1972).

10. A late eighteenth century country gentry family living in Durham had lice, fleas and ringworm. Yet they spent part of every year in London, for the season, where the father was in Parliament (Colburn-Mayne, 1929).

11. Over the years 'airing' has come to mean both letting air circulate and warming or drying. For example, one puts ironed clothes back outside on the line for a final 'airing' or 'airs' them around the fire.

12. Under the system of double-entry book-keeping *everything* that is encompassed by business activity is accounted in monetary terms: 'The essence of the double-entry system is that the value recorded in the accounts shall always reflect the balance sheet equation. Hence for every debit entry there must always be a corresponding credit

Leonore Davidoff

entry of equal magnitude, and for every credit an equal debit'. *Chambers Encyclopedia*, Vol.1, P.38.

13. It might be argued that the aim of the household is to expand over time through the generations, or at best to endure. However, except in very specific cases as in the aristocracy, this does not seem to follow empirically, or, according to economists, theoretically (Johnson, 1971: 37).

14. The resistance to rational calculation as part of woman's mission may be one of the reasons why girls are 'naturally' less able to do mathematics and technical subjects in *all* modern societies.

15. Other economists use the idea of 'non-pecuniary income' but, I believe, the same objections could be raised to its application. Under systems of barter — of services as well as goods — counting and recording do take place and must make use of some sort of unit of accounting, but surely the point is that this type of unit is not transferable from its very local associations.

16. This goes some way to explaining why, despite the introduction of labour-saving devices, time spent on housework has not decreased substantially in recent years. None of the housewives in Ann Oakley's study was working less than 40 hours a week, many were working 70 to 80 hours, 4 were working over 90 while the longest working week was 105 hours (Oakley, 1974b).

17. Hence the meaninglessness of recent attempts to 'cost' a wife, e.g. in the U.S. the average housewife works a 99.6 hour week doing 12 different jobs worth $8,285 p.a. or collectively $250 billion a year; 35 per cent of the G.N.P. *Chase Manhattan Bank* 'What is a Wife Worth?'

18. The existence of credit systems — from being carried on the tradesmen's books in the middle class to the pawnshop in the working class — complicates this picture but does not fundamentally alter the point.

19. This emphasizes the importance of the consumer cooperative movement, although this only affected the regularly employed, mainly in the north.

20. In 1945, 20 per cent of those in the lowest income groups (below £160 per annum) had to heat water for washing clothes in pans and kettles on the fire, stove or range. I am not underestimating the effects of tenancy patterns here, but I believe that landlords' interests were the immediate not ultimate cause of this neglect — a point which can be strengthened by looking at the amenities provided in council houses (Political and Economic Planning, 1945).

21. Personal control is crucial to the definition of who is a servant and 'a person is under the control of another if he is bound to obey the

orders of that other, not only as to which work he shall execute but also as to the details of the work and the manner of its execution' (Diamond, 1946: 1).

22. Nursery rhymes are an important source for the traditional sexual division of labour. 'It can be safely stated that the overwhelming majority of nursery rhymes were not in the first place composed for children' (Opie, 1952: 3).

23. 'For purposes of the theoretical definition of technical rationality, it is wholly indifferent whether the product of a technical process is in any sense useful'; and Weber cites the example of a supremely efficient machine for producing oxygen (Weber, 1968: 67).

24. In 1973 a French manufacturer began a sales campaign to push paper nappies in the English market — his efforts were unrewarding and the results of a market survey showed that resistance was not only on the basis of cost but also based on the belief that disposable nappies were not 'really clean'. Significantly, while a commercial nappy service has been attempted in large cities, a municipal nappy service has never even been proposed.

Husbands and wives:
the dynamics of the deferential dialectic

Attempts to account for the persistent subordination of women to men by the use of existing theories of social stratification have hardly been very successful. In a sense this is not surprising, given that the 'problem' of sexual inequality was not one that emerged from within the existing corpus of academic sociological theory, but rather emerged from outside it and forced sociologists interested in stratification to come to terms with it. For this reason, many attempts to explain sexual stratification have consisted of squeezing the phenomenon into pre-existing conceptual categories rather than developing them out of an analysis of the phenomenon itself. These attempts — both functionalist and Marxist — have until recently been, as Acker (1973) has said, just examples of intellectual sexism. Much discussion has revolved around such questions as whether, and in what sense, women are a class, or a caste, or a status group, or some other such concept plucked from the analysis of stratification in other contexts. Apart from being an interesting sidelight on the tendencies towards reification in sociological theory, this illustrates how an implicit concern has been to preserve the validity of existing approaches to stratification in the face of a potentially disconfirming instance, rather than to develop a deeper analysis of sexual inequality.

Equally disturbing has been the tendency to consider femininity as merely an extra *attribute* of the stratification system rather than to investigate the nature of male–female *relationships* out of which sexual inequality is derived. At best an explanation of inequality in terms of attributes in tautologous — women are subordinate because they are women — at worst it is false. We need instead to concentrate our investigations on male–female relationships, for an individual is only powerful or powerless in relation to another individual or individuals. This applies as much to the position of women, individually or in general, as it does to any other individual or group in a system of social stratification. Sexual stratification must, therefore, concern itself with the relationships *between* the sexes rather than the attributes of one sex or the other. It is all too easy once you are in possession of survey-generated data to be seduced into the manipulation of varyingly arbitrary categorizations of the attributes of individuals. Sex is only one of the most obvious of these categories. We, however, are concerned, with power and with relationships which seem to us to be two of the central próblematics in theories of stratification.

Needless to say an important arena within which male—female relationships occur is the family. It is, of course, not the *only* arena, as all too many sociologists seem to have assumed, but we would argue that within our society it is a *central* one, an examination of which will carry us a considerable way forward in our understanding of sexual stratification. At this point, however, a problem immediately arises: as far as existing theories of social stratification are concerned, the family has been regarded as the unit of analysis. Stratification within the family has therefore been overlooked. Goode (1962), for example, typically writes that, 'It is the *family* not merely the individual, that is ranked in the class structure. The family is the keystone of the stratification system, the social mechanism by which is is maintained'.[1]

Acker has questioned the validity of just this assumption. She notes (1973: 175) that once it has been decided that the family is the unit in stratification most sociologists have

> neatly dispensed with the necessity for considering the position of women in studies of social stratification or considering the salience of sex as a dimension of stratification. To put it another way, the fate of the female in the class system is determined by the fate of the male. Therefore, it is only necessary to study males.

She lists a series of embarrassing data (from the United States) for anyone who is totally attached to the 'family as basic unit' thesis — e.g. 11 per cent of the population over 18 is unattached, approximately two-fifths of households do not have a male head, in the sense implied by the traditional model of the nuclear family, and so on. Clearly there has been a blinding sexism in many sociological theories of stratification.

Yet statements such as that of Goode (and there are many like it) reflect something very close to the core of the culture and the ideology of industrial societies. One consequence however, has been to make it unnecessary for those interested in stratification to look inside the family. This is very significant (and not just related to the difference in 'importance' and 'prestige' of stratification as opposed to the family as a field of study in British sociology) and rather curious. Curious, because both in everyday language and in the metaphors and technical language of sociologists, explanations of hierarchical relationships have often been reduced to family analogies as though this in itself is sufficient. Weber, for example, refers to 'patriarchalism' and 'patrimonialism'. Studies of extremely powerless individuals have employed the term 'child-like'

Colin Bell and Howard Newby

(Bettelheim, 1943; Elkins, 1959). In particular we may note the frequent use of the term 'paternalism' without specifying the *content* of this relationship. It is unlikely therefore that the indiscriminate adoption of existing approaches to stratification is going to be sufficient when it comes to examining the nature of hierarchies *within* the family.

It is an examination of some aspects of these hierarchies that is our concern in this paper. We are primarily concerned only with the relationship between husband and wife, and not that between parents and children, though we feel that our approach may shed some light on this relationship also. Nor, it should be noted, are we centrally concerned with how extra-familial factors may affect the nature of husband—wife relationships within the family itself, which was the key concern of one well-known major contribution to the sociology of the family, Bott's *Family and Social Network* (1957). Not only shall we have very little to say here about husbands' and wives' extra-familial personal relationships but also, and more importantly and dangerously as far as theories of stratification are concerned, we shall tend to ignore the precise nature of the articulation between the productive relationships of society at large and the internal relationships of the family. We do so, not because this articulation is unimportant — indeed we regard it as an essential element in any understanding of the wider pressures and structures associated with sexual inequality within the family.[2] In this paper we wish to explore a dimension of sexual stratification to which less attention has been paid — the relational and normative means by which men (particularly husbands) maintain their traditional authority over women (wives) and, further, we wish to explore too the necessary strategies they employ in attempting to ensure the *stability* of their power. We are concerned here then more with the maintenance of sexual inequality than with its origins. We make this distinction because we are concerned primarily with the problem of the consciousness of wives of their subordinate position — and, by extension, the problem of feminist consciousness generally. Or, put another way, we are seeking theoretical answers to the question of why we see all around us the continued adherence of many, if not most, wives to a social system and a set of values that endorse their own inferiority

The deferential dialectic — a theoretical discussion

The Pauline doctrine, 'wives submit yourself unto your own husbands, as is fit in the Lord', would still seem to be descriptive of many marriages. The belief on the part of many wives that not only *do* their husbands possess greater power but that, in the last analysis, they *ought* to do so, is the kind of belief that occurs in other highly stratified social situations and with which students of stratification have become familiar. Here we are centrally concerned with the legitimation of power and the 'falsity' of consciousness. We may note that in most societies the power of the husband over his wife is legitimated by tradition in the first instance (employing this term in a Weberian manner as hierarchy that is legitimated by 'the sanctity of the order and the attendant powers of control as they have been handed down from the past' (1964: 34)). It is for this reason that the hierarchical nature of the relationship between husband and wife will appear 'natural' and even immutable. We wish to refer to this traditionally-legitimated hierarchical relationship as deference.

We realize that the term 'deference' has been so widely used and misused in the study of stratification that it has threatened to become meaningless (Kavanagh, 1971). However, the utility of the concept of deference can be rescued if it is considered as neither a type of behaviour nor a set of attitudes, but as a 'form', in the Simmelian sense, of social interaction.[3] Expressed in this manner the relational aspect of deference is more apparent and account is taken not only of the actor who defers, but also of the object of deference. No explanation of deference can dispense with either: thus definitions of deference which take account of the behaviour and/or attitudes of only the deferential actor, and not the individual who is deferred to, are, we believe, inadequate. Deference, therefore, is defined as the form of social interaction which occurs in situations involving the exercise of traditional authority. In this way, it is possible to move away from discussing deferential *relationships* — how these relationships arise, how they are maintained and why they break down — in a truly sociological way.

First, however, we need to develop the concept of deference further. The origins of deference lie in the processes of legitimation by tradition of the power of those in superordinate positions. Although some writers have suggested that power relations inevitably become moral ones over time (see for example, Durkheim, 1964: 287-291; Genovese, 1971: 92), there is no *prima facie* reason why this should be so. Clearly those in superordinate positions *do* have a vested interest in cultivating this conversion since all superordinates are normally concerned with stabilizing hierarchy and thus preserving their own positions. Thus legitmation, as Weber (1964: 124-5) recognizes, represents the process whereby the system of social stratification moves away from being based upon potentially unstable coercive relationships to one that rests upon a stable system of legitimate authority. *Stability* is therefore the keynote of deference, since deference to traditional authority is the most stable form of legitimation of the three types of authority outlined by Weber. For him, what legitimated power, and thus converts it into authority, is status. As he points out (Weber, 1964: 123),

An order which is adhered to from motives of pure expediency is

Colin Bell and Howard Newby

generally much less stable than one upheld on a purely customary basis through the fact that the corresponding behaviour has become habitual. The latter is much the most common type of subjective attitude. But even this type of order is in turn much less stable than an order which enjoys the *prestige* of being considered binding, or, as it may be expressed, of 'legitimacy'.

Status, then, is embedded within the existing power structure; it is an emergent property of the distribution of power, the basis of which lies elsewhere.

We thus regard status, and by extension deference, as outcomes of the stratification system and not sources of it. The deference of a wife towards her husband is not, therefore, an explanation of sexual stratification, but an exemplification of it. This seems to be the fundamental misunderstanding of those who have sought to explain the distribution of power within marriage by the use of exchange theory. Scanzoni (1972: 69), for example, has analysed the 'power politics in the American marriage' in these terms (following Blau, 1964: 22):

Power rests on resources. Husbands, because of their unique relationship to the opportunity structure, tend to have more resources (material, status), hence, more power than wives. And the husbands who have access to the sources of prestige and tangible rewards — those in the middle class — have more power than working-class husbands. 'Exchange processes', as Blau puts it, 'give rise to differentiation of power'.

Apart from the questionable empirical validity of this statement, the causal connection between power and status has become reversed.

Elsewhere Blau (1959-60: 157) has stated that: 'Differences in informal rank arise in social processes in which instrumental services are exchanged for deference.' The crucial question, however, is: what is the 'going rate of exchange' and how is it arrived at? How many hours of household drudgery are a bunch of flowers on the wedding anniversary worth? And who decides? Scanzoni, following Gouldner (1960), emphasizes over-riding norms of reciprocity, but this is to insist on a theory of social behaviour based not upon exchange, let alone power, but norms. Exchange theory cannot itself therefore provide an explanation of hierarchical relationships. Indeed it is based upon a misunderstanding of Simmel, for whom exchange *is* interaction not a theory of interaction (Simmel, 1971: 43). Deference, as any relationship, involves exchange but we need to know *what* is exchanged for *what*, how the norms of exchange are established or imposed. Deference derives from power, therefore, and is not a prerequisite of power. Deference can help us to understand how the distribution of power is stabilized between husband and wife, but in itself it cannot account for any change in the structure of power.

For Simmel all forms of social interaction were inherently dialectical in nature. It is, therefore, necessary to investigate the content of the deferential dialectic. Deferential interaction consists of two opposing elements both of which we will argue characterize, and can be found in, the social relationships between husbands and wives. The first is an element of *differentiation*. This is involved in any hierarchical relationship: by definition social stratification must involve social differentiation (though the reverse, of course, is not true). The second, and opposing, category is that of *identification*. Any interaction, even across a social hierarchy, involves at the very least a coming together, but more than this is implied. The stability which deference confers requires more than a simple interaction, or even interdependence, but rather a positive, affective identification. Hence involvement in deferential interaction is not simply calculative. Indeed, the identification is such that the relationship is not perceived as being between *morally* subordinate and superordinate individuals but is viewed as an 'organic' (in the Durkheimian sense) partnership in a cooperative enterprise.

It is the tension between these opposing elements of differentiation and identification from which contradictions arise which threaten the destruction of the deferential relationship. *Over*-identification — what we may call the 'familiarity-breeds-contempt' syndrome — may result in the denial of authority as much as over-differentiation. However, as we have already pointed out, deferential interaction does not occur within a social vacuum — it both derives from and is embedded in a particular distribution of power. The inherent tensions in the deferential dialectic are capable, at least in principle, of being managed by the superordinate individual. Thus, in the context of a hierarchical husband-wife relationship, the stability of this relationship, and the consequent continuation of legitimate authority, will depend to a large extent on the ability of the husband to 'hold the ring' — to control, contain or dissipate these tensions. Therefore, the continuation of deference implies success in 'tension-management', to be understood not in the functionalist sense of that term but as an active strategy by the superordinate to maintain the stability of the social hierarchy. The concept of deference therefore highlights some crucial areas for investigation into the relational and normative aspects of sexual stratification within the family, particularly with regard to the growth of feminist consciousness among women. It also enables useful analogies to be drawn with other social situations in which deference has been used to explain what occurs, for example, master—servant relationships (Davidoff, 1973), those between slaveowner and slave (Genovese, 1971), feudal lord and villein (Homans, 1960), contemporary farmer and farm worker

Colin Bell and Howard Newby

(Newby, 1972) — indeed wherever hierarchical relationships are typically legitimated by tradition.

It is noticeable that in all such situations, as in the relationship between husband and wife, the hierarchical relationship is a personal and particularistic one: that is, deference is given not just to some abstract ethic of traditionalism but to the embodiment of that ethic in a particular *person* (Weber, 1964: 341-2). In the family, therefore, the wife is most likely to subscribe to the traditionally-ascribed norms of behaviour where her personal ties of dependency are most ubiquitous. Tension-management will be most effective and most complete when based upon face-to-face contact (as between husband and wife) and where the superordinate (male) interpretations of her situation are the only ones available. As we know from many studies of the personal relationships (e.g. friendship and kinship) of individuals in industrial society (e.g. Young and Willmott, 1957; Bott, 1957; Townsend, 1953; Bell, 1968; Firth *et al.*, 1969) most if not all people spend their lives embedded in social milieux (which can be conceptualized as social networks) which are crucial social mechanisms for reinforcing both definitions of the situation and images of society (Bell and Newby, 1973; Bulmer, 1974). These social milieux will reinforce and add to the stability of both superordinates' and subordinates' interpretations of the situation. Barker (1972) has for example vividly described this process working on young people in South Wales who were about to get married. An additional and fundamental reinforcement comes of course from the whole culture of industrial societies as reflected in the mass media — the saga of Katie's OXO-loving family being only one of the most well known. This is too large an area for investigation here, but we should note that as Holter (1970: 183-214) has pointed out that the social situation of many housewives — isolated with young children, housebound (in suburbia) without a car — makes them particularly vulnerable and dependent for their social imagery and interpretation of their role on various mass media. For this reason alone we are glad to see that this topic is beginning to be explored.

Where definitions coincide or are commensurate — they usually are — then they will appear 'natural' or unalterable and so obtain the wife's own adherence. This needs to be explored further, but we are inhibited by the lack of data relevant to any consideration of the processual nature of tension-management. Particular stages in the life-cycle are likely to produce 'crises' in which deference and marital stability threaten to break down, leading, perhaps, to periodic reinterpretations of the content of the deferential dialectic. Therefore, we would need to incorporate into a full analysis of deferential husband-wife relationships a dynamic element from outside the deferential dialectic itself which will affect the *ability* of the husband to handle the inherent tensions. What we have in mind here are 'local' crises specific to a particular family — the birth of another child, the youngest child starting school or leaving home, extra-marital affairs being exposed, the use of overt violence becoming intolerable, or illness. Unemployment, too, as Marsden (1974) has shown, can have a remarkable effect on the deferential dialectic. 'Local' events rather than wider extra-familial social processes like the rise of feminism or changes in technology are clearly fundamentally important but are not our specific concern here. Though as Young and Willmott recently remarked in their *The Symmetrical Family* (1973) (the very title of which we would wish to disagree with and to which we shall return in our conclusions),

> feminism was in the long run an influence almost as decisive as technology[4] upon the growth of symmetry inside the family. Once it began to be denied that power should be ascribed to rulers solely by their birth into the station of life of a particular family, once elementary democratic rights had been granted to men, or some of them, once slavery had been abolished, once the claims of the individualism had been acknowledged for men, the same arguments could be used against men by champions of people born into a particular sex and so condemned by their chromosomes alone, to inferiority in society.

We would argue though that the growth of symmetry in the relationship between husband and wife is more apparent than real, despite some changes in the content of these relations. Nevertheless their comments indicate the importance of ideas — of consciousness — in accounting for the wife's unquestioning acceptance of her husband's authority.

Ideological hegemony

A degree of ideological hegemony over women must clearly be maintained if they are to continue to accept their subordinate position as natural and desirable, and the superior power of men as legitimate. In the management of the tensions inherent in the deferential dialectic it is apparent that, in this case, wives must be provided with a consistent and coherent set of ideas which interpret the dominance of their husbands in a manner that reinforces their legitimacy. Evaluative and factual statements must be made to elide — not only *do* men hold power but they *ought* to do so. Male interpretations must be taken to be correct interpretations, particularly in the area of defining rights and obligations, But how is this ideological hegemony to be achieved?

A degree of *totality* in the hierarchical situation is one way in which ideological hegemony may be achieved — there are simply no other

Colin Bell and Howard Newby

definitions available. A complete hegemony over a wife's beliefs is, of course, virtually impossible during adult life except in situations more isolated than that of the typical family, but during early childhood male ideological hegemony is more feasible and more apparent. It would be redundant here to reiterate the well known facts and arguments about sex-role socialization. What is crucial to us in this paper is that sex-role socialization — both within the family and later in agents of secondary socialization, such as schools — is a vital element in the achievement of ideology hegemony over women. Without becoming entangled in the debate about the biological origins of differences between the sexes, we know that families are 'people-producing' machines and further our culture tries hard to insist that as a social psychologist (Hutt, 1972: 70) has accepted 'Persons do not exist, there are only male persons and female persons — biologically, sociologically and psychologically.' A problem is, of course, as Brake in the companion volume points out, biological sex, sociological gender and psychological positivism do not always coincide. That male and female children are in many important respects treated differently from birth by all their significant others, in a manner that is consistent with the existing ideological hegemony, is a, if not *the*, vital social mechanism for the creation and maintenance of this ideological control.

Because deference to traditional authority is most easily stabilized in relatively small, face-to-face social structures, the corollary of this is an emphasis on a correspondingly small unity of territoriality — the home. The home represents, so to speak, the spatial framework within which the deference of wife to husband operates. The encouragement of ideologies of the home and home-centredness enables the identification of the wife with her husband's superordinate position to increase by emphasizing a common adherence to territory, a solidarity of place. A woman's 'place' is therefore in the home, partly because to seek fulfilment outside the home could threaten to break down the ideological control which confinement within it promotes. The ideology of the 'home' (like, in another context, that of 'community') is therefore a social control mechanism in the sense that escape from the home threatens access to alternative definitions of the female role, as Ibsen realized brilliantly in *The Dolls House*. It allows the wife to obtain 'ideas above her station' (to use a nineteenth century phrase often connected with the consequences of leaving the 'community') which identification with the home will prevent. We are not surprised by the religious and ritual overtones of phrases like 'the sanctity of the home'. There is, of course, a great deal of evidence on the segregation of sex roles of husbands and wives within the home and again, despite some changes, the notion of symmetry of sex roles within the family is a gross exaggeration. We know too from legions of decision-making studies within families[5] that major decisions are usually made by the husband. As Gillespie (1972: 147) concludes after surveying closely these studies, 'the equalitarian marriage as a norm is a myth. Under some conditions, individual women can gain power vis-à-vis their husbands, but more power is not equal power. Equal power women do not have'. The really vital decisions about the nature of a woman's 'place' — such as its location or whether to sell it, as opposed to the colour of the wallpaper — are taken by husbands not wives.

It is the essence of the ideological control implied by male tension-management that male authority must be expressed in an idiom sufficiently flexible to encompass the potential changes in the power base wrought by external economic circumstances and by the family life-cycle (such as those listed above). In other words, ideas about the Good Husband must be sufficiently flexible to cope with the tensions inherent in the deferential dialectic to be able to adjust the norms of the relationship where this is unavoidable. Direct empirical support for this is hard to come by because the changing norms of husband-wife relationships have hardly been systematically investigated. However, there is some evidence from studies inspired by Bott's investigations into conjugal relationships (Bell, 1968; Firth *et al.*, 1969; Bell and Healey, 1973). It appears that in response to emergencies external to the family what is considered to constitute the Good Husband has in recent years become increasingly redefined with greater emphasis placed upon companionship, home-centredness and shared activities. Yet we also know from decision-making studies like Blood and Wolfe (1960) that the power of the husband has remained largely undisturbed. In other words, whilst the norms of the relationship may have altered, the relationship itself has altered far less. Thus deference is retained because male authority is not expressed in an inflexible manner. What Barker (1972: 586) has referred to as 'swinging the norms' remains entirely feasible because deference is paid to a *person* as well as to an abstract tradition. It is for this reason that an individual invested with traditional authority may act in an untraditional manner and yet still retain traditional authority. We suspect that research into the history of ideas about the Good Husband would reveal continual change and yet this has not threatened the traditional authority of the husband over his wife. Swinging the norms of the relationship has enabled the identification of the wife to be retained whilst leaving the differentiation in power between husband and wife undisturbed.

Tension-management in action

The tensions of the deferential dialectic, between the opposition of identification and differentiation are too critical for their management to

Colin Bell and Howard Newby

be affected in a purely negative way; that is to say in terms only of the prevention of the loss of deference or in *post hoc* adjustments to potential threats to the stability of the relationship. Deference also needs to be maintained in a positive manner by the application of some substantive and/or symbolic form of reinforcement. Through family rituals and everyday interaction between husband and wife we are able to observe tension-management in action. The most appropriate method would be a form of action that combines exactly those identificatory and differentiatory elements that characterise deference. The best example of this is the gift.

The importance of the gift has, of course, long been recognized in anthropological studies of primitive societies and at a theoretical level the significance of various institutionalized forms of gift relationships has been summarized by Simmel (1971), by Levi-Strauss (1965) and, most notably, by Mauss (1970: 72):

> The great acts of generosity are not free from self-interest . . . To give is to show one's superiority, to show that one is something more and higher, that one is *magister*. To accept without returning or repaying more is to face subordination, to become a client and subservient, to become *minister*.

And yet to be benevolent to those further down the social hierarchy prompts feelings of 'faithfulness and gratitude'. For instance, we believe that traditionally charity was the gift that was exchanged for 'faithfulness' (or more nastily, subservience) among the British working class — most effectively in rural areas. It combines nicely elements of both identification and differentiation and was certainly seen by the givers of the gift as a mechanism of social control. So that any rejection of the ideological hegemony, say in the form of nascent class consciousness experienced in trade union activity, may be met by the regretful withdrawal and cessation of charitable activities (Stedman Jones, 1971: Part III; Harrison, 1965-6).

Within marriage the gift can be institutionalized around certain ritualized occasions like birthdays, wedding anniversaries and so on. However, husbands also present their wives with gifts on other occasions, often at frequent intervals — customarily bunches of flowers, boxes of chocolates, and so on. Typically the exchange of gifts is asymmetrical: it is expected that husbands are *more* generous in their gifts than wives — and of course because of their earning power and overall control of the family budget have greater economic ability to be more generous. These gifts, we would argue celebrate, symbolize and reaffirm the deferential dialectic. Gifts are therefore, in effect, a means of social control, analogous to charity or patronage.[6]

At a more fundamental level the husbands 'give' their wives a home, security and a whole way of life. This is inevitable with society still largely organized around what Gronseth (1970) has called 'the dominance of the husband—provider role' There is a great need here for a study of the 'micro-economics' of the distribution of housekeeping money between husbands and wives — we have much folklore and few facts.

Further we feel that we should at least refer to the dynamics of the sexual relationship between husbands and wives. That there is little reliable data does not mean that sociologists should for ever, as they largely have in the past, leave sex out of their analysis of the family. Husbands are said to 'give' their wives babies. And very significantly they are said to 'give' their wives orgasms. Elements within the Women's Liberation Movement were quick to realize the significance of this last point: the whole polemic about the precise location of female orgasms can be seen in part as a rejection of the gift aspect of sexual relations and all that it represents (Koedt, 1970).

Often, however, what is crucially important is not *what* is given but *how* it is given. This is merely to recognize the symbolic, as opposed to the intrinsic, value of the gift — 'it's the thought that counts'. Demeanour is, therefore, as crucial as the act of giving in itself. The significance of deference and demeanour in highly stratified situations of face-to-face interaction has been brilliantly described by Goffman (1972). Demeanour is of critical importance in conveying the correct balance between identification and differentiation in relationships characterized by traditional authority. All superordinate individuals in a deferential relationship are faced by a dilemma that reflects the contradictions inherent in the deferential dialectic: in the coming together involved in face-to-face interaction certain mechanisms must be employed that maintain social distance. What are these mechanisms? Some are ritualized and easily observable — bowing, curtsying, saluting and so on — whilst other mechanisms can be observed without too much difficulty — etiquette, forms of address, degree of physical contact, for example. The problem is that in the most particularistic of relationships, such as that between husband and wife, the norms of demeanour are extremely difficult to investigate. Even the more generalized attributes of demeanour referred to above are likely to be inappropriate. We need to know a great deal more about the obeisances, condescensions and ceremonial taboos which prevail between husbands and wives. We know that the behaviour of men and women is often different when members of the opposite sex are absent, whilst certain forms of behaviour, verbal and non-verbal, are traditionally taboo 'in front of the wife' (swearing, 'dirty' jokes, the explicit discussion of sex) or the husband (menstruation, 'dirty' jokes). But our knowledge is little beyond the level of social anecdote. The insights of Goffman need to be extended

Colin Bell and Howard Newby

beyond the mental hospital and the outermost Shetland Islands (Goffman, 1968, 1969) and brought into an examination of sexual stratification in the family.[7]

Ann Whitehead's paper (Ch. 9) provides a virtually unique account of husbands' and wives' behaviour in a social system where women are held, as she says, in 'contempt'. She has shown that detailed analysis along these lines, though difficult, is possible. Her observations of the 'finely balanced' situation lead her to a similar perspective to ours: 'while men have to control their wives' behaviour, if they behave too badly the wives will retaliate . . . at best they must be torn between the wish to establish a satisfactory marital link, and the desire to appear the boss' (this volume: 199). Her detailed fieldwork report and the analysis that emerged from it is an extremely important contribution to the sociology of sex roles.

So far we have been arguing that the relationship between husband and wife is a deferential one in that it is traditionally-legitimated and hierarchical. It appears both natural and immutable. It also has become — because it has been in the interests of those in the superordinate position — a 'moral' order. This 'moral' order is expressed through and by ideological hegemony. We have also argued that the contradictions within the deferential dialectic of identification and differentiation need careful if not constant 'tension-management'; and that there are a number of social mechanisms by which this is done — most notably by the 'gift'. Yet though 'might' has been turned into 'right' in most marriages, 'might' remains very close to the surface. Deference stabilizes the hierarchical nature of the husband-wife relationship, but we must emphasize again that the relationship is embedded in a system of power — and the naked use of this power can be, and is, resorted to if the relationship threatens to break down. Two sorts of power — both more direct and overt than those we have hitherto discussed — form the constant background to the deferential dialectic between husbands and wives. These are the power of the hand and the power of the purse.

Those who have been antagonistic towards the family as a social institution have fairly frequently pointed out that the family is the main area of deliberate interpersonal violence in industrial societies. More people are physically assaulted in a family setting than in any other. Clearly both adults assault their children, yet fairly few wives assault their husbands for what seem to be fairly obvious reasons rooted in biology. Men are bigger, and stronger. Yet as the recent experience of National Women's Aid has all too clearly demonstrated many husbands use extreme physical violence on their wives. And again as writers within the Women's Liberation Movement have been quick to point out, rape is legal within marriage. John Stuart Mill (1869: 35) wrote in a well-known passage in his essay, *The Subjection of Women*, published just over a century ago that 'people are not aware how entirely in former ages the law of superior strength was the rule of life: how publicly and openly it was avowed'. All that has changed is that it is less publicly and openly avowed. Physical coercion is, though, an inherently unstable basis for inter-personal relationships and whilst force is always latent in most relationships between husband and wife, this relationship must usually be a 'moral' one of deference if the relationship is to be stabilized.

It is well known that many wives do not know what their husbands earn — this is especially true of working class wives.[8] Further the earning power of most wives most of the time is far less than that of their husbands. This is, of course, especially true during the child-bearing and rearing stage of the family cycle. Such is the dominance of the husband-provider role that women have great difficulty surviving economically without husbands — as is graphically illustrated by Dennis Marsden in his *Mothers Alone* (1969). Within a marriage the husband has economic as well as moral and physical power, although there may be certain sections of society where this relationship could be reversed. Jane Marceau's paper (Ch. 10) shows that for at least a small section of the French middle class some wives bring considerable economic, social and cultural resources to the marriage that may be used to establish and maintain their husband's career.

Should, however, the deferential relationship between husband and wife begin to break down — say from increasing feminist consciousness or changing economic circumstances (as simple as the wife going out to work or the man losing his job) behind the morally charged, traditionally legitimate domination is savage force. The great benefactor can within a marriage also be the great persecutor. Where there is revolt from such relationships, as within marriage, the revolt is typically very bitter simply because the relationship is as morally charged and because previous identification had been so extensive. And equally the revolt is frequently put down without mercy. Such is the nature of deferential relationships that their sudden breakdown may release passions and violence stored up for years if not for generations. Tension-management, therefore, occurs *within* a context of power, and, while we have been concerned to explore the means by which this power is stabilized and maintained, this factor must not be overlooked — 'it must above all be remembered that ideal subordination is often proceeded by real subordination' (Simmel, 1950: 261).

Conclusion

In our introduction we emphasized that we were concerned with relational

Colin Bell and Howard Newby

and normative means by which husbands *maintain* their traditional authority over their wives. We think we have uncovered an extraordinarily resilient form of social relationship that will not be open to rapid change. Our conclusions are not, therefore, the too easily optimistic ones espoused by Young and Willmott (1973), who in their recent book stress over and over again a 'move towards symmetry' in the relationships of husbands and wives. We feel that they were only able to argue this thesis by concentrating on fairly superficial changes and by not confronting the form of the social relationship between husband and wife. By symmetry they mean for instance that 'there should be no monopolies for either sex in any sphere' (1973: 275), but given the exigencies of childbirth and the dominance of the husband-provider role it is unlikely that we will see major changes in the domestic division of labour, let alone the form of the social relationship between husband and wife. Indeed there is little evidence from their own data of any great change even in the former.[9]

Young and Willmott (1973: 278) go on to say in a major conclusion of their study that:

in this century wives have been doing a job outside the home that they did not greatly care for and the husbands a minor job inside the home that they did not greatly care for either — each therefore showing signs of the bonds that held them to the past as well as their partial recognition of the new order which they have been helping to bring into being. By the next century — with the pioneers of 1970 already at the point of the column — society will have moved from (a) one demanding job for the wife and one for the husband, through (b) two demanding jobs for the wife and one for the husband to (c) two demanding jobs for the wife and two for the husband. The symmetry will be complete, instead of two jobs there will be four.

If this is symmetry then it might happen. Yet of course there is no reason why this should necessarily upset the deferential dialectic. And we are certainly a long way from symmetry currently.

We find much more convincing the consequences of the deferential dialectic that Young has recently presented in a Sunday newspaper article. These data also illustrate the power of the purse within a marriage. Young and Syson (1974) reported the findings of a small investigation into the effects of inflation on the household economics of working class wives. They found that nearly half of the fifty women interviewed (all of whom were in the early stages of the family cycle)

had received no extra 'wages' from their husbands though almost all of the husbands were earning more. In these families the standards of living of the wives and children was bound to have dropped. They could not take action against their husbands as easily as their husbands could against the Government

Clearly far from a symmetrical family! We are sure that many of these wives would find it ludicrous to suggest that they should take such action and would have felt not only that they could not but also that they *should* not. Those women who were interviewed who were dependent upon the State were even worse off — again we would argue as a consequence of feminine deference. 'One reason why at all ages fewer women received the benefits they were entitled to was that they seemed even more confused than men about their rights. The widows and the deserted wives had always before left their husbands to deal with officials.' That the whole social security system is riddled with sex discrimination is not our concern here (though see Land's paper in the companion volume). But we should note that it was designed with asymmetry and deference in mind rather than the reverse. It was designed for people at work, drawing regular wages and paying regular National Insurance contributions. As was correctly noted in the newspaper article quoted above, 'the housewife was not thought of as being at work. She was paid by her husband, and so her rights were, in good part, derived from him. If he disappeared and left her with the children, she was unable to claim as of right a decent benefit either for herself or for them'.

Finally we would like to stress that the utility of what we have called the deferential dialectic was very much in its heuristic value. For traditional forms of authority remain, we would argue, prevalent in the relationship between husband and wife. And most importantly it seems to us that this is likely to be a central inhibitor of the growth of consciousness among wives of their subordinate position. Indeed it is in the family that this 'false consciousness' is both created and then supported. Apart from the traditional plea for more research along these lines within the family we would like to conclude by saying that the approach we have outlined here leads to a new and we believe more meaningful set of questions to be asked about the nature of relationships within the family and their relevance to more general problems of sexual stratification.

Notes

1. Multi-dimensional theories of stratification suffer most from this lapse; e.g., Lenski (1954 and 1966).
2. See for example Middleton's (1973) paper given at last year's B.S.A. Conference, and the papers by Brown (Ch. 2) and Gardiner (Ch. 6).

Colin Bell and Howard Newby

3. For an earlier conceptualization of deference which this paper supersedes see Bell and Newby (1973). A full discussion can be found in Newby (1975).

4. By technology here they mean the miniaturized technology of household consumer durables. But as Leonore Davidoff shows (Ch. 7) this supposedly rationalized technology is still used both for traditional goals and to support the traditional division of labour within the family.

5. For example, the so-called 'power' studies of Blood and Wolfe (1960) which inspired much empirical investigation into marriages. Not all of these studies show what they purport to show. See Gillespie (1972) and Safilios-Rothchild (1969).

6. It has been put to us strongly by Frances Korn in a private communication that husbands 'give' their surnames to their wives. Whilst we would not go so far as her in saying that 'nobody can expect anything but deference from people who are quite prepared to forget everything about one of the constitutive parts of their own selves by means of a legal ceremony' it is clear that a fuller analysis than ours would also have to consider the importance of 'naming' in the psycho-social process of identifying oneself as an independent entity.

7. Once again we should emphasize that what is important are the norms of this exchange and how they are arrived at as discussed above.

8. Young and Willmott (1973: 80-84) sum up the British evidence.

9. See for instance pp. 93-96 of Young and Willmott (1973).

Sexual antagonism in Herefordshire

In a rural parish in England where I did fieldwork in 1967[1] the worlds of men and women are segregated and opposed, as are gender stereotypes in which women are held in contempt. This cleavage affects the interpersonal relations of men and women with members of their own sex, and with each other in marriage. My observations suggest that men are both overtly and covertly hostile in their behaviour towards women, that the social control of all women and of particular wives is a burning issue and that some husbands and wives quarrel frequently and violently. Values of masculinity and virility, in which women are objectified, are cultural counters of male competition. This creates difficulties in establishing the personal bond between a man and a woman, which remains hesitantly and differentially held as a (submerged?) ideal in marriage.

What I describe is linked in part to the almost total barriers to women entering the workforce as well as to the nature of their husband's work. In this and a number of other respects the Herefordshire community could hardly be said to be representative of most families of advanced industrial society. Comparisons would be with less industrialized societies (see e.g. Davis, 1973; Campbell, 1964) and with what is fast becoming the largely inaccessible (and mythical?) world of the 'traditional working class' (in the restricted sense in which this is understood in British sociological writing) (for description see Klein, 1965; for discussion see Goldthorpe *et al.*, 1969).

Partly because of this and partly because, when we take away the familiar language of sociological analysis, the situation I describe in these pages is extreme and brutal, I have felt acutely that it can be used to support a prevalent notion that things have changed very much for the better. In some respects they have. In a recent book, *The Symmetrical Family*, Young and Willmott (1973) optimistically emphasize the reduction of male authoritarianism within the family, married women's increasing participation in the work force and the development of more joint marital roles. Women are seen as being increasingly freed from the burden of domesticity and as being progressively liberated. This buoyant assessment of the nature of the contemporary family is in stark contrast to

Ann Whitehead

some recent women's writing which sees women's role within the family as getting worse, not better (e.g. Friedman, 1963).

This paper focuses not merely on marital roles, but on the context of the wider relations between men and women within which marital roles are set. In particular it discusses the consciousness of sexuality as a dominant aspect of the behaviour of men and women. It also emphasizes the use made of women as a differentiated category to symbolize, express and maintain both solidarity and ambivalent rivalry between men. My material emphasizes that the complexity of social relations between men and women cannot be reduced to 'shopping lists' of who washes up, hits the children or baths the baby, nor of where men and women are in the labour force and how much they get paid. The content of marital roles may be changing. Gender stereotypes and the ideological use of gender differentiation remain.

This paper also implies that studying the family as itself a system of production, and studying the relation between the form of the family and the major mode of production within which it is embedded, while they are essential, are unlikely to be the entire key to understanding relations between the sexes and sexual antagonisms. Gender stereotyping, sexual antagonisms and their symbolic uses appear to be universal; the nuclear family and capitalism are (or were) not. An implicit question throughout this paper then is, what is the significance of the frequent use to which ideologies of gender differentiation and the symbolism of sexual relations are put, to express solidarity, submissiveness, inequality and control? And what is the link between this and the relations of production in which men and women engage? Readers familiar with a major published debate in recent writings on women, that between radical feminists (e.g. Firestone, 1971) and the rest (who did not like to call themselves feminists a few months back) will recognize this impasse. I find myself quite unable to deal with the implications of this at this time, but I offer instead this ethnographic romp to add to the complexity.

'Women suffer from petty jealousies'

The community I am discussing is a small parish (total population about 550) in the north-west of Herefordshire, about 6 miles from the Welsh border. The parish is not particularly isolated but is firmly rural in character. Mixed stock, grain and some fruit farming occupy half the men in some way or another. Farming is closer to the family farming rather than the large capitalist farming type (see Frankenberg, 1966). One-third of the farms are run by the household of nuclear family members only. Although 60 per cent of household heads were farm labourers 100 years ago, relatively few men are employed as farm workers today and only five head independent households. The non-farming occupations include shopkeepers, publicans and workers in transport and service industries, such as lorry drivers, delivery drivers, a railway worker, carpenters, builders and garage mechanics. A few men work in the timber trade as labourers on contract, and there are a number of other labourers working in tent erecting, scaffold erecting and for the County Council, as well as privately as gardeners or handymen. All these men work mainly in the local area. Very few travel to Hereford to work or have industrial occupations. Their fathers and grandfathers were farm labourers and skilled farmworkers, or smallholders and craftsmen. Many of the younger men who now drive lorries, or erect steel scaffolding, began their lives in farmwork and still turn their hands to it occasionally.

The parish is not an egalitarian place, but neither does it have a well-marked hierarchy of authority and deference, such as is characteristic of parishes which were more recently estates divided into a small number of tenant farms (see Bell and Newby, 1973) The members of the two major class groups (referred to in this paper as farmers and non-farmers)[2] do not interact on the basis of social equality. There are differences in life-style and control over resources, and intermarriage across this boundary is rare. There are quite substantial objective differences between families with farms of 150 to 300 acres and those with 40 to 80 acres, but these are not conceptualized within the parish. Farming is a unified and prestigious way of life, bringing a comfortable standard of living and access to community decision-making positions, which appears to be coveted and rated as superior by both farming and non-farming populations. Ideally farming status can be achieved by working up the farming ladder from farm worker to small farmer and then large farmer. One or two farmers have been spectacularly successful in this way, but by and large today's farmers are sons of farmers and/or they have married farmers' daughters.

Despite this stratification, I have argued elsewhere (Whitehead, 1971) that farmers and non-farmers share a number of aspects of culture and social organization, including some features of the relations between men and women. In this first section of the paper I shall discuss cross-gender contact in situations outside the household and farm for both farming and non-farming families. In the succeeding sections I shall concentrate exclusively on the relations between men and women and some aspects of relations between members of the same sex for non-farming households. In my view, an analysis of the same areas for farming households would entail discussion of the inadequacies and misconceptions in descriptions of women's position in the family when it is engaged in farming production, thus making the paper overcomplex.[3] (Scattered information on comparable areas for farming families can be found in Whitehead (1971).) Briefly, farming families share segregated

Ann Whitehead

marital roles, there is much joking and teasing between spouses, but there is much less overt marital conflict.

Outside the home, the situations in which men and women meet in Herefordshire are limited. With very few exceptions, non-farming men work in jobs where they are unlikely to encounter unrelated women. Timber workers, lorry drivers, labourers and so on work in exclusively male groups and rarely in organisations employing women in other tasks.[4] No women are employed on farms. The men and women who work together there are household and family members and in kinship or quasi-kinship relations.

As paralleled in other rural localities (Williams, 1956; Williams, 1963; Frankenberg, 1957), the communal affairs of the parish are run by a number of organizations which have largely segregated gender participation. The most important bodies concerned with public affairs are the Parish Council, the School Management Committee, the War Memorial Committee, the Flower Show Committee, the Parochial Church Council and the Women's Institute. The first three bodies are exclusively male. The Flower Show Committee has a separate women's committee which does not meet regularly, but which is responsible for catering. The Parochial Church Council has equal numbers of men and women on it, and these are usually listed in two sets, men followed by women. The Women's Institute is of course constitutionally confined to women. Both men and women conceptualize the differential gender participation in terms of their corporate solidarity. The men are extremely scathing about women's ability to organize. 'They quarrel amongst themselves. They suffer from petty jealousies and won't get anything done.' Men suggest that in the events organized by the Flower Show Committee and Parochial Church Council, those parts organized by men (the annual flower show, bingo evenings and the annual church auction to raise funds) are efficiently and competently handled in a spirit of cooperation, while the catering organized by women generates numerous neighbourhood feuds and squabbles. In my observation, none of the events mentioned occurred without serious disputes between men. (I have forborn to excise my sexist slip (?) of the pen which describes the men's disputes as 'serious', thereby confirming the men's view that women's squabbles are 'petty'.)

In the three organizations in which men and women 'combine' in some degree, women have had little success in moving out of the catering role. The major arena for women's political activity is within the Women's Institute, the definition of whose activities they more firmly (though not entirely) control. It is to the members of the Women's Institute, both collectively and individually, that men direct their greatest scorn. The initials W.I. are used to make a number of derogatory puns, and this hostility comes out in the Christmas party described below (pp. 111). The

W.I. is extremely active in parish affairs and has been responsible for raising each of a large number of recent political issues and forcing them upon the attention of the major decision-making bodies concerned — the Parish Council, the School Management Committee and the War Memorial Committee. (In the spirit of Frankenberg (in the companion volume), I note that this is described in detail in Whitehead (1971), with no comments as to its significance for women's corporate solidarity). The net effect of several years' agitation and political activity has been the election of a woman to the Parish Council, and the creation of two *ad hoc* bodies attached to and responsible to the Parish Council, on which men and women work side by side. Nevertheless, the woman elected to the Parish Council is an elderly class I immigrant with a minor title. Farmers' wives have failed in their bids to utilize the *ad hoc* committees as bases from which to get elected to the three male committees. On the other hand, male members with socio-economic statuses not traditionally associated with membership of the Parish Council have so succeeded.

If the communal affairs of the parish are not debated and decided upon by men and women acting jointly, many spare-time leisure activities also only bring together members of the same sex (with the exception, of course, of the courtship activities of adolescents and other unmarrieds). The Mothers' Union and the Sewing Circle are confined to women. Only one man attends meetings of the Over-Sixties Club, and only two attend W.E.A. classes. Men's activities are less well organized and they may 'shoot', go to watch football matches, follow the hunt, and together play darts, football and cricket. The sexual apartheid is not total, for both men and women go to whist drives, to church and to bingo (though not necessarily together) and, as we shall see below, some men and women come into contact in pubs.

At one level these examples of gender differentiated participation are a widely accepted form of social inequality leading to an absence of shared interests. At another, they add up to highly constrained opportunities for cross-gender contact. This goes together with a strong feeling that adult men and women who are not related and who do not stand in employer—employee relationships should not meet in private. The frequent callers to farms are rarely invited into the farm-house unless the husband is there and are instead sent off to the fields to look for him. It is considered most improper for a man to call at a house while the husband is away. To do so not only arouses the suspicions of neighbours but, if repeated, is taken as the only necessary proof that they have a sexual relationship. My attention was drawn by jokes to the visits an older, widowed farmer made to the homes of two middle-aged women whose husbands drank at the pub. As long as the husbands were not present at the pub, his comings and goings were always the subject of joking

Ann Whitehead

comment. 'There goes Charlie — Tom will be home from work in a minute', and gales of laughter when sure enough a few minutes later the husband did arrive. These visits did not simply create the opportunity for a laugh and gossip at somebody's expense. They were cited to me as *proof* that 'something' was really 'going on', with ribald references to the alleged impotence of one of the husbands.

When men and women normally only meet in defined situations, in which they stand in relatively formalized specific role relationships, what happens when they meet in more undefined and informal situations is extremely interesting. In general, in Herefordshire, these situations are characterized by joking and teasing.

Some leisure activities are specifically designed to promote such cross-gender contact as is required to choose a marriage partner and make the joint decision which marriage in this culture does demand. Most adults had met their spouses at a dance, at church or chapel, or at the Young Farmers' Club. The most popular form of Saturday evening entertainment for the unmarried, as for their parents, was still dancing, and dances were attended at village halls over a wide area. Farmers' children tend to go to and sit at these dances in mixed gender groups. Non-farmers' children almost invariably go out in single-gender groups. Girls go dancing with their peers from the neighbourhood or from school and occasionally go to a pub, especially if it has a juke box. Boys go drinking or to watch football with neighbours, friends from school or work. It is when they go together to dances that they are seriously looking for a girl. The teenagers sit in separate groups of boys and girls and the girls often dance together. The separate sets tease and flirt with each other. Boys and girls at first go home separately. Any relationship between an individual boy and girl begins and proceeds through the joking and flirting of the groups. The joking and teasing are about personal attributes and allegedly emotional intentions, about attractions and presumed likings. Boys and girls appear to have equal resources and skills in playing the verbal games. A boy and girl will eventually seek each other out from these groups, and in doing so bear the brunt of teasing from their friends. Even then, when they go out alone there seems to be little direct communication between them. Instead close friends are used to relay information about intentions and feelings and the boy and girl use this information and indirect signs and clues to interpret each other's behaviour and actions. When they are together in public they still joke and tease. The total number of boy-friends and girl-friends which any girl or boy has is usually quite small, and few relationships are experienced where a couple are alone together for any length of time.

Boys and men do not give up the old pattern of going out with their mates when they are courting, but often reserve special nights — Friday and Saturday — for their girl-friends. They spend the other evenings drinking with their peers, but once married they do not even reserve Friday and Saturday for their wives.

The licensed familiarity of the pub

Drinking in pubs was both ideally and in practice a man's privilege. Men, as we shall see, took care that it remained so. Nevertheless a few women could occasionally be found in pubs in the parish, or more often drinking in pubs outside it. For some men and women these dramatic encounters are some of their main experience of non-family, informal cross-gender contact; and I should like to describe them in some detail.

Patterns of drinking, in terms of who, where and with whom, were rather complex. For the men, farmers' frequent drinking was relatively socially invisible because it took place on market days in the numerous market towns of the area. The most socially visible drinking was that of a set of young married and unmarried non-farming men, in the semi-skilled occupations described above, who spent many hours drinking, both inside and outside the parish. A smaller proportion of older non-farming men and a few low-status farming men also spent quite a lot of time in the parish pubs. As to the women, older farmers' wives never drank, and younger farmers' wives rarely did so, unless they were taken for an evening out by their husbands to a more sophisticated pub on the main roads outside the parish. Among older non-farming women, one set, who would never set foot inside a pub, was hostile to those few older women for whom it was a pleasant source of entertainment, with or without their husbands. Young non-farming wives were occasionally taken to pubs by their husbands, but more usually went drinking with girl-friends. Most of this drinking took place outside their home parishes. The occasions when women are to be found in a parish pub will be described in more detail below.

On the drinking expeditions outside the parish which I shared with young married women, the women dressed and made up with care and elaboration, and drew a great deal of attention to themselves in the pub. They played the juke box, and criticized the other drinkers' choice of records; they pretended to dance together in confined spaces; they giggled and screamed and talked in loud voices; they called to men they knew slightly to buy them drinks (not taken up). On one occasion, when they had attracted the attention and advances of some travelling workmen (i.e. strangers), these men then tried to prevent us leaving by lifting the back of my car off the ground (showing masculine strength?), and then chased us dangerously along country roads. I am not sure how typical this behaviour is of all young married women out in pairs or groups. The giggling was not over sexual references and the behaviour was exaggeratedly coy and

Ann Whitehead

flirtatious. It is perhaps a more extreme form of that of young unmarried girls in the presence of unmarried boys.

Within the parish, my description is confined to a single pub, The Wagonner, which was much more exclusively a man's domain than any other. Groups or pairs of young unmarried women never entered it. In line with the secrecy surrounding boy–girl friendships, none of the unmarried regulars at The Wagonner ever brought a girl-friend for a drink there. One evening a young married man (not a real regular) brought his young unmarried girl-friend, who was subjected, in his presence, to a barrage of increasingly hostile comments about the length of her skirt. There were special circumstances: the man was already married and still living with his wife; he was wealthier and had a higher if more ambiguous status than most of the drinkers; he lived outside the parish (although many of the regulars did too). I do not know whether any other accompanied unmarried woman would have had to run this gauntlet, and the comments may have been largely directed at her companion. Nevertheless she was considerably embarrassed.

The only unmarried woman who drank regularly at The Wagonner was the anthropologist. My class and stranger position, and my general eccentricity (by Herefordshire standards) made my first visits tolerable, but my access to the pub was only finally gained after one young married lorry driver whom I knew well pronounced the facilitating formula: 'Ann and me, we're like brother and sister. She's like a sister to me.'

Apart from the wife of the landlord, who was in her forties, two or three older married women (i.e. they had young grandchildren) drank regularly in The Wagonner. Two were sisters, with homes close to the pub, whose husbands also drank there. One, a retired tradesman, very active in parish affairs, drank with his wife and her sister in the top bar, while the second husband, a former skilled farmworker and now a factory worker, drank in the bottom bar. He was a core member of the male clique and a renowned teaser (see below). Although both these women drank in the top bar, the lay-out of the pub was such that conversations and verbal exchanges were often general between the bars. These married women seemed to participate symmetrically in much of the exchange in the pub. They swopped ribald and obscene remarks with each other and with most of the men, although this was more often with men of their own age group. There was a certain amount of avoidance of sexual jokes and the exchange of obscene banter between them and the young married men.

The symmetrical behaviour was similar to that at the Christmas Party for the Women's Institute, to which members' husbands were invited. Apart from eating and drinking, most of the evening was taken up with uproarious party games. Many of these had explicit or implicit obscene or sexual overtones, which were not lost on the participants. On the contrary, it seemed that the greatest fun was had in games where men and women got themselves in positions which simulated or symbolized sexual intercourse.

In the pub, the older married women were often the initiators of teasing and joking against bachelors, both old and young. Young unmarried men were sometimes teased about their lack of sexual experience, but older bachelors were subject to a great deal of teasing and the source of much amusement in the pub circle.[5] No older bachelor was ever in the pub while I was there without being jokingly and challengingly offered me in marriage.[6] Quite elaborate plans for taking me out were drawn up for some of the more wealthy farming bachelors. Married women would promise to 'go away with' bachelors and one or two older bachelors were observed in several prolonged bouts of 'horse-play' with the landlady — chasing her about the bar, hitting her with a rolled up newspaper, fighting her, etc.

The young married men who drank at The Wagonner rarely brought their wives to the pub. As I shall describe below, their husbands' involvement in the pub was a bitter source of complaint for their wives, and the social visibility of events in the pub and in the marriages of its regular drinkers affected events in both arenas.

The response of some wives to their husbands' drinking was never to enter The Wagonner at all. One evening, when a particularly good and boisterous time was being had, with everyone still drinking at 2.00 a.m., a thunderous knocking was heard at the back door. Here the landlady was greeted by a wife, who, remaining firmly outside, wanted to know whether her husband was coming home that night, as one of his children was ill. This wife never set foot inside the pub even when she had to make odd purchases there. Other drinkers' wives are the women described above who drink with each other outside the parish. Their husbands occasionally brought them to a special evening at The Wagonner, such as the annual pheasant supper, or over Christmas.[7] When they did so the husband and wife dressed in their best clothes and drank in the top bar. When I was staying in the home of one of the drinkers he took me and his wife to a darts match in the pub. His responsibility for us two women prevented him from engaging in the normal jokes and banter with his male friends, and the experiment was never repeated.

Those wives who do drink rarely if ever went directly to The Waggoner, but nevertheless during the fieldwork period some of them often became involved in a tangential way in the pub. Thus on Christmas Eve the landlady of the pub asked Stella, a young married woman whose husband was a core member of the pub clique, to make a fancy table arrangement for her. Her husband stayed at home to babysit and told her not to be too long. Stella stayed on and on and describes what happened:

Ann Whitehead

There was a few of us there in the end very late, still drinking. When it came to midnight Peggy went round kissing everybody under the mistletoe. She said 'Come on I'm going to kiss everybody.' There was a lot of larking about. Then they turned on me and said 'Come on, Stella, we're going to kiss you now.' I wouldn't let them. 'I'm not having that' I said. Mike [the landlord's eighteen-year-old son] chased me all over. He jumped over the bar where I was hiding. They were all egging him on. He'd had quite a bit to drink and of course he's not very old. He was silly. In the end I spoke seriously to him and said 'Don't be silly, you can't kiss me' and he stopped then. But not the others. One of them got me on a stool and pressed me right back saying they were going to kiss me. 'You're not' I said. I was struggling so somebody held me back and Stan tried to kiss me. I said 'No' and he said 'I'll give you a love-bite then' and he got me in the neck. A minute or two later I felt it rise up and when I looked in the mirror there was a mark as big as a half crown on the side of my neck.

This tale, told me with a mixture of laughter and tears, sounds like a mild(?) group assault by the male drinkers on a female interloper. Apart from the unnamed man who held her down, the rest of the drinkers gave at least verbal encouragement. I hardly need point out that a love-bite is both sexual in implication and more permanent in its effects than a kiss. Positioned on her neck, it was difficult to conceal throughout the Christmas holiday. Stella had to bear the brunt of teasing comments from male neighbours casually met (not members of the pub clique) and to explain its origins to both her own and her husband's family. This incident was surrounded by a complex set of other happenings in the marriage and in relation to the pub, so that there were possibly many reasons why her husband did nothing about the man 'responsible'. Stan had rather few links with the rest of the drinkers and with her husband, for whom he was not a close friend or mate.

An equally tangled set of complexities surrounds a second case, which I shall only outline. When the landlord and his wife went away for a summer holiday they left their son and his teenage wife in charge of the pub. In their absence, Stella's husband and a close friend were largely responsible for initiating one or more evenings of increasing ribaldry and obscenity. The conversation was full of sexual jokes and jibes which discomforted the young wife, and her husband, who was unable to control it or support his wife. The situation got quite out of hand. An older 'respectable' bachelor told me: 'I was disgusted. She's hardly left school. I know she has two little kiddies, but it's not right. I wouldn't repeat the kinds of things they were saying.' The joking and obscenity were in part directed towards the husband, who was rather a mild young man who hardly ever drank at the pub, but the detailed rumours just after this that the young wife had been walking her children up in the woods to meet some man who had been working there are unlikely to have been coincidence.

These last two incidents are the most hostile encounters of young married women that I observed. They can be seen as situations in which 'joking' abuse is used by men to control the behaviour of women. Among other things the drinkers may be expressing their disapproval of Stella's presence in the pub, of her drinking outside the parish and of the 'walks' of the second young wife.

Had I not read Alwyn Rees's account of a Welsh parish and its young men's group (Rees, 1950), I might have been less amused at the following more elaborate jokes to control women, in which it is my own behaviour that is being sanctioned. After a few months in the parish I moved to live alone in a cottage in a small wood which was off the beaten track. Most women I met expressed the view that they would rather die than live there alone, and everyone declared that at the very least I should have a dog. I had only been living in the house a few days when, in the gathering dusk, I received a visit from a group of young men in a van, who shouted and made animal noises and menacing gestures from the track across the stream, which was the nearest approach to the house. They rapidly made off at the appearance of my father, who happened to have just arrived on a visit. Some weeks later an unaccompanied young man, driving a rather ostentatious car, came to spend a few days at the house. We were soon met at the entrance to my lane by the policeman from a neighbouring parish, who said he had reports of our being seen in an unlicensed car (untrue). In the first case definitely, and in the second case probably, these visits were initiated by, if not carried out by, young men from the pub, after discussions amongst the entire company.

Nevertheless it would be a mistake to end the analysis of these incidents by categorizing them as the social control of particular aspects of women's behaviour by men. The whole range of behaviour and the content of the joking cannot be ignored. What I have described are a number of situations in which men and women meet in which their behaviour often includes joking, teasing, banter and sometimes obscenities and horseplay; some cross-gender relations are marked by physical, as well as verbal abuse. The situations range from quite gentle reciprocal teasing between individuals, to more hostile and boisterous teasing between gender groups, and even more overtly hostile and physically abusive attacks on individual women by groups of men. These more overtly hostile elements should not be separated from the ambivalence being more generally signalled by joking.

Ann Whitehead

When we turn to social science literature for the analysis of parallel situations, we find there is a notable lack of observations in industrial societies of the informal behaviour of men and women towards each other outside marriage and courtship situations. An article by Sykes (1966) describing cross-gender relations in a factory is the major relevant account known to me. In this, as we might expect, Sykes turns to the set of writings on joking relationships in African societies (for references see Douglas, 1968) which centres around criticisms and extensions of Radcliffe-Brown's analysis (Radcliffe-Brown, 1952). For Radcliffe-Brown, joking relationships are an important category of relationships in which both elements of hostility and friendliness are present. He describes these ambivalent relationships in which there is a 'real friendliness and a pretence at hostility' associated with 'relations of conjunction and disjunction'.[8] Radcliffe-Brown is thus using 'joking' in a special sense. Sykes's analysis is notable for the distinctions he draws between categories of cross-gender joking behaviour: whether it is coy and flirtatious or obscene; whether there is any physical abuse or horseplay; whether it is symmetrical; and for the close attention he pays to who is interacting in terms of age, gender and marital status. By making these distinctions Sykes shows that one kind of joking and teasing, although not that characteristic of the Radcliffe-Brown category of joking, occurs between potential sexual partners, or who are potential sexual partners but are 'non-available', have 'joking-relationships'. Sykes (1966) wishes to refute his generalization of the African studies viz:

> It is generally assumed that joking relationships between people of different sexes are found only between people who are potential partners in marriage or in sexual relations; there is an avoidance relation found in those who are in a tabooed relationship to each other as regards marriage or sexual relations.

Sykes points out that in the factory coy, suggestive behaviour with no elements of obscenity and explicit sexual reference is characteristic between people who are potential sexual partners. Thus between young men and young women all exchanges were lighthearted, coy and suggestive and young girls were impossible to engage in serious conversation. Sykes singles out obscenity and banter as characteristic of cross-gender relations where the participants are not potential sexual partners, in this case between 'old' men and 'old' women. He finds that there is horseplay and gross obscenity in relations between persons who are potential sexual partners but who are 'non-available'. The greatest licence was in the public behaviour of old men to young girls. It included petting and gross obscenity, but any sexual relation between the young women and old men was ruled out. He suggests that within the factory these men and women were brought together in a situation which provided sexual contact and opportunities which were exceptional compared with those in their private lives. 'In these circumstances the behaviour patterns which regulated sexual relations required strong emphasis. Hence the crude but powerful nature of the joking relationship.'

As a generalization about the African literature, it would not be too much of a distortion to say that joking relationships occur between the genders when they are members of different exogamic groups, or between persons of the *same* gender of the same generation who are involved in marriage exchanges — i.e. when they are also members of different exogamic groups. That is to say, joking relationships occur between persons who are potential partners in marriage or sex, or between persons who are involved in relationships in which the control of women's sexuality is being transferred. This serves to emphasize Sykes's point that in these societies, too, cross-gender joking is commonly associated with possible sexual relationship and sexual availability.

The content of cross-gender joking in Herefordshire argues a consciousness of gender difference between the participants and a consciousness of sexuality. When non-related men and women get together in informal contexts they joke in a variety of ways. Flirtatious behaviour, obscenity and sex as a source of humour in this joking, suggest that consciousness of sexuality and of gender differences are irreducible elements in this interaction; men and women cannot be non-gender-specific friends (e.g. women's friends are always either girl-friends or boy-friends).

The Herefordshire incidents can be considered in the light of Sykes's categories (see Table 9.1). Coy, suggestive behaviour between young unmarried men and women, the tendency towards avoidance, or placing into quasi-kin categories, and gentle teasing about being unmarried suggest that unmarried girls are potential marriage (and therefore sexual) partners, and that reference to their sexuality is tabooed. Reciprocal obscene banter (characteristic of relations between persons who are sexually active, but who are not potential sexual partners) occurs between old married women and old married men and to a lesser extent between them and young married men. The most sexually dangerous encounter which has to be dealt with appears to be that between men and young married women. Horseplay appears to be particularly characteristic of the behaviour of some unmarried and most married men to young married women. This is not only in the pub. I observed (in front of the husband) prolonged games involving hiding keys and throwing possessions out of the window between a young wife and her husband's friend when he had called at their house. As far as the men are concerned young married (i.e. sexually active) women are desirable, potential sexual partners, but they are not available

Ann Whitehead

to them. Young married women bear the burden of the danger of potential but illegitimate sexual attraction, associated with double standards in attitudes towards and the practice of non-marital sex.

Table 9.1 Cross sexual joking and teasing in Herefordshire*

	Young unmarried woman	Old unmarried woman	Young married woman	Old married woman
Young unmarried man	coy flirtatious (non-sexual) teasing		horseplay /teasing	avoidance /teasing
Old unmarried man	?avoidance/?		?/non-obscene teasing	physical abuse horseplay suggestive /tease
Young married Man	avoidance/ 'like a sister'		avoidance horseplay	obscene banter
Old married men	mildly suggestive/?			obscene banter

*Symmetrical behaviour patterns have no bar.
 Where there is a bar, men's behaviour to women is tabulated first.

†There are no observations of behaviour between old unmarried women and other categories.

As far as premarital sex is concerned, the situation may be summed up as 'boys can, girls can't'. Boys' masculinity is dependent upon their sexual escapades, whilst girls' femininity is dependent upon their maintenance of a reputation of virginity. In extramarital sex, too, 'men do, women don't' Men sometimes had girl-friends, usually unmarried women.

This is a serious marital wrong and on discovery women regard it as the breakdown of the marriage. Close friends (and probably the entire male clique) cover for men having affairs. I do not think women are ever sexually unfaithful to their husbands, but they do have elaborate running away fantasies which they discuss with other women. These are often centred on men who do not live locally but who do pass regularly through the area. Women refer to assignations with these men and say that they are going to leave their husbands. These arrangements are probably set up in the joking context of 'I'll be in next week. Mind you're ready for me now.'

The pub ·is a special context promoting dramatic verbal encounters between men and women both because it may provide a licence for behaviour which might not be acceptable in other contexts and because it is associated with sexual availability. The pub as situation exaggerates the ever-present element of sexuality in male-female relations. Outside joking contexts, comments on young married women who went out drinking were that they 'only go out for one thing . . . she's after a bit of . . . what else would a married woman go out for?'. Indeed, when women do go to pubs outside the parish and behave in the way that they do, then, given the nature of relations between men and women, it appears highly probable that some of the pleasure of going to a pub for married women *is* the opportunity to enter into the excitement of premarriage patterns of flirting. Were it not for the fact that the theme of the consciousness of sexuality and of gender differences runs through all other encounters, the sexual content of behaviour in the pub could be due to its being a situation of sexual meetings, and behaviour in the pub could be regarded as primarily social control. Nevertheless, considering the whole range of joking situations between the genders does bring us full circle. Most of the men and women who behave in antagonistic and ambivalent ways towards each other as gender categories, are themselves husbands or wives to individual members of the opposing category. This raises the problem of what social and personal relations are like within the major institutionalized form of cross-gender relationship: marriage.

Till death us do part [9]

In Herefordshire the achievement of adult status is dependent upon forming a permanent contractual and intimate relationship with a member of the opposite sex. There is a strong moral component in the attitude towards being married. For both men and women, being unmarried is regarded as peculiar, pathetic and involves negative estimations of honour and esteem. Conversely, marriage is the normal and ideal state for adults. There is a strong suggestion that those who are not married are irresponsible and immature; and that men and women are not really fully adult until they are married and have the responsibilities of home and children. Everyone *ought* to be married. The moral component cannot be over-emphasized.

Ann Whitehead

Marriage coincides with the setting up of a new household both ideally and in practice. The stress on setting up a new household at marriage is linked to the fact that children do not leave home until then, and that while they are at home, whatever their age, they owe a considerable measure of obedience to their parents. A bachelor in his thirties was ribbed in the pub by being asked if he had been chopping wood again. Later it was explained to me that his father made him do all the work about the house and would not let him out otherwise. The subordinate relationship of the child—adult at home conflicts with the notion of the authority that a man has over his wife, and the independence and adulthood which marriage should bring. The importance of marriage is also linked to the derogatory attitude towards bachelors and spinsters in the community at large.

Marriage in Herefordshire is an asymmetrical partnership in the sense that husband and wife have roles which are different and indispensable to the household as a unit. One reason why all women had to marry if they were not to remain in their parental homes was simply financial necessity. No farming wife had ever taken employment outside the home. The only jobs open to non-farming women in the parish were domestic work or work in a family trading enterprise, such as a shop, post office or pub. Married women could have worked in shops in the nearby town, but did not. Women, like men, could only have worked in Hereford if they had had their own cars. In fact the involvement of women in the workforce at any stage in the life-cycle was very limited. The work experience of older women was almost exclusively in living-in jobs in service which had often taken them to live away from their home parishes. Some of the youngest and most recently married women had stayed at home after leaving school until they married. The majority had taken non-residential domestic work nearby. One or two had taken a job in a shop and two others had worked briefly for a trouser-making factory in the nearby town which had since closed down. The current jobs of the married women of husbands who had class IV and V occupations were exclusively in part-time domestic work, which the majority of wives did (in 1967 at 3s an hour or less).

I have no material on attitudes towards married women working. Few wives expressed any desire for a job at all. Two women articulated 'fantasies' about jobs — one wanted to be a nursery nurse, the other to take up painting or 'art work' of some kind. In both cases these appeared to be linked to getting away from the whole business of being married, living in the enclosed world of the parish and the daily round of housework and child-minding.

Of the women I knew who did part-time domestic work, most kept the money themselves and controlled its use. One wife saved all the money she earned working a few mornings a week for a farmer's wife in the Post

Office Savings Bank until she had enough to buy a small van. In another case the money was usually spent on clothes for the wife and her child. In at least one other the husband's wage was so poor (and his spending on drinking so large) that her money went on feeding and clothing four growing sons.

Where there is so little actual and conceived possibility of earning, the financial dependency of being a woman is one of the most significant aspects of marriage. This financial dependency is something which farmers' wives share with non-farmers' wives. There are farmers' households amongst the older generation in which the wife is provided with little personal or housekeeping money and the farmer pays all the bills. The elderly smallholder who still bought (i.e. went to the shops and chose, as well as paid for) all his wife's clothes was considered rather old-fashioned. Some farmers' wives indicated obliquely that decisions about major domestic financial outlays were a source of conflict. These references occurred in less than a third of the cases.

It is not surprising then that the husband's role of provider was stressed in the responses I received to a question about what is it that makes a good husband: 'Someone who will work hard and bring the lolly in.' And in reply to a question about why someone had moved to the parish, 'I followed the wage-packet.'

I knew no women whose husbands gave them the wage-packet, although many women were able to give a rough idea of their husband's earnings. A wife is normally given a fixed amount from which she has to meet various expenses, although she makes the decisions about spending it. One wife who was a self-confessed poor manager of money relied entirely on her husband to budget and to decide her shopping lists — but this was extremely unusual. Because men's earnings are often irregular a wife may often not know how much 'the family' has received in any particular week. For those married men who did casual work, these earnings were almost always used by the husband for his personal consumption. It was my impression that in about a quarter of the non-farming families there was a serious shortage of money over which husbands and wives quarrelled. In some others, wives grumbled over the amount of money the husband spent on himself.

The husband's role is not (quite) ended with his work outside the home. The ideal husband 'when he comes home from work, stops at home, doesn't go to the pub all the time, is good to the children and helps me if I'm not very well'. Some wives demand personal qualities as well, 'one who'll talk it over quietly with you'. The domestic roles of men also include doing a number of jobs around the house. Bringing in firewood, carpentry and electrical work are men's jobs. Decorating is mainly done by women. Being the provider goes with a quite natural organization of the

Ann Whitehead

home around a man's daily routine. The husband expects a meal to be ready when he gets home and for his wife to have finished her work. Her work is to shop, cook, wash-up, clean the house, wash and iron the clothes and to take primary responsibility for the children.

Herefordshire husbands appear to be unusual in that they do not regard washing-up as occasionally a husband's job. Most fathers appeared extremely fond of their children and quite willing to take them out. They play with them at home and help feed younger children. In the ordinary way Herefordshire husbands help their wives at home hardly at all. Indeed, men are mostly considered incapable of domestic tasks. This is borne out in the fact that not one single husband had ever stayed at home and looked after himself when his wife delivered a baby. All wives had arranged for their husbands to be looked after by other women during their childbirths. They often went to stay with their own or their wives' relatives.

The inviolability of the segregation of domestic tasks is typified in a piece of domestic spite in which the morning after a young husband had quarrelled with his wife, before he left for work, he dug up a spadeful of garden earth and threw it on to the polished sideboard. A later domestic retaliation also indicating the strict segregation of tasks was the wife's refusal to light a fire since her husband had not brought in any wood from the wood pile. It is domestic services which wives sometimes withdraw as sanctions when they are annoyed with their husbands' behaviour. The state of some of the marriages are deduced by both men and women, principals and audience alike, from the domestic performance of the wives. A young married woman told me, 'It's not going well between Jim and Betty. She hasn't cooked him a hot dinner all week.' The dutiful performance of these obligations may also be stressed when couples are in dispute. A mother-in-law complaining over her son's wife pointed out, 'He's a good husband — he's built her a lovely cupboard in the kitchen.'

The extreme emphasis on her domestic capabilities is also shown in the qualities of an ideal wife. *Nine* out of ten replies included 'a good cook' and in some cases this was the sole qualification needed. All the replies referred to domestic activities. She 'keeps the house nice, has the meals ready and keeps the clothes clean'; 'likes their home and family and puts them first'; 'the only thing a man worries about is a full stomach and a warm house'; she 'runs the house, looks after the children and helps in the business'. In no families was the division of domestic labour a source of dispute. Women, as well as men, accept the segregation of male and female tasks. Many of the replies citing domestic or culinary competence as the only qualification for being a good wife were from women.

Women's motivations, value or esteem were bound up in their domestic roles and they were extremely competitive about their domestic competence, their children and husbands. Because of the close-knit and rural nature of the community, the esteem from these rewards was not wholly confined to the home (cf. Littlejohn, 1963). Domestic competitiveness was displayed most fully on those occasions when women are responsible for the refreshments at meetings, sales and occasions of one kind and another. Every member of the Women's Institute, for example, took it in turns with two or three others to provide the refreshments at the monthly meeting. They strove hard to outdo each other in the quantity, quality and originality of the food provided. A large section of entries at the Flower Show was devoted to cooking and home-making arts, which was well supported, especially by farmers' wives.

What I have described is a fairly uniform pattern of the allocation of domestic division of labour which fits the segregated conjugal role ideal type outlined by Bott (1957). This kind of division of labour between husband and wife has been reported in a number of studies and some of their findings will be discussed below in the light of the Herefordshire material.

Some of them have, however, pointed out that one of the consequences of segregated domestic roles is that husbands and wives have relatively little in common within a marriage and that they are more likely to spend time with their own gender category. The joint interests in child-rearing and such shared interest in the home as there is (home is, after all, not simply a place to sleep in and eat at, to keep clean and maintain, although it must often appear like that), is not sufficient to bridge the gap. By and large a wife is less interested in what happens to her husband at work and out drinking than she is in her own daily round, while the husband finds the things his wife is interested in equally boring. In Pisticci, Davis notes that husbands and wives tend to talk about family matters, which are weighty, while gossip and hilarity take place in same sex groups (Davis, 1973). Komarovsky (1962) argues that 'the gulf of interests between the sexes is sometimes so wide that neither could serve as a satisfactory audience for the other. They repeatedly missed cues', and when they did understand each other's concerns they found them trivial and boring. Dennis, et al. (1957) say: 'As the years go by and any original sexual attraction fades, this rigid division of labour between husband and wife cannot but make for an empty and uninspiring relationship.' Komarovsky suggests this absence of shared interests was a substantial barrier to marital communication. There is not much to talk about and for what there is, husbands and wives do not always share the same language.[10]

The studies cited differ in how they evaluate the significance of the absence of shared interests and talking about things. Komarovsky points out that a substantial proportion of her blue collar marriages did not

Ann Whitehead

expect much marital communication. 'The ideal of friendship in marriage is not likely to emerge if the mode of life makes sharp differences in the interests of husbands and wives.' She also found that heavy involvement in single-sex networks did not prevent the achievement of considerable marital satisfaction and happiness, so long as wives and husbands did not expect a high degree of verbal communication. She makes the same point that Young and Willmott (1973) make, that involvement in their own inter-personal networks contributes to the stability of marriage. 'The equilibrium of marriage is maintained by the availability of close relatives and friends who fulfil for both, but especially for the wife, functions lacking in marriage.'

While Komarovsky's families show that it is *possible*, the evidence from Herefordshire is less sanguine. What is striking here *is* the frequent, socially visible quarrelling in marriage, especially in the child-bearing years. The marriages of non-farming women were rent and rift by rows and events; men (and women) were locked out of the house by their respective spouses; women (and men) refused to perform their respective domestic chores; kin were called in to make one or other of the partners behave; there were physical fights when husbands 'knocked' their wives about; women or men threatened to leave their spouses, either alone or with another partner; rows were followed by bargains as to which partner could go out when; women threatened to (and in some cases actually did) go home to mother. The day-to-day lives of many of my friends were full of quarrels and abusive exchanges. Some of the quarrelling (and abusive joking) was the idiom in which the relationship between husband and wife was expressed, and much of the verbal conflict was not as serious as it sounded. Some mock conflict in verbal exchange served to express the individual relation of affection between a husband and wife in a situation where men and women were socially defined as opposed. Again, although not all marital quarrels are destructive some can actually strengthen a relationship: 'Free remonstrance ... is a safety valve, letting off steam which, if confined, might blow up the boiler' (quoted in Scanzoni, 1972: 76). Quarrels may clarify motivations and help redefine the relationship, but this depends on each spouse liking the motivations of the other. Some clarification may reveal things best left unsaid. Despite the quarrels it should be pointed out the marriages were stable; where stable is taken to mean they lasted. Permanent separation and common law marriage were very rare. I knew of no cases of divorce. In this context then it appears that 'Mum' is not such a source of succour that she provides a haven for a daughter from an unhappy marriage.

Whether men and women were 'really' dissatisfied with their marriages and whether they were 'really' unhappy can be left aside for the moment. The quarrels were real. What were they about? The wives' dissatisfactions largely turn on how little they see of their husbands, and some voiced complaints that they never went out as a couple as they used to do when they were courting. Stella (of the love bite) complained that she and her husband had only been out together alone twice since they were married (four years before). She wanted to go out dancing in the way they had before they were married. It is difficult to see how they could have enjoyed a dance, since the teenagers in segregated sex groups would not be well known to them, and they would have had to spend the evening entirely together, which was not what happened before they married. Stella had persuaded her husband to go out once with another young couple where the husband was his friend. She said she would never do it again: 'We had an awful evening. Peter didn't know how to behave. He complained all the time. It was very embarrassing.' On another occasion, Stella and her husband went out drinking with a couple with whom each was separately on very friendly terms. 'It was terrible. They weren't speaking to each other and you could have cut the air with a knife. We came home early.'

Mainly, however, the complaints were about the husband's absence from home. 'Some days I have breakfast, dinner, tea and supper by myself.' The hours of work of some men were relatively long since a high proportion did jobs which required travelling about the area. The main reason why little time was spent at home, however, was because time was spent in pubs drinking. Both men and women expected the husband to spend some of the time when he was not working in the pub, playing darts or air gun shooting — but mainly just drinking. This was a husband's right. Some husbands confined their drinking to the evenings after they had been home after work to have tea. Others had a drink on the way home, and this could easily turn into an evening's drinking. For some men there was relatively little distinction between work time and drinking time. The hours of 'work' not taken up with working were spent in the pub. Many husbands also did casual work in the evenings and weekends. This also took them away from their homes and was centred on the pub. Some young wives found that the marriage they dreamed of, with evenings spent in front of the fire with a chosen companion[11] turned out to be a succession of evenings spent alone with the television and the baby and the husband's dinner drying up on a plate over a pan of simmering water. The desire for more of a husband's company is not a contradiction of the segregated division of labour. You do not have to conceive of a husband as a friend, or similar to yourself, in order to want him in the house. What is wanted perhaps is the sense that your work in the home is valued. 'A woman does all these things for love and for children. Some women could keep on a marriage just for the children, I couldn't do that. There has to be love.' This woman regarded willingness to spend time

Ann Whitehead

invested in the marital relationship as a proof of love, and absence from home (from which context this quote is taken) as proof that her husband no longer loved her.

I had little opportunity to discuss with men in private the quarrels they had with their wives. I cannot tell either what complaints they made in private to their friends, nor what dissatisfactions they expressed. Men were, however, by no means indifferent to marriage and women's behaviour. On the contrary, it was women's behaviour and women indirectly as sexual partners which formed the major items for conversation in The Wagonner. It is arguable that what happened when no women were present is of greater importance in relations between men and women than the incidents already recounted when women do venture inside it.

'We Come Here to Have a Good Time'

The bottom bar of The Wagonner, already referred to, was a special arena of social affairs in a number of senses. Situated in the centre of the parish, The Wagonner drew most of its customers from the immediate locality, and was the pub with the least number of ephemeral or unconnected visitors, although some of its core customers were from outside the parish. All its customers rank lowest on the parish's status and prestige dimensions. Some regulars are gardeners, timber workers, lorry drivers and labourers; a number of men work irregularly on timber work or casual jobs; of the three prominent farmers who drank regularly there are two bachelors who work for brothers; the farmers with smaller acreage are the least successful, or have retired early.

The links between the customers outside the pub are complex and dense. Some of them work together in their ordinary jobs, many of them are neighbours, a few of them are distant kin or affines, some of them spend much of their spare time together. There is a high degree of overlap in these separate links, so for the set of men at the pub there is little spatial or temporal segregation of separate segments of activity and relationship from each other. Work and non-work life are intimately intertwined. The links often reach into other areas of men's lives, especially their homes and marriages, so that all the drinkers have problems of information management. The pub also functions as a clearing house for various forms of casual labour, bringing together men who are seeking casual work and men who seek labour. Many married men who drank at The Wagonner spent much of the time outside their regular employment in these jobs. Men meet to go off to jobs from the pub, and return to it after they have finished. 'Working' at the weekend or in the evening is thus synomymous with spending it drinking.

A day in The Wagonner was a long round of coming and going, with scant attention paid to licensing hours. The first drink of the day was often dispensed at 7.30 a.m. and the last not until midnight or later. The drinkers positively defined the situation as one of gregariousness. No one drank alone. The chairs, tables and benches were arranged in such a way as to encourage conversation between all. The customers and landlady thought of it as a friendly pub where you come to have 'a good time'. Men who wanted to talk privately did so outside — either publicly or covertly by going outside to the men's lavatory together. Business matters and matters of conflict were not discussed. The drinking was largely reciprocal exchange between equals. There were only two customers — both farmers who frequented the bottom bar — who did not interact with the others in terms of defined broad equality ('Boss' and 'Uncle').

In the pub men were brought together into focused interaction (Goffman, 1961), in a situation of defined equality in which drinking sustained and made possible a whole set of other activities. Certain personal psychological and social characteristics were left behind on entering and a premium was placed on other kinds of behaviour and activity (cf. Szwed, 1966). Within the pub, activity might be focused on darts, on quoits, or on a card game, but the primary activity was verbal. This provided other rewards than simply those of companionship and the stimulus and pleasure of drinking. The pub was a place where men gathered, passed on, appraised and assessed news and information about events and people they all knew. The customers also took a great interest, disguised and undisguised, in the affairs of other drinkers. Frequently, however, the conversation developed into a highly characteristic set of exchanges in which joking and humour were uppermost. The joking, teasing and humour might be subtle or crude, but it was all pervading, continuous and almost impossible to convey. No opportunity was lost of making a witty remark, no statement went unchallenged which could form the subject of a joke, no suggestive remark or obscene interpretation escaped, no action or comment went unseen or unheard. At these times the pub was an unparalleled situation of social drama. It was a circle of recreation and entertainment in which the conversation proceeded by allusion and innuendo, brimmed over with laughter and jokes and was full of banter, obscenities and long competitive exchanges.

I must stress that not only was there more joking and teasing than in any other social situation in the parish, it was unlike that, for example, at the other pub, in that it was not joking of an anecdotal or archetypal kind involving the use of universal humorous situations. The joking depended for its humour on reference to matters which were internal to the set of men in the pub. The dynamic of the exchange involved finding a point of vulnerability in another customer (either present, just left or about to) and

Ann Whitehead

pointing to it by a remark which made everyone laugh. Even ribald exchange and obscenities were funny because they were applied to the people present. A ready subject for joking was stereotyped references to the characteristics associated with certain statuses — farmers, older bachelors, young men without sexual experiences. Some of this joking among other things serves to demarcate statuses and reaffirms the importance of these status differences. A brief and pointed repartee may also serve to remind people of uncomfortable transgressions, or to signify that the general company was aware of other events.

One evening in the pub, for example, the young, well-dressed and slightly reprobate son of the wealthy owner of the former estate in a nearby parish had been standing at the bar where he had had a boasting conversation with the landlord. As he left he bought a 'Babycham'. Whereupon one of the other customers said, 'What's that, a peace offering?' and another added 'Only one?.' He replied, 'If one won't do the trick, it's no good taking two', and walked out to yells of laughter.

The dynamics of this briefest of exchanges are complex. He was married but had a girl-friend. The state of his marriage was of interest, and the original question was a joking attempt to get a reaction. The intervention of a second speaker directed the episode against him for it referred to the fact that he had a girl-friend and a wife; but the victim triumphed for he managed a joke with sexual overtones and walked out.

The only response to joking was to joke about the weakness and vulnerabilities of your opponent. Men only scored in such joking, however, if they pointed to roughly comparable vulnerabilities. It is only prestigious to compete and verbally overcome someone if he was of equal status to yourself, and if you did not exploit weaknesses over which he had no control. When a low status timber worker, who was a little pompous, and had a discrepant status position due to his marriage to a farmer's daughter, joked at the expense of a half-witted man visiting from a neighbouring parish, although there was laughter, it was not considered very funny and the joke was not considered in good taste. Quite a lot of this joking is relatively innocent and light-hearted in purpose; much of it is barbed and pointed and constitutes a guise under which men may say outrageous things to each other.

Much could be said about the source of the ambivalence which is being expressed in joking (see Whitehead, 1971). Here I want to concentrate on the use made of women as counters in joking currency. Within the pub, men's standing in general was associated with their ability to joke successfully, and, importantly, not to get into a victim situation. In joking situations the joker and the victim are at least momentarily opponents, and the joker is united with the audience. Success at joking is a complex matter (cf. Kapferer and Handelman, 1972), but at least in part it depends on the willingness of the audience to force defeat on the victim. Men would joke against men with whom they had relatively few direct relationships, and, as I have pointed out, joking was often about ascribed statuses. Some joking was thus indulged in for the sake of the rewards being successfully brought, rather than as an expression of a particular relationship. In joking sequences of this kind the choice of victim often changed frequently and an overall balance between the drinkers was maintained. Stereotypes about women and relations between men and women in general could be an important weapon in the battery of items used. Men who were status equals often engaged in prolonged and competitive joking and teasing in which there was mock abuse and the belittling of an opponent. It was not a big step from joking exchanges of these kinds between status equals to prolonged hostile joking and teasing about much more serious matters. The hostility is recognized for what it is. 'They teased my husband blind yesterday at the pub. They've been on to him at work as well. It's his own fault — he's a terrible teaser himself.' '[My husband] came home early last night — saying "the buggers will have me walking barefoot yet".'

The major content of teasing of this kind was the degree of control that a married man exerted over his wife's behaviour. The men acted as if a married man should be able to do just what he liked after marriage. He should be able to come to the pub every day; to stay all evening after 'calling in' on the way home from work, and to stay out as long as he liked. He could and must row with his wife, hit her or lay down the law. Rows and quarrels in which he had the upper hand brought a man esteem, but if his wife rowed with him, locked him out of the house or refused to cook for him, he lost esteem. If he babysat while his wife went out he lost face.

For many months the pub was taken up with what was going on in some of the men's marriages. Men were always subject to ribbing when their wives had been known to have gone out drinking. Attitudes towards the amount of freedom a young wife could have were changing and in general husbands could not expect to exercise the same amount of authority as their fathers. The young couples whose quarrels were most socially visible were wives who were either trying to establish rights to go out by themselves, or to have more of their husband's company. The social visibility of quarrelling may be part of the wives' tactics. The husbands of wives who simply did not go out, did not seem to stay at home much more (apart from one or two with very low wages). The drinkers who were not at risk (either because they did not have wives, or whose children were grown up) took a great delight in promoting difficult situations for the younger married men. The landlady arranged a series of friendly darts matches that 'coincidentally' occurred on the same night as bingo.

Ann Whitehead

Husbands appear to have been made extremely insecure about their control over their wives' sexuality: when a husband picked a quarrel with his wife, back from bingo twenty minutes later than expected, she said, 'He thinks I went behind a hedge with someone – in weather like this.' (It was early February.)

Although control of sexuality is at the core of a husband's dislike of his wife going out, the key assessment which is often being made in the exchanges in the pub is which of the partners is in control. This may be articulated through the symbolism of threatened loss of sexual control. The other major piece of wife's behaviour which invariably, although often indirectly, sparked off joking and teasing, was her evening at bingo. Bingo evenings had not been run very long in the parish, and almost every week there would be a conflict in one of the marriages of the drinkers around which of the couple should go out and which babysit. (For reasons discussed below there is a constraint on the use of parents as babysitters for some of these couples.) One evening a week when a husband could not go to the pub seems rather little to the wives, but, because of its repercussions when they get into the pub situation, men were loth to allow even this. Thus after a particularly bad and protracted quarrel lasting a couple of days (during which the husband twice locked his wife out of the house), the couple agreed that she should not go to bingo any more, and that he should drink shandy at the pub. (Note *she* must not go out; *he* must moderate his drinking. This latter condition indicates the extent of nonunderstanding of the man's world at the pub. Shandy?) That marital power was partly the problematic thing is also shown in that when it has become known outside the pub that wives have done such things as lock husbands out, or not cooked a hot dinner all week, these too spark off joking in which the husband is bound to fail.

There is running through what I have said a distinction to be drawn between teasing and joking. Teasing is about real things that have happened. Joking is not about such real things, but the joking often has a sexual content. I have not been able to establish the circumstances under which men would be teased about real events in their marriages, and the circumstances in which the real events were only the initiation point for becoming a victim of joking which did not overtly refer to these events.

What goes on in the pub is obviously rewarding and exciting, but it is a finely balanced game. If men can gain temporary esteem through successful joking, they can easily lose it. Men are made vulnerable by their wives, but the agents of their vulnerability are often their closest male friends. The drinking situation is an arena of public confrontation in which men come together and engage in verbal competition. The content of the exchanges is such that information about the personal lives of other drinkers is at a premium. It is close friends who often have most inside knowledge, and who may eventually use this knowledge to be successful within the joking situation. As the teasing and joking ebb and flow, so too does the men's relation to the pub and its other customers become closer or more strained as they are subjected to, or become the protagonists in, the most extreme forms of teasing. Investment in the encounter situation of the pub makes for ambivalence in relations between men. Eventually men lose such face that they have temporarily to leave the pub and withdraw from close contact with other drinkers. Thus friendships blow hot and cold and men who have been constant companions for some weeks will avoid each other. (See Whitehead (1971) for detailed accounts.)

The Wagonner then is a major locale for verbal games whose performance brings considerable psychological rewards for the members of the male clique. Women appear in these exchanges in at least three ways. Much of the language is obscene and vulgar; it is concerned, that is, with sex and sexual relations. The everyday use of obscenity in our culture presupposes, I would assert, a certain attitude towards women and their role in sexual relations.[12] In addition, much of the exchange uses an ideology of gender differentiation as a source of humour in which stereotypes about women are, at their worst, contemptuous and degrading. Finally, control over the behaviour of specific wives is one counter in the apparently perpetual competition for male standing.

'The Secret World of Sisters and Mothers'

There are some obvious costs to wives and women when they are used in this way. It is difficult for men to treat their relationships with wives as relationships with people when wives are used as objects in another arena. At best men must be torn between the wish to establish a satisfactory marital link, and the desire, or necessity, to appear the boss. At worst, the establishment of the marriage must be subordinated almost completely to the demands of the male clique. Involvement in some kind of male clique (or male single-sex network) is frequently found associated with segregated domestic roles of the kind I have described. One of the recurring arguments in studies of the situations in which the two are found together is that the men's membership of cliques has to be counterposed to their wives' involvement in women's networks largely peopled by kinswomen. In Young and Willmott's version (1957), men are actually excluded from the intimacies of this circle and from the home itself by the close-knit bonds between mothers and daughters and sisters, which are forged in upbringing and maintained as adults by their joint interests in domesticity and child-rearing. Rosser and Harris (1965) and Fallding (1961) refer to the 'compulsive' (compelled?) domesticity of women which is associated with kin based networks. ('The more domesticated the women . . . the

Ann Whitehead

greater the likelihood of a sharp division of roles between husband and wife inside the home and the greater the chance of their involvement in frequent contacts with *relatives* (my italics) in their kinship network' (Rosser and Harris, (1965: 208). These arguments have been taken up again in recent work in the women's movement, where evidence is being sought for alternative women's ideologies (Davin, 1972), and in some social science analysis. Frankenberg (in the companion volume), for example, argues: 'The weakness of *Coal is Our Life* is not that it overdoes the oppression, but that it fails to take account at all of the fighting back at home or in the community at large.' He sees bingo evenings as important assertions of some financial independence and the right to free time.[13] He points out the enhanced position of women during the depression when men's role in the industrial division of labour was denied them. He also sees corporate female solidarity as founded in the structure of the relations of production associated with child-rearing — Sigal's 'secret world of sisters and mothers' (Sigal, 1962). The assertions here have to be carefully supported. Female personal networks are indeed a potential basis for feminine solidarity, and are structures within which alternative ideologies may develop. We need to examine situations of social action to see if the members of these networks do behave in solidary ways with each other, *and against husbands*, when faced with marital conflict, and to see what kind of alternatives, if any, are the ideologies they hold.

This is much more easily said than done. I have extensive data on the personal networks of men and women (Whitehead, 1971), but much less extensive data on the conversations of women when they are at home. The secretness of the women's world is an indication of its powerlessness. From this data it is possible to conclude that men and women have primary and other kin links available to the same degree to form the basis of personal networks. Men seem to visit or see their kin as frequently as do women. Male kin form a source of mutual aid and exchange (for tools, garden seeds, shopping for these items, job information, etc.) as do female kin. The *relative* importance of kin in the personal networks of men and women is substantially different because women spend much more time in solitary pursuits in the home than do men, who as we know spend their time in the pub.

Several generalizations emerge about the content of links in the women's networks. It *is* largely primary kin and close affines who form the source of mutual aid and exchange and companionship, not only in domestic activities, but in other activities (which are few), such as going to bingo. Those women who do not have these kin living nearby often appeared isolated. Up to one quarter of married women did not have kin of the same age living near enough to be companions or sources of aid. These women often complained that they were lonely. In a number of cases there were women of the same age and status living nearby who helped in emergencies, but it seemed difficult for a young woman to form a close companionship relationship with a neighbour. There also appeared to be constraints on the development of friendships. The content of the exchanges between daughters and mothers, and between sisters and sisters-in-law was limited in at least two respects. The mother-daughter tie was largely one of the exchange of mutual domestic aid. Mothers and daughters rarely went out together, say to bingo. A young woman is more likely to go with her sister and sister-in-law than with her mother. Nevertheless women kin of the same generation (i.e. sisters and sisters-in-law) were not drinking companions. Drinking companions were usually described as 'girl-friends' by those women who went drinking, although they might also be neighbours.

These patterns can actually be related to the part which close kin play in the marital quarrels I have described. Parents and parents-in-law cannot ignore the quarrels of their offspring, especially as they rapidly become public through their effect on incidents in the pub. A number of crucial incidents occurred in the homes of the married couples whose conflicts have been described earlier, into which parents were drawn. Their invariable role was to support the marital bond, rather than their son or daughter. Parents are in fact at pains not to appear to favour their own child in these disputes since this is 'interference' (and is likely to be counter-productive). Advice, threats and domestic sanctions were exerted over both husband and wife by their parents, but although equally sanctioned, the norms of marital conduct are themselves unequal. Those young women who are attempting to establish greater freedom, or to obtain more of their husband's time, company and emotional energy, are either trying to change marital norms, or are engaged in a struggle which their mothers have long since given up. In the private and family discussions about behaviour within the marriage, then, it is the wives who are most often deemed to have done wrong. Mothers as well as husbands try to control young married women.

The young wife who kicked her husband out of the pub (see below) is also the wife whose husband threw soil on the furniture and whose husband was discovered with a girl-friend. Their quite new marriage was the most crisis-ridden one that I knew. Just after the birth of her first baby this wife bought a small van which meant that she was very mobile. She visited about the parish during the day and sometimes persuaded a girl-friend to go out with her for a drink. In the beginning her mother looked after the baby. Before long women were saying that she was neglecting the baby and her mother began to refuse to babysit. She eventually confided to me that she would not babysit any more; that she was worried about the marriage; and that although the husband should not

Ann Whitehead

go about with another woman, her daughter ought not to go out but should stay at home. That this was not an isolated case is shown from my systematic data on choice of babysitters, which shows that relatives are used much less frequently by non-farming wives than by farming wives, even though there is no difference in proximity or ease of access for the two sets. This data reinforces the impression that the mother–daughter tie is more complex than the notion of the women's trades union (Young and Willmott, 1957; Stacey, 1960) allows. Mothers and daughters do not have the same values and the mother may damp down her daughter's demands rather than support them. It has been suggested to me that this does not have to be seen as the act of a woman who resents freedom which she does not have, but that the older women may be more aware of the quite serious consequences for women if they do not toe the line. That women cannot support themselves financially is only one aspect of a number of psychological and physical consequences (battered wives, the incidence of mental breakdown) which might lead to accommodatory ideologies.[14]

A particular family ideology then is deeply entrenched in Herefordshire. The information on women's networks emphasizes the obvious point that the necessity for cooperation in the industrial sociology of child-rearing reinforces an ideology of gender differentiation and gender-specific role-differentiation which in its Herefordshire form provides opportunities for tightening the screws of social control on young wives. The major basis for women's solidarity turns out to entrench them further in deference, powerlessness and, in many cases, personal misery. If there is fighting back it is not from the solidarity between mother and daughter. Relations with sisters and sisters-in-law are probably equally ambivalent. The apparent constraint on close female kin being drinking companions for women can be traced to the same source. Sisters can be too easily accused of aiding and abetting each other. I found sisters tended to compete about their success at achieving marital harmony and the extent to which their husbands fit the Herefordshire ideal.

One reason why there is no development of an alternative women's definition is that there is no physical basis for solidarity. As Bell and Newby (Ch. 8) point out, 'deference', or rather unequal power, is lived within a small face-to-face unit within the four walls of the home. Mothers and daughters visit each other's homes when the husband is out, but rarely get together outside it. In the earlier material on contact between non-related men and women it is apparent that where women as individuals encounter men in groups they are unable to retaliate against mild teasing, or the informal and fairly brutal expressions of male solidarity. Where both sexes are in groups, as in the courtship situations and the Women's Institute Party, there seems to be no inherent reason why women are not equally successful at 'putting down' by joking and teasing. An intermediate form of social control therefore is to prevent young women ever being in groups, and to prevent the development of solidary relations of support. Friendships are frequently located in going out activities for women, for women can only go out at all if they can get someone to go with them. For the husband, then, his wife's friends or her closest relations with her neighbours are a threat. Husbands appear to make bargains which often include that their wives should see less or nothing of their girl-friends. These links are a further threat in that they represent a most dangerous channel of communication. If the wives tell each other about their marriages, this information may be passed to a husband. Where the first husband is also a drinking companion of the second, this information may be used in pub disclosures. This may explain Stella's abortive attempt to go out with another couple where the friendships criss-crossed in this way. The problem of friendships, and to some extent also neighbouring relations, does not in fact leave women much else *but* the links with female kin. Where these are absent she may lack many interpersonal links and aid, as some of the case histories demonstrate. While they may welcome the support and interest in domesticities which the female kin network apparently provides, wives will find its moral censure the more trying because they are more confined within it.

Nevertheless, the young non-farming wives who appear in this account are fairly obviously fighting back. While men have to control their wives' behaviour, if they behave too badly the wives can and will retaliate. Thus one husband left the pub for several weeks after his wife had come into the pub early one evening and dragged him out. The story was that 'she kicked him up the arse as he went through the door. He never even finished his pint'.[15] Only the wife can assess whether the bruises that she sported for several weeks after this were worth the victory. The secret nature of other attempts to fight back confirms the importance of the absence of any corporate base. Women appear intermittently to have made futile attempts to limit the pub's activities and their husbands' drinking. Another parish pub is immediately opposite the small council estate in the village, and is the 'local' for men who live there. Two wives were rumoured to have been responsible for a raid by the local police, whom they had summoned anonymously by telephone when they had become too fed-up with waiting for their husbands to come home. A very involved story, which I never completely worked out, of another anonymous telephone call, this time exposing the poaching activities of the landlord of The Wagonner, was probably another example of women's attempts to get their own back.

The most significant aspect of fighting back is, in my view, ideological. I have referred to the accommodatory, resigned view of older

Ann Whitehead

women about their marriages. At first, I found the hold which the ideology of romantic love had over the young married women whom I knew disturbing in the face of the realities of marital power and their everyday married life. Nevertheless, those women who cling to the ideologies of love (as in the quote on p. 189) are themselves holding out against the realities of marital power. To the extent that love is deemed to be the basis for successful marriage, and successful marriage involves choosing to spend some time with a spouse, then the behaviour of young husbands is also being subjected to some social control. They too, in the pub even, are being taught to relate across the antagonisms which divide gender categories. Although a potential ideological basis for making demands on husbands, the ideal of romantic love is itself a double-edged weapon. For an unsuccessful marriage is thus one in which love has died, and when that happens, where can a wife go and what can she do?

Postscript

It is tempting to see the Herefordshire semi-skilled workers as ethnographic exotica. It is equally tempting to see these families as an empirical example which comes particularly close to an ideal type of family structure within the capitalist mode of production. I have myself emphasized here the extreme economic dependence of wives whose husbands are breadwinners in an earning situation described elsewhere (Whitehead, 1971) as characterized by economic insecurity, interpersonal competition and firm ceilings within the local socio-economic structure.

In addition to the arguments that men are squeezed out of the domestic circle, the husband's involvement in male cliques has been explained as compensation for the brutalizing nature of some men's work under capitalism (Dennis et al ., 1956; Young and Willmott, 1973), and as involvement in a compensatory area of rewards when the husband cannot for economic reasons establish himself in the husbandly role of provider and so finds no esteem at home (Komarovsky, 1962; Rainwater, 1974; Liebow, 1967). An ideology of sexual differentiation in which women are held in contempt[16] appears to go with male cliques of this kind (cf. Komarovsky, 1962).

In my earlier analysis of the reasons for ambivalence in relations between men in the pub and for their continued involvement in these exchanges, I pointed out the individual nature of the competition in their permanent and casual occupations, and implied that virility was a source of competition because there is nothing else in terms of which to compete. If we rely on the published writings of social science, these generalizations appear tenable, tolerant, liberal. They are also sexist nonsense.

If instead we turn to our everyday experiences as women (and men) and the increasingly published collective experiences of women, much of the behaviour I have described is not by any means confined to other places, other times, another class. 'Bird', 'on the job' and 'screw' are a few words in the language in which sexual relations are described. Men do not expect women to shout to them in the street: 'Hallo, sailor, I wouldn't mind half an hour with you.' I remind you of the extraordinary court case now (Autumn 1974) proceeding against a group of women whose only crime seems to have been having a drink together in a Fleet Street pub and being unwilling to respond to the 'joking' advances of the male drinkers. Men's drinking groups occur in senior common rooms, the Houses of Parliament, the Inns of Court, Board rooms, recreation clubs, and in pubs, bars and clubs with a variety of clientele, as well as in Fleet Street and Herefordshire.

Where I take issue with the recent work on the companionate family (Pahl and Pahl, 1971; Rapoport and Rapoport, 1971a; Young and Willmot, 1973; Bloode and Wolfe, 1960 and Scanzoni, 1972) is that in all these studies the relevant arena of social action is taken as the home for women and the market place for men. These studies certainly show that domestic marital roles are changing, with a wider range of tasks and chores being done by both partners, and more married women going out to some kind of work. But there is little material on what kind of behaviour occurs between husband and wife at home. Herefordshire families have a variety of techniques to maintain social distance between husband and wife when they are occupying the same physical space. Some of the Rapoports' dual career families seem to 'organize' away domestic contact. Little effort has been made to see what kind of relations occur between men and women in their work situations, although secretaries and nurses are, in our everyday experience, often more subject to the kind of sexual joking and insults that I have described than is the secluded mother at home. Young and Willmott's (1973) evidence suggests that if anything there has been an increase in gender segregated leisure activity (i.e. an increase in male leisure groups to drink and joke). There is no data at all on whether attitudes towards sexuality are changing. It is often suggested (Douglas, 1966; Ortner, 1974) that ideologies of gender differentiation, and the language of sexual relations, are used as metaphors for something else. But they also 'say' something about relations between men and women. It is not only in Herefordshire that men and women are caught in concrete and ideological structures which reinforce and perpetuate sexual antagonisms.

Notes

1. The research on which this paper is based was supported by grants from the Dartington Hall Trust and the Rowntree Trust made to the

202

Ann Whitehead

School of Social Sciences, University College of Swansea. My thanks to Professor W. M. Williams for obtaining these grants and for supervising the research. I should like to thank Prue Chamberlayne, Mike Cushman, Susannah Handley, Sue Lipshitz, John Maclean, Jenny Shaw, Wendy Smith and Doris Virgoe, and members of the London Women's Anthropology Group for help in preparing this paper.

2. The terms non-farming and farming broadly speaking correspond to membership of the Registrar General's Class IV and V, and Class II and III. Whitehead (1971) contains a detailed description of the local stratification system. Non-farming will be used throughout this paper to refer to men whose occupations are as listed in the previous paragraph.

3. A start on this analysis has been made by Frankenberg (in the companion volume).

4. Lorry drivers entertain the pub with stories of the invariable sexual availability of the few women they encounter.

5. Bachelors are built into the developmental cycle and pattern of inheritance in farming. They often work for married brothers, and are more like farm workers (Whitehead, 1971).

6. Am I being treated as a married or an unmarried woman in these exchanges?

7. Two wives who had been left at home by their husbands came together to one of these evenings. They were made to feel so uncomfortable by their husbands and husbands' friends that they left, declaring that they would go dancing in a better pub nearer Hereford.

8. As Loudon (1970) points out, there has been little investigation of situations where the hostility is at least as real as the friendliness.

9. What I say in what follows about marriage may appear in some respects excessively one-sided. This is in part because marriage is a relationship of privacy and intimacy. A rounded study requires prolonged interviewing of a more systematic kind in these areas than I carried out. It is also one-sided because amongst the families themselves the conceptualization and articulation of emotional relationships is relatively undeveloped. I had no satisfactory conversations with men about their personal lives. Their wives told me a lot about what they saw as going on in their marriages, but it was rarely focused on the meaning of behaviour, or on the nature of the emotional tie. It was instead often focused on the rights and obligations of each side. My own lack of language and lack of experience affected my ability to collect this kind of information. Komarovsky (1962) reports a similar absence of self-conscious

awareness amongst blue collar families which led to marriage relationships being discussed 'with few distinctions of kind or degree'. I want to emphasize that the one-sided picture that I present is as accurate a portrayal as my fieldwork methods allow, of marriage among the couples that I knew best for that part of their lives that I shared for 20 months. I offer my apologies to those men and women who manage to establish and maintain relationships of mutual respect, affection and esteem in these unprepossessing circumstances.

10. Drunkenness itself is not likely to promote marital communication. This is one reason why husbands and wives appear to talk so little about their sexual relations and contraception. My information on contraception is very unsystematic, but in the couples whose quarrels I knew best, the husbands were unwilling, often brutally so, to allow their wives to practice contraception themselves. Not all of their wives were as totally resigned as one 22-year-old who confided frequently to her friend that the greatest fear was that she would become pregnant again, and there was no way to make her husband 'take precautions'.

11. This image is not my own, but an ideal version of their marriages distilled from my conversations with young wives.

12. Readers who doubt this might like to analyse the view of women which is revealed in the jokes collected in Legman (1969).

13. Frankenberg (1974) is undoubtedly right to draw attention to the fact that our sisterly solidarity is made more problematic by our membership of antagonistic classes, but his reference to 'even intellectual women's attitudes towards bingo' is gratuitous. Bingo appears as a focus for conflict within marriages in Whitehead (1971) without, as far as I can judge, any evaluation of it as 'mindlessness'.

14. My thanks to Sue Lipshitz for this point.

15. Versions of this story differ. Another one was that he had followed her out of the pub and pretended to cycle up the road until she could no longer see him in the driving mirror of her van. Whereupon he had gone back to finish his drink. I did not witness this incident. I have always been puzzled as to quite why he left/how she managed to get him out.

16. I do not regard the 'on a pedestal' or 'saintly' mother stereotypes as compensating for what I have described.

Marriage, role division and social cohesion: the case of some French upper-middle class families

This paper describes and analyses marriage behaviour and role division amongst some French upper-middle-class families and links these to the maintenance and acquisition of elite positions by the individuals concerned. The linkage is set within a wider framework of social stratification and economic change and, more specifically, of educational and professional reconversion strategies developed by members of older elites to prevent social regression.

The study is based on file and interview data gathered from French students doing the equivalent of Master of Business Administration courses at an international business school in France, and their wives. It was originally designed to be a complement to studies by Bourdieu and his colleagues of the major engineering and commercial *Grandes Ecoles* in France in the light of their theory underlining the relationship between education and the 'reproduction' of the existing social order.[1] The study examines the social origins, educational and professional experience of the students of the school concerned, to discover the principal reasons that lead apparently highly qualified young men (and a very few women) to add a specialist business diploma to their list of degrees — and in many cases to do so after some years in business life. After analysis of the file data on past students a pilot study was carried out in June 1973 and then 60 of the 63 French students of the year 1973-74 were interviewed at length. During these interviews it became evident that for many of the married students the part played by their wives in the decision to attend the school was very important. The study of the wives reported in this paper is based on a secondary study springing from information gathered in the major enquiry and this is the reason for certain limitations in the data.

The social and educational origins of the husbands

The students of the school in question are recruited in the great majority from very limited sections of the population — each year between 75 and 85 per cent are the sons of members of the liberal professions, of senior executives (State and private sectors) and *patrons* of industry and commerce.[2] The proportion of the latter is particularly striking, constituting about 30 per cent of the total 1973-4 (French) student body and 40 per cent of the categories mentioned above. While one might expect such concentration in a business school, it is clear that their presence is partly the result of subtle processes linked to economic and social changes.

Over the 15 years of the school's existence the educational background of the students has been changing. In the early years the highest proportion held diplomas from commercial schools (*Ecoles de Commerce*), many in the provinces but also the major Paris schools — H.E.C., E.S.S.E.C. and E.S.C.P.[3] — with a relatively low proportion of engineers (*ingénieurs*) and men with legal and political science training. Since then there has been a gradual changeover to the reverse situation and there is now a majority of engineers, a rise paralleled by increases in the numbers of lawyers and political scientists and a commensurate fall in numbers of men with commercial education.

French employers are notorious for their use of a person's educational background as a criterion of recruitment to management positions, and especially in the early stages of a career, fine gradations as between schools and type of speciality are recognized (and reflected in salaries offered, as can be seen from the list published each year by *L'Expansion*). Further analysis of the engineering diplomas held by students at the school studied here reveals that many are from the less prestigious Paris schools or from provincial schools, or are for the less prestigious subjects, such as chemical engineering, with only about one-eighth from the really top *Grandes Écoles*. In recent years too the school has developed a policy of recruiting principally people with some experience of professional life. Hence many students have had time to savour the disadvantages attaching to their diplomas or their experience. Several when interviewed complained of their lack of promotion, or their 'relegation' to technical departments. This picture needs to be more finely drawn but it represents clear tendencies. It should perhaps be emphasized here that throughout this paper we shall be talking about tendencies rather than explaining individual cases.

Changes in economic structure and changes in diploma demands

The evolution outlined above would appear to be linked to more fundamental economic changes occurring in France in the 1950s and 1960s.[4] The nature of the industrialization process involved major changes in the type, size and location of profitable industries and often meant that regions of previous prosperity suffered economic decline. The typical case is the textile industry in the northern areas of France, where many

Jane Marceau

family-owned and run firms folded or merged. This evolution was accompanied by an ideological change, favouring industrial and commercial operation by managers rather than by owner-bosses. The change came with both the influx of American investment and American management techniques and predilections, and many businessmen felt the pressure for more efficient use of resources to stay in business or to organize larger productive and distribution units.

The same period saw the 'boom' in consumption and the creation of profitable opportunities in the tertiary sector. The employment this offered needed not so much engineering and mathematical skills as those of accounting, marketing or publicity. Together these changes mean that the demand from firms for managers has become centered more on men with qualifications in the commercial field, although students from the top few engineering *Grandes Écoles* are still much in demand. Similarly, men with law and political science degrees began to find their qualifications insufficient to ensure them the jobs they had expected to obtain on graduation. To distinguish oneself from the rest and acquire the sort of position one has been brought up to expect, it has become necessary to hold a new and specialist business diploma. Thus the social classes who have for long most used the education system are forced to use it still more, but those who had used it relatively little, the *patrons* of industry and commerce, are also now forced to rely on the school to ensure the occupational success of the sons they can no longer place with their own economic and social capital alone.[5]

In short, many of the French students at the business school find themselves in a relatively new position. They have in the main been brought up in families with high expectations (as evidenced by the diplomas held by and the occupations of their fathers and siblings) and they thus hold high expectations themselves. The great majority of those interviewed stated that they were aiming at the top of the management hierarchy, the *direction générale*, but somehow either in terms of the schools they entered or the posts they managed to obtain, these expectations had not been fulfilled or had been promised too far in the future, while the career paths of their fathers were closed. These then are mainly elite students who are or feel themselves to be threatened with relative regression socially or occupationally.[6]

The marital roles and social characteristics of the wives

What then of their wives? What role do they play? Thirty-five of the students in the sample were married and of these wives twenty-one have been interviewed. Thirteen wives could not be contacted, either because they were not with their husbands near the school, continuing to work elsewhere; or because their hours of work made it impossible; or, in three cases, because they refused or they did not reply. The numbers interviewed are very small so of course the resulting analysis is only very tentative. However, the distribution by social and educational origins of the husbands is very similar to that of the total population of French students of the school and it seems likely that the situation does not change markedly from one year to the next.

Bourdieu in earlier works (1970 and 1971) has discussed the importance of different kinds of capital — social (networks of relationships), economic and cultural (diplomas and *culture génerale*) — in the reproduction of the social order. The objective of the study of the wives reported here is to assess the extent to which the marriages contracted could be considered, objectively, as strategic alliances from the point of view of the husband for the maintenance or improvement of his social and economic position. Further, within that general framework, we wish to examine the extent to which the 'traditional' division of roles as between the husband who has a career and the wife who stays at home, looks after the children and is 'available' for her husband's needs, is both maintained in the young generation and, more important here, serves the interests of the husband's career. We are interested then in the social economic and cultural capital brought by the wives to the marriage and which hence falls to some extent under the control of the husband, or at least may be considered as accretions to his social personnage, which may be 'used' by him either directly or indirectly to improve or maintain his social and occupational position.

When we compare the wives' social origins with those of their spouses, as measured by the education of their fathers,[7] we find that virtually half the contacted wives are from the same social circle as their husbands, while a further seven are from higher social origins, with only four from lower socio-professional categories. These four are only 'lower' in terms of diplomas held and not necessarily in terms of occupation, as one of them is the owner of a major department store and the other two are also in business as *patrons* of industry and commerce. The uncontacted wives show a clear tendency to be of higher social origins than their husbands (8 out of 13),[8] and it is interesting that virtually all these wives are either working in or studying for the more demanding professions, which suggests that they may be intending to pursue a career in contrast to their maritally more conformist sisters. Table 10.1 shows more precisely the origins of both spouses in terms of the professions of their fathers.[9]

The table shows clearly the predominance of industrialists among the fathers of the contacted wives. The four military fathers are of interest, too, as in France such a career is (or was) often undertaken by 'younger sons' for whom there was no room in the family business,

Jane Marceau

Table 10.1 The professions of the fathers of husbands and wives*

	Contacted		Uncontacted	
Occupation	Wives	Husbands	Wives	Husbands
Industrialists + wholesalers	8	6	–	4
Other business posts	4	9	5	3
Military (colonel, etc.)	4	2	–	2
Medical (inc. 7 who began)	2	1	2	–
Liberal professions, etc.	3	2	5	2
Manual or non manual working class	1	3	1	2

* There are more professions than persons in some cases because of
  changes in occupation; for example, after early military retirement

suggesting that in the grandfathers' generation there may have been even
more *patrons* in industry or commerce. The fathers of the husbands, on
the other hand, are to be found more in salaried posts. It is perhaps also
significant that none of the uncontacted wives have industrialist fathers
but that their fathers are more concentrated than their husbands' fathers
in the liberal professions, medicine and other business posts, suggesting
families of greater education since one cannot, for instance, become a
doctor without training at a high level — which may be important as a
stimulus to study on the part of their daughters. As we shall see below, the
uncontacted wives were 'more' educated and probably more inclined
towards following a career seriously.

Social capital   In terms of social capital the most frequent contribution
of the wives is the consolidation of social respectability. This they provide,
for example, by maintaining the previous level of the husband's family, as
in the case of the wife who 'brought' a father who is a doctor to the son of
a military officer, or the daughter of the owner of a large chain of stores
marrying the son of a senior executive. Or they may bring improved social
capital through the network of relationships they possess through their
families of origin. Thus, for example, the alliance between two Parisian
families, one with a retail business and the other an industrialist. While the
linkages are not necessarily used, at least in the short term, they are
potentially useful and can always be activated later. This is perhaps

particularly the case in the cross-profession marriages, where the marriage opens up a whole new field of social relationships and networks, especially important because the interviews showed the families of the husbands to be fairly 'isolated'. Many husbands had few or no contacts through marriage or blood relatives with members of other sectors of the economy and society and their fathers themselves tended not to hold positions in more than one section or field of power, a situation that contrasts with the 'captains of industry' analysed by Bourdieu *et al.* (1973: 76-7). When there were linkages they tended to be with members of older sections of the economy, such as the wine-trade or the textile industry, and not with the higher civil service, the university or the political world.

The number of such relationships potentially available through the families of the wives should not be underestimated. If we look, for example, at the siblings, the wives have more than the husbands: the contacted wives have between them 68 siblings, 35 sisters and 33 brothers, most of whom will marry, probably into similar families in terms of social origins and connections; the husbands have only 21 sisters and 17 brothers. Thus the contacted wives come from considerably larger families (average 4·2 children) than do their husbands (average 2·8), which suggests that they come from even more bourgeois and well-established families.[10] The figures indicate at least greater possibilities for wider social networks on the wives' side then on the husbands'. Since the majority of the wives' siblings' occupations are concentrated in the liberal professions (law and medicine) and business, the potential advantages of such links may be judged important. Given further that the families on both sides tend to be 'family' oriented, in that they exchange regular visits and holiday frequently in property belonging to members of the family, the chances of effective interaction are considerable.

On the other hand it should be noted that the uncontacted wives come from smaller families, not only smaller than those of the contacted wives but also slightly smaller (average 3·2) than those of their husbands (average 3·8). Such a reversal is interesting, and is perhaps linked to the same group of factors which made them marry less orthodoxly and pursue their studies and their careers with greater tenacity. More detailed analysis would seem necessary here but was unfortunately not possible within the confines of the present study.[11]

Economic capital   The economic capital brought to the marriages by the wives is considerable and takes several forms. It may be brought to the marriage 'at one go' in the form of a dowry or an advance on inheritance. Five of the wives interviewed declared that they had had a dowry in money or shares, while others had financial aid in the form of 'loans' or gifts in kind — such as a houseful of furniture or a complete trousseau of

Jane Marceau

linen, though not all had had such valuable presents. Many of the wives had only been married 1-3 years, had often travelled and had relatively few children, so it is hard to assess the amount of occasional present-giving, but it seems likely that there is important family help when needed.[12] Some couples had been offered flats in family houses after marriage and some aid is linked to presence at the school — certain of the men declared that they had loans from their in-laws (and many from their own families) and one for example was living rent-free in his father-in-law's weekend house near the school (1972-3 student).

The capital may also be brought through inheritance at different times during the life of the marriage. The importance of the economic capital involved in the marriages may be gauged from the kind of marriage contracts drawn up on family and legal advice. Only five couples had the *communauté de biens* which is the automatic form and which means that the couple hold all their property in common with the exception of inheritances given specifically to one or other partner. Twelve of the couples had the *communauté réduite aux acquêts* which gives each partner the right to keep at death or divorce any property he or she brought to the marriage; and four had the contract of *séparation de biens* under which all property, acquired both before and during the marriage, remains that of the spouse concerned. The latter is particularly important where there is a business to inherit, as it remains the property of the spouse concerned while it is doing well, while limiting the responsibility to that of one spouse in case of bankruptcy so that the other partner's property remains intact. The formal separation of property in this way does not of course mean that the husband does not benefit from his wife's property during the life of the marriage and he may well be involved in its management.[13]

The economic capital brought by the wife may be and probably most frequently is in the form of income acquired through the professional activities of the wife or the latter's private means. Of the wives interviewed, 14 were working at the time and 2 of the others had worked before their husbands went to the school. Of the 5 who did not work, only 2 had no income of their own, thus suggesting that they had private resources. The majority of the wives (14) used their income for the family's living expenses and 1 saved hers. It seems likely that at least half of the husbands would have been unable to attend the school, pay the heavy fees (about £2,000 for nine months, including board) and live as well as they did, had it not been that their wives worked, especially since the 'style' of the school 'requires' considerable spending on ancillary activities, such as sports, entertaining, etc.

Cultural capital Cultural capital can be measured either by the educational diplomas held by the wives, which could be turned into economic capital by taking a job, or by what the diplomas yield in terms of general or feminine cultural assets, or by the contribution made by activities such as reading, interest in art, etc., to the *culture générale* of the couple.

Where the diplomas are concerned, most seem to be in line with their holders' education as women and indeed women of a certain class. Most hold what might be termed 'feminine' diplomas, giving access to service careers such as teaching or nursing and which yield feminine skills appropriate to the female roles to be played by members of the upper-middle class.

The cultural capital brought by the wives is varied. In the main they read literature of the 'lighter' kind, although a striking number read *Le Monde* and reviews such as *L'Express* and thereby keep themselves (and their busy husbands?) up to date on newsworthy matters. Where cultural matters outside the home are concerned, the cinema predominates, although some wives go regularly to concerts and exhibitions and a very few to the theatre. Their chief recreational interests seem to be music and manual crafts. On the other hand, by French standards[14] they practise a wide variety of sports — skiing (10), horse-riding (6), tennis (11), sailing, etc. — most of which they do with their husbands, some of whom only started such sports after meeting their wives. Most of the wives also speak at least one foreign language, a useful asset for men working for international companies or going abroad frequently. It seems likely that neither husbands nor wives came from families which took a particular interest in developing the more intellectual side of French culture. For the daughters, at least, their moral and religious education seems to have been in the forefront (as we shall see below) and social labelling in these milieux is perhaps more dependent on the sports one practises, the languages one speaks, the holidays one takes and the practising of one's religion, than on presence at theatres or discussion of exhibitions.

Role division and marital power

What then is the type of role division and marital power structure prevalent in these families? Where the power structure is concerned it had been expected from the reading of the (scanty) literature on French and other European family power structures and role divisions, and the American studies which had served as the inspiration for the European ones (Blood and Wolfe, 1960; Heer, 1963; Safilios-Rothschild, 1967; Lupri, 1969; Michel, 1972), that the power structure would rather favour the husband in such established middle-class families, especially where financial matters were concerned.

Originally we had planned to use the questionnaire to gather data on

Jane Marceau

the division of household tasks. Closer inspection of the population, however, revealed that, given the particular circumstances in which the couples were placed — that is young married, few children, heavily work-burdened student husbands, transitional period of the year at the school — this would yield relatively little of interest while making the survey instrument unnecessarily heavy. Moreover from a theoretical point of view it seemed more valuable to concentrate on the analysis of marital power structure and on the division of roles between the sexes over the crucial areas of career and home and the attitudes of the wives in relation to their role as wives and mothers and to their role in relation to their husbands' careers. Then, in the light of this information, to set the whole back in the original social context by examining the place in the social structure held by the husbands (as we did in the early part of this paper) and to examine the antecedents of the wives' attitudes (as we shall do below) in terms of their education, upbringing, etc.

Given this general orientation, we took two criteria of marital power: that of control over income and other financial resources, and that of participation in decisions concerning the husbands' careers — discussion with the wife of possible jobs and of work problems, the decision to attend the business school, etc. Questioning on this revealed considerable equality and indeed independence of the wives in financial matters and important participation in husband's career and educational choices.

We also took one criterion of role division — that of the working wife or the wife-mother in relation to the husband's career, now and in the future. Analysis of the replies to these questions showed the reverse of the former situation and lack of independence.

(a) **Financial independence** We have seen above that only 2 wives among those contacted had no income of their own. We have also seen that 14 wives used their resources for the family's living expenses. They continued in fact to control their income — more than half (12) had their own bank accounts into which they put their money and another 3 had both their own account and a joint account; only 6, including the 2 with no income, had a joint account alone (and they include also the two 'richest' wives in terms of personal economic assets). Those with dowries controlled them either themselves or in conjunction with male members of their own families. Almost all the couples took important financial decisions jointly and the budget (where there was one) was run by both.

(b) **The wife's participation in the husband's career decisions** Virtually all the wives interviewed discuss with their husbands the latters' career and the choices to be made. Almost all felt their opinion to be important and they were unanimous in feeling that their spouses would not accept a job against their wishes. Indeed several of the wives, both working and at home, were engaged in a preliminary sorting of the job advertisements in *Le Monde* (perhaps this is the reason they all read *Le Monde* so assiduously?) for their husband's decision about which to apply for and to show him the state of the market. Moreover most expressed themselves enthusiastic or very enthusiastic when their husbands began to think about investing a year in business education, only one having been presented with a *fait accompli*. The social backgrounds from which they come and their knowledge of education and the business world may be gauged from the fact that 14 of the wives interviewed already knew of the school when their spouses first talked of it and they knew what it offered. Some had a clearer picture than others but some knew it very well: one had had a cousin at the school, others knew alumni (as friends of their brothers for example), the father of one had advised the husband to go and one had in fact intended to go herself. Their backgrounds too make them highly aware of the subtleties of the hierarchy of schools (*Grandes Ecoles* and university) in the French system and they know that in the early days of a career at least the schools attended are reflected in earnings. They have mostly brought this knowledge to their marriages and it is reflected in their participation in their husbands' career decisions.

(c) **The working pattern of wives** Fourteen of the 21 wives interviewed were working at the time. Of the remainder 1 was a full-time student and 2 had worked before their husbands went to the school, which involved a geographical move. As we can also see from Table 10.2, these are mostly educated women, a majority of whom have a diploma involving study after the *baccalauréat*. Most had jobs, or at least had had jobs before moving, which they enjoyed and which they seemed to feel were commensurate with their abilities and qualifications (except for the two who felt they were at turning points and two reduced to being assistant teachers at the local *lycée, faute de mieux*). Yet of these 14, 12 said that they would stop working when they had a child, or, in two cases, a further child, sometimes with the added proviso of 'when my husband earns enough', or 'if we go somewhere I can't get a post easily'. While no husbands seemed to disapprove actively of their wives working, only three wives (including the students) said that they definitely intended to work after having children and these were clearly the most unusual wives in terms of the diplomas held and professions exercised. Two further wives who already had children (one each) and who were currently working to enable their husbands to attend the school were thinking of giving it up for lack of job satisfaction but felt that they would in fact probably continue. Most thus seemed attached to their professional life to only a small degree and all (with no exception) said that their husband's career was of far greater

Jane Marceau

Table 10.2 The wives' diplomas and professions

Contacted Wives		Uncontacted Wives	
Highest Diplomas	Current Professions*	Highest Diplomas	Current Professions
home economics	asst. teacher	M.A. hist./geog.	hist. teacher
½-deg. langs.	stud. + teacher	B.A. langs.	lang. teacher
deg. maths.	maths. teacher		
½-deg. physics	lang. teacher		
		secretarial	secretary
		sec. (trilingual)	secretary
sec. (bilingual)	secretary teacher		
baccalauréat	secretary	commerc. sch. +	notary's clerk
		notary sch.	
dentistry	dentist	M.A. letters	librarian
nursing	nurse	M.A. hist/geog.	interpreter
pub. rels. documtary	specialist in educational	CAPES hist.†	organizer of permanent
training	cinema		education courses
baccalauréat	designer		

Contacted Wives		Uncontacted Wives	
Highest Diplomas	Current Professions*	Highest Diplomas	Current Professions*
Dr economics	runs own firm	–	mannequin
Agron. engin. + M.Sc. biology	technical executive	stud. pharm. doctorate stud. medicine	student student
M.A. langs.	student preparing *agrégation*	prep. M.A. (lettres) prep. *baccalauréat*	student schoolgirl
nursing	—		
lab. asst. dip.	—		
lab. asst. dip.	—		
speech therapy	—		
½-deg. sociology + sec.	—		
baccalauréat	—		

* Except for the students and the wife with half a degree in sociology, all the wives had worked at some time.
† Certificat d'Aptitude Professionelle à l'Enseignement Secondaire

Jane Marceau

importance than their own. Even the wife with her own flourishing business emphasized that if her husband's career demanded it she would give up her professional life, although they would try hard to reconcile the two. Most underlined the predominance of the husband's career when being asked about their own and it was clearly something of salience to them (perhaps this is a sign of a certain conflict?). Their own working lives were seldom seen in medium or long-term perspectives — none discussed the kind of career pattern open to her in any but the vaguest terms and few discussed it at all. Although several said they would probably return to work 'later', when all the children were at school, only one said that by then she would have to do a refresher course. Moreover, these wives nearly all want quite large families, similar in size to their families of origin — 8 want 3 children; 7 want 3 or 4; 2 want 4; 1 wants 5; 1 wants 6; and only 2 want 2 — so that returning to work after all the children are at school will mean 10 or more years out of the professional world. Since the average age of the wives is 25.5 years, this brings them easily into their middle to late thirties.

These considerations bring us to an important 'contradiction'. Although the wives studied here have a conjugal relationship in which they are independent in financial matters (largely controlling their own revenue, etc.) and in which they have a participatory—egalitarian position in relation to decisions about their spouses' careers; in terms of their own professional activities, career orientation and development they remain voluntarily the dependent wife who prefers to remain at home at least most of the time with husband and children and who wishes to remain 'available' whenever her husband needs her. For the majority this is the essential part of their role. While many are contributing materially to the household budget they view their outside activities as basically secondary and/or temporary. In short, they show a set of attitudes which tend to be essentially supportive of their husband's role and in no way in competition with his aspirations. Their financial independence and participation in decision-making do not 'flow over' to influence their behaviour in other spheres. This 'contradiction' suggests that it is insufficient for wives' 'liberation' for them simply to acquire greater economic, social or cultural power. The issue is a deeper one.

Power, resources and attitudes

What then is behind this contradiction? Where power is concerned, Blood and Wolfe (1960: 12) suggest that

> The sources of power in so intimate a relationship as marriage must be sought in the comparative resources which the husband and wife

bring to the marriage . . . A resource may be defined as anything that one partner may make available to the other, helping the latter satisfy his needs or attain his goals. The balance of power will be on the side of that partner who contributes the greater resources to the marriage (1960: 13) and control over future resources is especially crucial, since decision-making involves the allocation of resources within the family. The partner who may provide or withhold resources is in a strategic position . . .

The theory has been refined to include not only resources brought to a particular marriage but those *potentially* available through a new alliance (Heer, 1963). The original and refined theories have been tested many times both in the USA and in Europe with a considerable degree of homogeneity of result. We have seen that the wives studied here bring appreciable resources to their marriage, particularly social and economic capital, and we suggest that this is the origin of their power and independence in the conjugal relationship where financial and husband's career decisions are concerned. They allow the husband to reinforce a possibly unstable social and economic position as seen in comparison with their families of origin and their expectations.

On the other hand the ideological posture of the wives is such as to preclude them from prolonged and serious attempts to play roles after marriage other than those of wife-mother and almost entirely precludes them from playing roles which might bring them into competition with the career aspirations of their husbands.[15]

Blood and Wolfe themselves mention, and Rodman (1967) and Safilios-Rothschild (1967) underline, the importance of cultural factors in determining the exact constellation of power, attitudes and role division. The internalization of norms presented directly or indirectly by the family of origin is likely to be of particular importance in relation to overall role division of the kind discussed in this paper in analysing the reasons why behaviour considered appropriate in one sphere does not 'flow over' into the others. We may also consider the specific issue of the wives' working in terms of the 'facilitators' or 'barriers' they encounter. As Hoffman (1963: 36) says:

> Another group of factors which may operate as barriers or facilitators to the mother's employment includes the attitudes of her family, her community and herself . . . Attitudes about children are also important, for example, attitudes about how essential the mother's continuous presence is to the child's development . . .

The French wives discussed here have attitudes very similar to those of the American wives described by Poloma and Garland, who conclude

Jane Marceau

that even in 1970 most American women had little interest in a career and who found that both husband and wife may give the wife's career a high priority early in the marriage but with time her career takes more of a back-seat to her husband's. The husband is seen in the role of provider and status-giver and the wife is very reluctant to do anything to usurp his position (Paloma and Garland 1971: 131-2).

Sources of role images: values, norms and education.

Where then do these role images come from? The wives discussed in this study come mostly from very 'traditional' families in terms of values and upbringing.[16] Twelve out of the twenty-one wives interviewed had spent their entire period of education, both primary and secondary, in religious schools, as had most of their brothers and sisters. Another three had been in religious schools at primary level and another three entirely in private though lay schools. Only three had had an entirely public lay education. Moreover, when asked about the education of their own children, seven proposed to put them into religious schools and another two were undecided. All the wives without exception had been married in church and all but one (undecided) either have baptized or propose to baptize their children. Several spontaneously described both themselves and their husbands as religiously *très pratiquants* (very practising). While taken alone religion may mean little (Blood and Wolfe, 1960), but in the context discussed here it forms part of a wider constellation of attitudes.

In terms of non-formal education, when asked who principally dealt with their upbringing and social education, 12 replied that it was their mothers, including 4 who were brought up by a governess as well and one other by a governess more or less alone. Seven said both their parents and one an older brother. This lends support to the suggestion made by Rapoport and Rapoport (1971a) about the influence of the early years, for almost none had mothers or indeed any close female relatives in the previous generation who worked, or if they did so, it was by necessity, for example, unmarried aunts, rather than by conviction. Almost all the female roles presented in the early years included few or no voluntary professional ones for women of their class. Further, 7 reported that their mothers would not have liked to work even if it had been socially or otherwise possible, being happy to be wives and mothers. Of those who think their mothers would have liked to work, most think of it as for now and not for when they had small children and they are clearly referring to occupations rather than continuous careers.

Finally, asked if their own parents and parents-in-law approved of their working, 8 replied that both their parents and parents-in-law approved, 3 that one set of parents disapproved while 5 had both sets of parents against them. The remaining 5 said that their parents were either dead or indifferent or that it was none of their business (1). In other words, 8 had either both or one set of parents against their working while 8 had full support. Of the latter we find the owner-manager of her own firm, the agronomic engineer, the dentist (the only girl among a family of boys, all medical), and the girl preparing the highest level teaching examinations (*agrégation*). These were the most qualified wives, and they included two of the few who intend to go on working after having children, i.e. the most committed to the work situation. Among the 8 who have either no support or only partial support, we find 3 who do not work (and who have children), 1 student, and 3 who work but who will stop on starting a family; only the designer has an artistic vocation strong enough to withstand the disapproval of her family.

Most of the wives, however, do work or have worked at some time. The trend (see Table 10.2), more clearly marked among the contacted wives but evident among the others, is to remain in typically feminine occupations or in occupations with a high female population (teaching, nursing, secretarial work, home economics, laboratory technicians, librarian, mannequin, etc). Four of the contacted wives had had no higher education at all, 6 were early segregated or 'relegated' into courses leading to posts where they would play essentially subordinate roles to men (for example, the laboratory assistants) or to higher grade service careers such as nursing where they are again subordinate to men and which include an ethic of genteel self-sacrifice. Eleven of the contacted wives had had some university education but of these 4 had not finished their first degrees and 1 had done a basically lower-level course. The uncontacted wives did rather better, with 9 out of 13 having had and completed university-level diplomas. That they seem to be more attached to their own careers may well be associated with their educational achievement and may account for their other unorthodox behaviour in that they more frequently married 'down'. It certainly contributes to giving them a status independent of that of their husbands. Of the contacted wives, then, most were either early segregated into 'feminine' courses or were channelled into degree courses which could be valuable without the acquisition of the final diploma, such as languages, because of the social value of such skills. On the whole they had either left the male-female competitive and egalitarian sections of the education system fairly early, or they had not been sufficiently motivated to compete on equal terms so that the change from such a system to that of the role of wife with a subordinate professional life was relatively easily made (cf. Rapoport and Rapoport, 1969). Indeed it should be further noted that the type of occupation entered by the wives or potentially available to them on the basis of the diplomas they hold, in some ways presupposes their marriage — and marriage to someone in their own social

Jane Marceau

and economic class — because they are not in the main professions that would generate sufficient income for the women to maintain themselves in the manner to which they were accustomed in their families of origin.[17]

Conclusion

Objective examination of the marital strategies of the high-level business students discussed here shows the potential gains from and systematic advantages of the marriage alliances made. These gains include accretions of social, economic and cultural capital and the 'acquisition' of a wife who provides both practical and 'moral' assistance but whose own role aspirations rarely conflict with those of her husband. The solidity and appropriateness of the wives' social and economic backgrounds and the values and social conformity they bring to their marriages support the reconversion strategies of their husbands, often members of older and in some ways marginal elites, preventing social regression and helping to provide a baseline from which new social ascension is possible. This at least is the case for the contacted wives. Detailed analysis of the uncontacted wives' marriages has not been possible here but there are indications that they have more frequently married 'down' and they thereby constitute an important mode of upward social mobility for their husbands. With numbers as small as those here, such a study can only be takèn as a pilot investigation, indicating a path and a framework for further work, and it is in fact planned to extend the analysis by sending questionnaires to the wives of the school's alumni at the same time as their husbands are contacted in the next part of the present study. It is also suggested that the following would be interesting avenues for further exploration:

1. Frequency of family visiting, holidaying in family property, etc., and other forms of gift-giving between the generations, such as providing capital for house purchase, guaranteeing loans for business ventures, etc.
2. Analysis of the occupations and educational diplomas of the extended families of the wives (so far we have only done it for the husbands) to assess how well-established, economically central or marginal the families in fact are.
3. Examination of the actual use by the husband of the potential networks his marriage makes available — analysis of the acquisition of jobs, business links, mutual aid in non-directly business affairs, etc.
4. Further probing of the way in which female role images are built up in this milieu and the influences on occupational choices. Mechanisms of control over the marital alliances of the daughters.

5. Deeper investigation of the images and expectations held by the wives of their husband's careers.

6. Analysis of the public and local community positions held not only by the parents of the wives but also by earlier generations of alumni of the school studied here and, most important of all, their wives.

Notes

1. Many studies in France, including those of the Ministry of Education, show a close 'fit' between the prestige of a school or a subject and the social composition of its 'public'. The process of selection begins in the secondary schools, with clear social differences between, for example, the pupils of the *lycées* and those of the technical schools, and later between faculties, such that those of medicine, pharmacy and law are much more 'bourgeois' than those of literature and especially the natural sciences. Within the *Grandes Ecoles* the most prestigious, *Polytechnique, Centrale, Mines,* etc. have very few students from humble homes, the percentage increasing proportionately as the prestige of the school declines. The gradations between subjects, schools, faculties and *Grandes Ecoles* are well established and from a hierarchy recognized by teachers, pupils and employers alike. The education system thus both reinforces and legitimates the social and economic hierarchy.

2. The women tend to be from even more restricted social origins than the men.

3. *Ecole des Hautes Etudes Commerciales, Ecole Supérieure des Sciences Economiques et Commerciales, Ecole Supérieure de Commerce de Paris.* Political science studies are carried out in the *Instituts d'Études Politiques,* notably in Paris.

4. For a detailed analysis of the economic changes see in particular Carré *et al.,* (1972).

5. For a more detailed discussion of this see Bourdieu *et al.,* (1973).

6. Only 15 per cent of the 1973-4 French students were from artisan or shopkeeper origins and only 2-3 per cent from the homes of manual workers, so we are essentially not concerned with them here.

7. This is only a rough guide as the fit between diplomas and professions is not perfect.

8. The only information available to us on the uncontacted wives concerns the diplomas and professions of the wives and their immediate families of origin, as this was gathered from the husbands.

9. We are aware of the limitations of assessing the social position of a family through the occupation of the father, especially when dealing

Jane Marceau

essentially with variations between families of similar social class. Additional information given in the text below will enable the reader to situate the families more accurately. As most of the mothers do not have a profession we are obliged to situate them by reference to the husbands.

10. The average family size of the interviewed wives is 4·2 with the mode at 4 (8 cases) and including 14 families of 4 or more children. On the other hand the husbands come from families of an average size of 2·8 with the mode at 2 (6 cases) and including 4 families of only 1 child, of whom there were none amongst the wives, and no families of over 5 children, whereas the wives' families included one of 6, one of 8 and one of 11. Of the husbands' families half were of less than 3 members while of the wives' only 4 contained less than 3 members.

    In France upper-class families tend to have larger numbers of children than other sections of the population, except the unskilled manual workers. See Bourdieu and Darbel (1966) and *Informations Sociales* (1973).

11. More information on the wives of alumni of the school will be available shortly as the next stage of the study includes the mailing of questionnaires to all the French alumni and their wives.

12. The level of family aid potentially available may perhaps be guessed by a glance at the wedding receptions provided. All had held wedding receptions for more than 50 people and 13 of the 21 for more than 100 people, including 2 of 300, 2 of 400-500 and 1 of 2,000. With a probable minimum outlay of £10 per head a reception for 100 people costs £1,000, for 500, £5,000. Consider further that each wife had on average 1·7 sisters for the parents to provide for in addition.

13. It is perhaps interesting to note that the property inherited by daughters is frequently different in kind to that inherited by sons, being more often 'moveable' rather than 'immoveable' property — that is, shares rather than a business as such — and the daughters control their property relatively less than their brothers. Further, the nature of the education of the girls tends to mean that they rarely have the skills necessary to make the best use of their capital.

14. See, for instance, Pitrou (1972).

15. This does not of course mean that they do not take part in activities outside the home in their 'spare' time, but 'spare' is a crucial adjective.

16. It is interesting to note here the apparently limited nature of the 'real' marriage choices open to these girls. Of the 21 contacted wives, 7 have married friends of their siblings and 1 had married a person

with whom the family had arranged a meeting, 5 had met their husbands through common friends, 1 had married the brother of a friend, 3 had met their husbands at a dinner party or other *soir*ée, while only 2 had met 'by chance' on holiday, 1 at school and another through a common activity (scouts).

17. Those women who did have some private income, probably did not have enough to enable them to maintain their accustomed life-style unless they married (though we do not have exact information on this point). On the other hand, those wives who seemed likely to be the 'richest' in their own right are those most determined to work, e.g. the agronomist-biologist and the girl with her own business.

Purdah in the British situation

Purdah is an extreme form of sex role differentiation. The word itself is Urdu, meaning curtain or screen, which reflects the segregation, restriction and covering associated with the system.

The main purpose of this paper is to illustrate how an understanding of *purdah* in the British situation necessarily involves an understanding of the system as it is found in Pakistan. In the last section of the paper further considerations which arise from such an analysis of *purdah* are outlined, together with some implications for the position of women in general and the position of ethnic minorities.

It is perhaps relevant to note here that the dearth of material on *purdah* in Britain and in the many societies in which it is found is due to the tremendous difficulties associated with fieldwork (Papanek 1964: 160). In such a Muslim society a male researcher cannot hope to gain entry and acceptance into the woman's world. A female researcher, of whom there are still relatively few, may only do so by adopting the life expected of a woman and thus restricting her movement in the man's world and even in certain other sections of the community (see Maher in the companion volume). As an outsider she may assume a certain flexibility which can be manipulated to her advantage, but this involves a careful management of impression to maintain a consistent picture of herself.

The work reported here is based on research among Mirpuri families in Bradford and their relatives in the villages of Mirpur, in Azad Kashmir — the Pakistani held part of Kashmir.[1]

Purdah in Pakistan

As a land of contrasts between rich and poor; between towns of the twentieth century and villages of a pre-industrial era; and incorporating different ethnic groups and languages, it is hardly likely that the observance of *purdah* is uniform throughout Pakistan. Any system of sex role differentiation cannot be understood in isolation from other social, economic and ideological systems of the society concerned, to which it is intimately related.

Pakistan is an Islamic society which, however, manifests many characteristics associated with the rest of the Indian subcontinent, reflecting its relatively recent origin as a nation-State based on a religious ideology. Pakistani society is patrilineal and patrilocal. The family is typically three-generational and subject to the authority of the eldest male.

Although an Islamic society is ideally egalitarian,[2] Pakistan has retained many features of the caste-system, and has a marked socio-economic stratification. The fundamental institution regulating Pakistani life is not, however, class or caste but the kinship system. A man or woman must be conceptualized as existing in a complex network of rights and duties which extend from the central core of his immediate family to a wide set of paternal and maternal kin relations. He, or she, is not an individual agent acting on his or her own behalf but exists only in relation to family and kin. Reputation or status is dependent on this network, and on the fulfilment of the rights and duties inherent in a position at any particular time. To concentrate on personal, financial, educational or occupational achievements to the detriment of the loyalties and duties to one's family and kin involves a loss of reputation and can eventually lead to rejection. The individualism and independence so valued in the West, appears selfish and irresponsible to the Pakistani living in this context. To move out of this network involves forfeiting the mutual aid, trust, support (emotional and financial), inheritance rights, etc., which are the right of any member.

In a society where elders have a monopoly of authority, where boys and girls do not mix freely after puberty and where marriage is a contract between two families, to reject or be rejected by one's family also entails forfeiting the only acceptable form of marriage. All men and women are expected to marry; family and children have the highest priority. In Pakistan, as in many Muslim countries, marriage traditionally takes place within the kin group, and the preferred marriage is with a patrilateral or matrilateral cross or parallel cousin.[3]

For explanatory reasons it is possible to outline a *purdah* system which, although observed in actuality by relatively few Pakistanis, is relevant in that it is the ideal to which the majority aspire.[4]

The basic rules of this 'ideal' system are four. First, interaction between men and women is limited outside a certain well-defined category of people. This category is the immediate kin as outlined in the *Quran* (XXIV: 31). Secondly, the sexes are segregated before or at the time of puberty. Boys and girls no longer play together and must maintain the required social distance, or avoidance. Thirdly, there is a division of labour. The women's work is in the house, cleaning, cooking and caring for the needs of her children and husband. The man's work is outside the house, gaining the livelihood of the whole family. The division of labour is evident from the age of puberty. Fourthly, women must at all times be modest in dress, movement, attitude and expression to avoid attracting the opposite sex.[5] They must be virgins at marriage and must remain chaste thereafter. These rules must be observed in their respective ways, by both men and women.

As the relationships between people are highly restricted the devices of *purdah* form a very important non-verbal communication system, a symbolic system coding messages to the participants which enable them to interpret their next move (whether they should move, stay, sit, stand or speak and if so in a familiar or formal tone). Gestures, clothing and different physical contexts are signs in any society to aid people in their interpretation of the situation. *Purdah* is maintained basically by the division of physical space, and the use of certain articles of clothing: dynamically it works through people's relation to physical space and by their manipulation of these articles of clothing.

The household is divided into male and female sections. The men of the family spend a lot of time with their women and children in the women's part of the house but when a guest arrives their separate worlds come into existence. If men come to visit, the male family members receive them in the men's part of the house (*mardana*); if women come to visit they are received into the women's quarters (*zanana*). A close relative of either sex will not cause the family grouping to split, unless it is a senior male relative, or the men wish to talk business. The formal and highly ritualized interaction between the two worlds is balanced by the relaxed atmosphere in each separate world. As it is believed that relations between the sexes would, or should, be strained, the device of separate physical domains allows for a much greater freedom and privacy than otherwise possible. The *burqa* and the *veil* act in a similar way.

The *burqa* is traditionally a large white cotton sheet of cloth covering the whole of the body. It is traditionally an urban phenomenon. It is tailored to fit over the head, and has a panel of small holes over the eyes so its wearer can see out, but no one can see in. This is known as the 'shuttlecock' *burqa*. The more modern styles are found in the cities where the covering is usually made of a black silken material and falls to the waist or knees. It has sleeves and a button-up front and can be loosely fitted or carefully tailored. A panel of cloth which falls over the face can be thrown back easily when it is not needed. It is another device which, by restricting social contact, allows a greater freedom of movement than otherwise would be possible if the rules of the *purdah* system are to be observed. Without it women would be confined to their homes. It enables mobility by literally disguising the woman. Under her *burqa* she is a no-body, a non-person in no need of recognition, nor of participating in social interaction. Unlike the veil which can regulate the degree of social distance it is a device which prevents the initiation of a relationship in the first place.

The traditional *burqa* is effective in its main function of covering the female form and preventing any means of recognition. However, the newer styles seem to neglect this original function. The traditional *burqa* could not, admittedly, hide pretty hands and shoes but the newer styles not only reveal the style and quality of the girl's clothes but also her figure. A great variety of colours (often black, white, brown or pink) and trimmings (buttons, lace, etc.) are found. The different *burqas* and their changing fashions are an obvious sign-system, indicating the socio-economic background and the degree of traditionalism of the wearer.

The veil is a more complicated device for regulating social interaction between the sexes. It sets distance: it may function so as to maintain maximum social distance, or a restricted social distance, or the minimum distance associated with the 'natural' modesty of, and respect due to, women. There are many variations of the veil. The traditional form, worn by the old and by villagers, is more a shawl as we know it. It is called a *chaddar* and is placed over the head (to cover the hair) and then one end is drawn across the shoulders to cover the chest. It differs considerably in size, shape and colour. The *dupatta* is most often seen in the cities. It is a thinner and smaller piece of long muslin cloth which is also draped over the head and chest. The more traditional wear it permanently on the head and covering all the head; the less traditional wear it on the shoulders, across the neck and leave the two ends dangling down the back. And the ultramodern wear a gesture of a veil, or no veil at all. The way the *dupatta* is worn immediately indicates (since it is a symbol of female modesty) the wearer's attitude to the place of women in society or her degree of conformity to tradition.

But a girl or woman does not wear her veil in one position all the time. Even the ultra-modern girl who does not place it on her head in the presence of elders (particularly men), nor when walking in a town, will put her *dupatta* on her head when the *azan* (call for prayer) is heard from the mosque. (This illustrates the dimension of respect, as well as modesty, in its use.) All women frequently alter the position of their veils during the day according to where thay are, and who is present.

There are other devices which support the system of *purdah* which are found typically in the urban areas allowing women a certain mobility in a very large and diffuse population. They are particularly obvious in means of transport. There is an unstated but carefully observed law of seating in buses, which divides men from women; usually women are at the front (so that the men cannot turn round and stare). Many taxis and some private cars have curtains over the back windows. Trains have separate

Verity Saifullah-Khan

second-class compartments for women. In the upper-class there are no separate compartments but the reserved seats are invariably shuffled about so men are next to men and women to women. In some cinemas there is a *purdah* partition dividing the audience, in others a modified system of families and groups of women sitting in the balcony and men downstairs.

There are many other occasions when devices are used. Some, like *purdah* mornings at some elite swimming pools are rare; others, like two-stage meals (men first, women later) at weddings are customary. And each has variations according to the class, degree of modernity, place of residence of the peoples concerned.

The explanation of *purdah* given by those who practise it is usually simply that it is a part of their religion, or a custom observed by their forefathers and thus to be maintained. More specifically they see it as a control mechanism: a mechanism that is necessary to ensure orderly and acceptable relationships between the sexes. Their argument is based on the observable fact that disorder and disgrace do arise (in traditional terms) if it is not observed. But there also seems to be a fundamental belief in the weakness, or lack of self-control in human nature — that is, that both men and women are likely to succumb to sexual temptation. If a man and woman who are unrelated are left alone it is believed that sexual activity will inevitably follow. Some stress the predatory nature of men, or their physical strength, others that women deliberately entice, or are physically or mentally too weak to resist.

Variations on the ideal *purdah* system result from three basic variables; cultural, ideological and socio-economic. It is the last variable which is particularly relevant to this paper, but first the relevance of the other two variables will be outlined.

Variations in the practice of *purdah* in Pakistan result from regional and cultural differences. The vast majority of Pakistanis are Muslims, but they include several different ethnic groups associated with different regions of the country.[6] The differences in their observation of *purdah* are clear, besides the differences relating to socio-economic position and ideology. The rules and devices outlined in this paper are based on Punjabi culture, to which Mirpuris belong, but a greater understanding of the nature of *purdah* should involve comparative analysis of the different ethnic groups. For example, the Pathans, of the North West Frontier of Pakistan, are renowned for their strict form of *purdah* which relates to their emphasis on certain features which are also evident in Punjabi society (a woman's incorporation into her husband's lineage, and the notion of honour, *izzat)* and also to the relatively underdeveloped nature of their Province.

Differences in ideology may also account for the differing degrees and ways in which *purdah* is practised. Although it is not easy to distinguish any obvious difference in the observance relating to the different Islamic sects[7] there are obvious schools of thought with different values and beliefs relating to the importance of *purdah,* the status of women, and the general interpretation of the Islamic tradition. A division between a 'traditional' compared to a 'liberal' school of thought does not neatly correspond to the distinction between village and city life.[8] In the village the priest's or *mullah's* wife is likely to be more circumspect in manner and restricted in movement. In the city the most traditional of families will shun the increased importance given to the education of girls (which is proving to be a strong force of 'interference' in the observance of *purdah*) and the employment of women (which is still largely restricted to the fields of education and medicine). But there is much support for the argument that Islam cannot, and does not, survive in its original form in a modern, urban setting.[9]

The 'liberal' school of thought is associated with city life, however, where the period of adolescence, the questioning of parental authority, the value of education and the existence of co-educational colleges and an increasing number of 'love' marriages are major changes in the traditional scene.

These ideological positions may not, of course, remain constant throughout a person's lifetime. Children learn traditional Islamic teachings at school or in the mosque but when they grow up these beliefs may be relaxed as they interact in the outside world. This is particularly true of the men, whereas women, less influenced by conditions outside the household and involved in the socialization of their children, are more traditional. The guardians of tradition, and particularly of *purdah,* are the old women. Having borne and brought up a large family they acquire status and authority, particularly over their daughters-in-law. A young woman intending to modify her observance of *purdah* knows that it is not her husband, but her mother-in-law who is likely to object most.

The socio-economic variable is of obvious importance. The ideal *purdah* system outlined above necessitates a certain standard of living, the *purdah* household requiring more than one room and servants or children to maintain contact between the two worlds (in the form of food, messages, etc.). Complete seclusion of the women similarly requires servants or the men to collect water, fodder and shopping. It is therefore a small percentage of the population who can maintain the ideal. Invariably they are from the higher socio-economic strata, the wealthier city dwellers and the landlords of the villages. As an ideal that only the wealthy can maintain, social prestige is associated with strict observance. It is adopted by those who have, or aspire to, raise their status. The majority, about 80 per cent of the population of Pakistan, however, live in villages and practise a subsistence economy.

Mirpur District borders the Punjab, which lies to the south and west,

Verity Saifullah-Khan

but the land is hillier and less fertile. There is only one city and a few small towns in the district. The majority of the population are, therefore, subsistence farmers living in small villages, but the nation-wide processes of economic and social change and the particular effects of a large volume of emigration from the area, are rapidly altering the traditional scene.

By force of necessity, *purdah* is relaxed in the villages, but the fundamental rules remain evident. The women's work is still centred around the house, caring for the children and the needs of her husband and keeping the house and domestic animals in order. A man's work is out of the house, working the land or in an inherited craft. Women have to leave the confines of the courtyard to collect water, to do the washing in the river, to cut the fodder, to take meals to the men in the fields and to help them during the busy harvest period. Only a few wealthy families have servants, tenants and tube-wells within the house and can forfeit the economic contribution of their women and thus gain prestige. When the woman leaves her house, however, she still observes the code of female modesty and places her *chaddar* well over her head and stops to talk only with those with whom she is well acquainted. She is not, in fact, venturing into the unknown or likely to meet unrelated men. All villagers are seen in a brother-sister type relationship, even if they are not related. Everyone knows everyone else and although fellow villagers who are not close friends or not related maintain an accepted social distance there is no necessity of total seclusion. Reputations result from the common fund of knowledge about a person's behaviour and attitude and when in public the villagers intend to avoid blemishing their reputation. Community control thus maintains the social control which in a more diffuse setting are maintained by the strict *purdah* devices. Where a woman is likely to come into contact with unknown men, for instance, in another distant village and particularly in the city, she must cover herself completely with her *burqa.* Gatherings and festivities are often between relatives and fellow villagers and therefore men and women are not separated into different quarters but may sit and talk together or, as often happens, congregate with their own sex. The village houses have two or three rooms but the large family unit and limited space prevents a strict division of the house into male and female quarters. At puberty boys and girls seek more of their own sex's company, which results partly from the division of labour which has begun by this time. At marriageable age (15 for girls and 18 for boys) they do not mix freely except with certain close relatives and neighbours.

Village women do not gain the prestige associated with the observance of *purdah* of their urban sisters, nor is their power reduced as it is for urban women who do not contribute to, or control the household budget because of the physical restrictions of *purdah* and the existence of a wage economy in the cities.

Purdah in Bradford

There are approximately 15,000 Mirpuris in Bradford out of a total population of Pakistanis of about 25,000.[10] Many Mirpuris in Bradford came to England directly from their home villages, never having lived in a city in their own country. They depended on the migration 'chain' established by pioneer migrants between their district and certain cities in Britain. Invariably coming to their relatives and to areas with a concentration of Pakistanis, they found comfort and support, not only from their friends and kin, but from the goods and services available (the mosque, the *hallal* butcher, the Pakistani cinema, restaurants, shops, banks and estate agents) and from the presence of their countrymen in the work situation. A sense of security and identity so often in jeopardy in migration between such different worlds is a positive result of the re-establishment of the traditional institutions of village-life.

Like many other Pakistani women in Britain, the Mirpuri women in Bradford observe *purdah*. They do not go out of the house more than is necessary and many of the first women to join their husbands in England, and even some today, do not leave their house at all, except in the company of their husbands. In these cases the men, or children, do the family shopping and errands. Nowadays most women do go out to nearby shops (often owned by Pakistanis or Indians) and to the doctors or to visit friends living nearby. Besides these occasional excursions, the rest of the day is spent indoors. At weekends particularly, and sometimes in the evenings, they go with the whole family to visit friends and relatives. Only very recently has one heard of Mirpuri women going out to work, but this remains a rare occurrence, much criticised by other Mirpuris.

The restriction on physical movement is also evident in the social and physical organization of Mirpuri households. In the terraced houses in the streets of Bradford the back-room is the domain of the women and children and the front is reserved for guests and menfolk. The family when alone will remain in the back-room and may not disperse if close friends or relatives visit. If a large number of visitors come, or male visitors not well known to the wife, all the men move to the front room and food and drinks are served separately. During this time it is only the young children who may move between those domains, and who can therefore serve as messengers between husband and wife.

In the back-room, even when friends and relatives congregate, the seating arrangements indicate the observance of *purdah*. A married couple occasionally sits on the same sofa, but more often men sit on one side of the room and women on the other. When someone enters the room and the only spare seat is among the wrong set, someone moves or the chairs are reorganized. Needless to say this is a natural and automatic gesture and not accompanied by embarrassment.

Verity Saifullah-Khan

The modesty expected of women in dress and manners is also maintained in Bradford. Mirpuris in Bradford always wear the traditional *shalwar-kamiz* (a long tunic top and wide baggy trousers), keep their hair plaited and their *dupatta* or *chaddar* over their head when in company, or out of the house, and occasionally the head-piece of the modern *burqa* is worn. The positioning and movement of the women's veil symbolize the social distance and relationship with those present.

The Mirpuris in Bradford come from the village life outlined above, where observance of *purdah* is relaxed due to economic circumstances but supported by the social control of a close-knit community. From the earlier outline it is obvious that *purdah* in Bradford is stricter for the Mirpuri than it was in her home village. This is due to a combination of factors.

First, the city of Bradford, like any city in Pakistan, is an alien world to the villager. The immediate neighbours in the street and surrounding areas are not known to the family; there is no common way of life. Even if there are many Pakistanis in the area very few are likely to be kin or fellow villagers. The Mirpuri woman, therefore, must observe *purdah* from all these unrelated men, and most particularly from other Pakistani men, because Pakistani men, unlike English men, are seen as part of the system and are known to operate by the same code of behaviour.

Secondly, the Mirpuri women can no longer help the men in their economic activity, which is now separated completely from the household. Nor have they cause to go outside for water, firewood or fodder. They cannot go out to work in such an alien world and there appears initially to be no necessity, since the husband earns far greater wages than he would have done at home.[11]

Thirdly, something must be said about the purpose and intentions behind the Mirpuri migration to Britain. Like many villagers from other parts of Pakistan, but unlike the more educated urbanite, the Mirpuri has come to earn and to save as much as possible so that he may return to his home to buy land or to retire comfortably or start a small business. Everything he does in Britain is in terms of these intentions which, although hindered by the presence of his family and the rising cost of living, are foremost in his mind. Accepting the loyalties and duties due to his family and kin (and his very existence in Britain often results from their decision and financial aid), and accepting that the motive of migration was to raise his and thus his family's economic and social status back home, the migrant is not primarily concerned with the quality of his life in Britain, nor with altering his life-style to accommodate to new features in that society. Close contact with home and the maintenance, with minimal modifications, of his traditional life-style are facilitated by close kin and village ties established in Britain, and the goods and services provided by the Pakistani community at large. Their existence negates any justification for using the facilities of the wider community. Whether a Mirpuri is aware or not of the difficulties he would experience if he tried to integrate, he is certainly conscious that any gesture he makes signifying a relaxation of traditional loyalties to family, kin, religion and country would be open to severe criticism from Pakistanis in Britain and at home. In brief, the Mirpuri does not wish to alter his behaviour or values more than is essential and their preservation facilitates the achievement of his goals.

Fourthly, and following from the last point, the importance of the traditional or home frame of reference means that the Mirpuri is seeking symbols of his success in traditional terms. The importance of acquiring property even if it is very old and in need of repair, rather than renting accommodation or living in a council flat, is but one example. The main source of status in Pakistan is ownership of land, and in the British context this extends to ownership of a house, which also brings a certain degree of security and independence. The stricter observance of *purdah* in Britain may be due to a considerable extent to the new context in which Mirpuris find themselves, but it is also related to its importance as a status symbol. Strengthening the pride of the Mirpuri, it also indicates to others in Bradford and in Pakistan, his acquisition of a new and valued status.

The new features of *purdah* in Britain

The significance of the maintenance or adoption of *purdah* in the British situation can only be grasped with reference to the traditional system in Pakistan. But in certain important aspects it differs from the situation there.

The Mirpuri women in Bradford may well be proud of their newly acquired status and of the amenities (cooker, bathroom, electricity, etc.) of a *pakka* (brick-built) house, but the observance of *purdah* in Britain takes on different and sometimes painful proportions. Its observance in Britain may lead to loneliness and anxieties which can have a serious psychological consequence.

It is often not apparent in the literature that this highly segregated society involves two worlds; that of the men and that of the women. In Pakistan women are always in the company of family, friends or neighbours due to the nature of the extended family and the community nature of the village, or *mohalla* (neighbourhood) in the city. Women in strict *purdah* are never alone, nor do they seek so to be. Privacy as we know it is not highly valued. In Britain the Mirpuri woman not only misses the company, but also the psychological and physical support of family and friends. This is particularly so for the new bride arriving in England.

Verity Saifullah-Khan

For the women, village life involves joint responsibility for child-caring, decision-making, work and relaxation. In Britain she is alone and restricted to the house. She has more household cleaning and washing (nappies and layers of clothing are necessities in Britain's climate) and little help or company to lighten the load. Children are at their mother's feet for much of the day, the danger of traffic and bad weather restricts them to the back yard and house. There are very positive advantages therefore for women who live in an area with many of their own people, or when two or three families live in the same house.

In Pakistan the woman's world involves her exclusive responsibilities in the domestic domain, regulating the elaborate rituals of gift-giving, the major part in the socialization of her children and the intricate and lively social world which 'compensates' for the restricted interaction with men. The interdependence of the sexes due to their participation in exclusive worlds and the very existence of this alternative world beyond the private conjugal and family relationships, results in a far greater amount of bargaining power for the women than is usually acknowledged. What appears to us to be a lack of choice to determine her future and develop her 'individuality', is equally true for her husband. In the final resort it is he who decides whether she does or does not observe *purdah*, yet his decisions are subject to his father's, and in this case particularly his mother's, decisions, and the overriding rights and duties of his position.

The new features of *purdah* in Britain initiate new dimensions and potentialities in the relationship between husband and wife, enabling the development of a closer relationship more independent of external control. A woman in Britain may not only feel this new independence in her relationship with her husband, but also in a greater control over the socialization of her children and the running of the house, due to the absence of his mother and other older women of the household. In the extended family no one relationship must jeopardise the harmony of the whole. The affection and attention paid to the bride by her husband must not be at the expense of his relationship with his parents, and thus publicly it remains formal and time together is limited. An increased emotional dependence between husband and wife is likely when the alternative men's and women's worlds are considerably restricted and when more time and privacy are available. The lack of emotional and physical support usually received from others of the same sex is perhaps also a contributing factor to the strengthening of relationships among kinsmen and fellow villagers in Britain.

Besides these new features of her situation, the woman is involved in dealing with tradesmen, shopping, using a bus and handling relatively large sums of money (i.e. household money) whereas in the subsistence economy she had full charge of the household resources, mostly grain and a little cash. This may initially cause considerable anxieties but usually results in increased confidence and self-assurance. This new-found freedom may cause tensions between husband and wife if the husband feels threatened or insulted by his wife's increased capabilities in dealings which were once his domain. A further source of tension may result from the restriction of another feature of village life. In the village the men and women of a family work and relax in the same place but in Britain the husband works long hours, often on night-shift.

It is obvious that the nature of *purdah* in Britain may be considerably changed in the Mirpuri households, with wide repercussions in social relationships. The degree to which these new pressures modify *purdah* depends on the composition of the particular family and the personalities involved. It is difficult, however, to predict their actual relevance without following the situation over a longer period of time. There are perhaps two obvious changes which are likely to have a major effect. Although it is rare for a Mirpuri woman to work outside the home, a few are already doing so and it seems probably that their numbers will increase. This will be partly due to the changing age composition with more women passing the child-bearing and -rearing stage and partly due to the changing pattern of migration.[12] The ever-increasing expenses (due to the rising cost of living, and children born in Britain) means the family saves less and their departure to Pakistan to settle recedes into the distance. Some men have sent their wives and children back to Pakistan with the intention of joining them after a few more years of hard saving. But others become disillusioned when they visit Pakistan and worry how their British-born children could adapt to conditions there. Many families see the advantages in Britain for their children and accept a postponement of their plans to return for their benefit. It is very few of these latter families who have braved the criticism and let their women go out to work.[13] The choice appears to be one of more Mirpuri women returning to Pakistan or going out to work.

The second obvious change relates to the next generation. Most of the first generation women, including the new brides arriving from Pakistan, are likely to maintain *purdah* to some degree. The children of these women, however, are already experiencing some of the pressures of modern urban life and a Western education. However orthodox a girl's home life is, she is also influenced by life at school: mixing with friends who discuss boyfriends, going to the cinema, talking about fashions, etc.; and she is also taught to question and to develop her individuality. Many Mirpuri parents have not appreciated the strength of these pressures until their effects are noticeable in their own children. Others who have learned from the experiences of friends or relatives may leave their daughters in Pakistan or send them back to live with grandparents. Some see the answer

Verity Saifullah-Khan

to be a single-sex or Muslim school in Bradford. For the truly orthodox, however, this can only be a partial solution. Girls will still be subject to the 'corrupting' influence of the Western society outside the school, unless they are completely secluded.

Further considerations on the social functions of *purdah*

Purdah is a system of social control, a mechanism that regulates relationships between the sexes. And it is a non-verbal communication system which, through an immediate and simple sign language, allows maximum communication when other interactions — physical and verbal — are restricted. *Purdah* aims to maintain in an overt manner the moral standards of the society by reiterating and thus reinforcing accepted values. Through constant expression in the elaborate ritual of social interaction, the moral order is strengthened and maintained where it might otherwise weaken under external and internal pressures. *Purdah* is a public performance, set on an established stage and open to the scrutiny of a discerning audience. The elaborate ritual interactions and the command over every sphere of life act as a statement of something important; something to be held sacred. It is backed by supernatural sanction (the *Quran*), and the sentiments of shame and disgrace resulting from a breach of code reflect its moral worth. The reality of everyday life is thus constantly related to the ideal and sacred order, outlined in the scriptures, accepted by custom and supported and repeatedly verbalized by the deeply religious.

From comparative work in Islamic and non-Islamic societies[14] it appears that it is not an Islamic or any other religious ideology which is the prerequisite of *purdah*, but a strongly patrilineal and virilocal society. Where a woman leaves her natal home to join and produce children for her husband's family, the husband has control over her and her reproductive powers. She is sacred and respected in her capacity to perpetuate the group (i.e. as a mother) because children are highly valued for religious and economic reasons. This capacity is, however, often interpreted as a danger. She has the power to defile the 'pure' blood of the group, and this is often used to legitimate the strict control over her movements.

In its function as a symbolic system the observance of *purdah* in Bradford can be used as an indicator of many features of the Pakistani population in the city and in the country as a whole. A few will be suggested here.

Its observance in Bradford indicates the values and intentions of the different Pakistani sub-communities. Basically it is the villagers from Mirpur and Punjab who maintain it and (due to force of circumstance and an increased income) observe it to a greater extent than in their home village. Pressure to conform to group norms, but particularly the intention to return to Pakistan, leads to the preservation of traditional values. The observance of *purdah* in Bradford is a demonstration or statement of conformity and of acquisition of a superior religious and social status for the participants and the community in Britain and Pakistan. It thus involves a feeling of belonging, of security, and of pride for the villager who knows he is of the lowest social strata in his home society.

It is the more educated Pakistani, usually from an urban background, who often had already observed a modified form of *purdah* before migration, who relaxes or abandons the principles in Britain. Such migrants illustrate a different set of values or intentions. More equipped for life in a Western society, often with fewer obligations to kin in Pakistan and keen to settle in Britain, they are more prepared to leave aside customs that will restrict their acceptance. It is, in fact, the so-called 'leaders' of the Pakistani community who come from this group and who appear to the British to represent the majority of their countrymen. Often professional men or successful entrepreneurs, their wives may go out to work (as teachers, or social workers) or organize Pakistani women's associations. They rarely observe *purdah* and are likely to accept that their teenage children will have to mix with the opposite sex and will have a greater choice of marriage partners. The ambiguity of their position is obvious. Their assumed role as representatives of the villagers, who are concerned to maintain their traditional life-style and values, contradicts their own beliefs and practices.

The observance of *purdah* among the different sub-communities based on region of origin is also well illustrated in Bradford. The Punjabi and Mirpuri are in most ways similar in their observance of *purdah* and in the percentage of their women living in Britain. The Pathans are a much smaller group, possibly numbering around 400, who keep very much to themselves outside the work situation. The percentage of women among the Pathans in Bradford is far lower, due to their tradition of leaving wives behind when the men migrate. Pathan women are more restricted than the Mirpuri, but their close grouping in certain streets and areas of the city reduces their isolation. A few Pathan women wear a *burqa* when outside the house.

The clothes associated with *purdah* are also a useful indicator of change. The abandonment of the *burqa* appears at first sight to be a remarkable compromise in an alien land. It does not relate to a fundamental change, however, but an acknowledgement that its function of hiding the woman is lost in this new context in Britain. It becomes an oddity that attracts attention and amazement from the local population. There are other forced changes which have little relevance. The wearing of coats, socks and gloves are necessary in a new climate though the resistance to wearing socks and closed shoes illustrates the reluctance to

Verity Saifullah-Khan

change. There are other changes in the style and quality of material which not only indicate the availability of new types of cloth, but also the increased socio-economic position of the wearer. Resistance to this trend may indicate a more traditional view which is critical of shiny and tightly-tailored clothes. The adoption of the English head-scarf is an interesting adaptation. As yet it does not replace the *dupatta*. The head-scarf is worn by some women while they are out of the house, but if they expect to visit someone else's house they take a *dupatta* to replace it while indoors. A relaxation of the use of the *dupatta* or an adoption of bell-bottom trouser suits may eventually occur among Mirpuris, as it has for most other Pakistanis. However, it may not indicate a major change but result from the realization that these are now widespread in the cities of Pakistan.

A structural approach to *purdah*

The more obvious functional explanations of *purdah* have been emphasized so far. An attempt will be made to provide the beginnings of a structural explanation.

Just as *purdah* functions to avoid ambivalent relationships by restricting relationships only to those who are out of 'the marriage market' (i.e. immediate kin, and members of one's own sex), so structurally *purdah* is closely related to the ambiguous status of women.[15] The restrictions on social interactions and the maintenance of social distance enable the continuance of social life in the face of the striking ambiguities that underlie the system.

In a society where male pride (*izzat*) is so important and the patrilineal kin group the fundamental institution, the 'symbolic shelter' (Papernak, 1971) of one's women maintains the notion of male control. Though the man is dependent on his women (due to the division of labour, the importance of children and to preserve his status) in the outside world, this dependence bears no recognition when the outside world is his domain and the domain of other men. Acknowledgement of this dependence contradicts the notion of male pride.

Somehow related to this aspect is the further ambiguity in the tension between the family group (and the kin group) and the outside world. Existing in a world of ascribed status and with the close inter-dependent relationships of rights and duties to family and kin, the family remains an exclusive entity. Outsiders are intruders, and the lack of any binding loyalty leaves them open to suspicion. Women in their exclusive domain of child care and domesticity are the core of the family. They produce the sons who perpetuate the family and they produce daughters who will eventually leave the family as they once did. There is shame or a kind of embarrassment for the father who has to hand over his daughter to another family. She can no longer remain part of his exclusive world. Both her own and his reputation are vulnerable at the hands of 'outsiders'. The father who receives a daughter-in-law into the house loses no pride, and gains a certain power or influence over the father who loses his daughter. From the day a girl is born, both parents prepare their daughter to uphold the reputation of the family by strictly adhering to the norms of the society. *Purdah* ensures she will taint neither the honour of her natal family nor that of her affinal family. She is the weak link in the family's exclusiveness. She leaves their protection and she and they must ensure that her husband's family have no cause to insult her parental home. Concerned for her *izzat* and their own, her parental family (whether parents or brothers) give her presents throughout her lifetime (Eglar, 1960: 97 and 188). It is she who eventually becomes mother-in-law and, with the men of the family, become guardians of the women who have come from outside.

The frailty and the powerfulness of the link between those who give and those who receive daughters is considerably reduced in cousin marriage. Endogamy within the kin group (*biṛadari*) and a preference for cousin marriage results in a highly compact and exclusive kin group which does not separate kin from affines. Marrying a member of the kin group decreases the bride's unfamiliarity with her new home and her family's uncertainty of the treatment she will receive. A certain familiarity and trust is already established. The bride retains rights in her parental home and strengthens an already established relationship between the families; ensuring an added stability. However, when conflict or disagreement do arise, the resulting divisions in the kin group have far more serious consequences. So long as the marriage remains stable the father of the bride 'loses' less when he is contributing to the strength of the kin group.

A girl may play in her childhood with a cousin she will eventually marry. After puberty, if the two families agree to the alliance, the girl will observe *purdah* from the boy until the day she is married.

Conclusions and hesitations

It has been argued in this paper that to understand the existence and workings of *purdah* in Britain it is essential to see it in the context of Pakistani society as a whole, from which it originates and to which its practitioners in Britain remain orientated. Without reference to *purdah* in Pakistan, and its inter-relation with other institutions of the society (e.g. arranged and early marriages, the authority and respect structures) its importance as a status symbol, and its stricter practice among villagers in Britain, would have been lost.

Verity Saifullah-Khan

The illustration of these rather straightforward points also highlights important questions in the field of race relations and the women's movement.

Like millions of other migrants throughout the world, the Mirpuris in Bradford are 'urban villagers'.[16] They have come to this alien land, as they see it, to work hard and improve their lot. They happen to be in Bradford (rather than Marseilles or Frankfurt, for example) and to be employed as they are (mostly on night shifts in textile mills) because of our colonial past and the social and economic stratification and discriminatory ideologies of this society. The migrants' move is not simply a journey of 6,000 miles, but a journey across centuries and cultures and thus, invariably, involves adjustments and uncertainties and the revaluation of past hopes and future plans. Many aspirations are realized, but as many new problems arise, most notably the difficulty in returning to settle in 'the old life' or deciding to settle in Britain, and the resultant problems involved in bringing up children in this country.

Changes are taking place which to the outsider appear infinitesimal but to the participant they are of major consequence. If we are to condone, even to hasten such processes by direct policies (e.g. dispersal by slum clearance, ignoring the demand for single-sex schools) we must be prepared for the effects felt by those uncertain of their roots. As yet these effects are far more noticeable among West Indians in Britain. The 'adjustment' or 'integration' some so earnestly or lightly advocate will inevitably involve considerable emotional cost. Positively to encourage the westernization of Pakistan girls, who at present return to Pakistan to marry or are likely to marry a man from Pakistan, introduces added tensions to an already stressful situation. Does not our desire for a multi-cultural or plural society contradict in part attempts to rid this society of racism and sexism?

This paper serves also perhaps to remind us that to understand another culture implies suspending or suppressing our own values and presuppositions. A particular feature of one culture is not directly comparable to its equivalent in another culture, without reference to the full systems of which they are a part. The recent trend, of which the conference and this book of essays is a part, to attempt to counteract the lack of attention paid to the more uninstitutionalized but equally important institutions of the woman's world in anthropological and sociological literature, must not concentrate on its task to such a degree that the position of men and status of individuals in general in the society in question are not taken into account. The women in Asian society may well be 'dominated' by men, yet men too are subject to the power of the elders (both male and female) and the authoritarian hierarchical nature of the society as a whole. Any change in the position of women necessarily involves a change in the position of men, but any fundamental alteration is impossible without liberation from the exploitation of the extended family and other social institutions which maintain the *status quo*. However, the provision of welfare, medical, nursery, banking and other services are at present, for the masses of poorer villagers, performed only by family and kin.

There is a disturbing arrogance and 'cultural' imperialism underlying many of the most valid aims of the women's movement. The movement is based on concepts such as individuality and independence, which are essentially Western concepts. It applies little time and energy to delve below the submissiveness, conformity, dependence, exploitation and lack of individuality which it characterizes as fundamental to the Asian, and many other ways of life. In our society the state of the old and the mentally ill indicate but two examples of our need to learn from the altruism, and the notion of duty which are equally fundamental elements of Asian culture.

To the Asian, the Westerner's stress on independence and individuality appears immoral, selfish and irresponsible, although it may well foster innovation and creativity. Freedom is not identified with self-assertion and emancipation must surely be attainable without Westernization. It is arguable, I think, that Asians do not see the status of men and women as comparable, and thus not in competition or conflict. If the word status is used it is not used with the connotation of ranking and thus it has a different meaning in Asia. Western society believes that men and women are comparable, that is they belong to the same 'league', having fundamentally the same characteristics and resources while manifesting them in a differential manner. The subsequent ranking presupposes an accepted value system (which the women's movement claims is a distorted all-male value system arising from the nature of a male-dominated society). Asians, I deem to suggest, do not conceive of men and women as members of the same 'league'. Each have their own 'equal' status, but their statuses are different, with their own unique characteristics and resources. Comparison and competition make little sense.

The foundation of the women's movement developed in the seventeenth and eighteenth centuries when (Rowbotham, 1972: 35)

> the values associated with early capitalism, the questioning of authority, the idea of individual responsibility and conscience as a guide for political action, the elevation of activity, the notion of control and change of the outside world, and its corollary that those changes in turn affected the characters of human beings, were as relevant for women as they were for men.

These values are certainly evident and fast developing in the cities of Asia and city women are increasingly conscious of the powerlessness of the

Verity Saifullah-Khan

urban woman in strict *purdah*. As a status symbol she is restricted from participation in, and the rewards of, economic activity and is subject to the physical and psychological effects of lack of exercise, fresh air and mental stimulation. As a cash economy reaches traditional village life and an increased social mobility results from the migration process, so the village women may lose their command over the household's resources, their physical mobility and bargaining powers. But, although pride is felt in the acquisition of a *purdah* household, it will be increasingly difficult to maintain because the influence of the mass media, the rebelliousness of the younger generation, the importance of female education and other processes associated with 'Westernization' and modernization will be increasingly felt.

These forces are equally evident for the Pakistani villagers now living in Britain's cities and in both contexts it is an interesting and important question to consider whether some compromise between Eastern and Western values and life-styles can further the cause of the emancipation of women, or whether (as in the days of the Empire) we are to maintain our sense of moral superiority, and indeed whether we intervene or leave others to work out their own destinies.

Notes

1. I lived in Bradford for 1 year, 6 months of which was spent in one Mirpuri household where I became a member of the family, participating in their interactions with friends and relatives. My acceptance in the family involved a considerable disassociation of myself from the English world around us, and my becoming more Pakistani than a Pakistani girl to ensure their respect and trust. I observed a modified form of *purdah* (at times becoming an honorary male) which enabled a considerable insight into the woman's world, but forfeited a detailed understanding of the more economic and political activities of the men. The loyalty due to my adopted family also restricted my interaction with their 'out-groups', within their own community and with other Pakistani groups in general.

   In the winter of 1972-3 I left for Mirpur to stay in the villages from whence 'my' family and other contacts in Bradford had come. There are innumerable difficulties experienced by a Western woman doing fieldwork in a Muslim society but I found it refreshing, at least, to be away from the dual existence which the Bradford situation necessitated. Details of my fieldwork in Pakistan and Britain and the problems encountered are found in Saifullah-Khan (1974).

2. That is, Islam assumes the equality of men, the 'brotherhood' of Islam, but it does not stress equality between the sexes. Many Muslims argue, however, that Islam gave a great status to women, because prior to Muhammad men could have many wives, divorce them easily and they bought their wives from the girl's father, or captured them in time of feud to demonstrate their prowess. Islam raised the status of women and the family by restricting the number of wives, restricting women from the eyes of other men (through *purdah*) and giving *mehr* (dower paid to the bride). Had this 'spirit' of Islam been upheld in subsequent centuries the position of women would have improved through reforms as conditions changed, but 'the word' established when the conditions of life were so different, has been maintained at the expense of 'the spirit' of those Islamic injunctions. In law the woman remains half the worth of a man (e.g. she is entitled to half her brother's share of inheritance). For further details see Fyzee (1949).

3. By preference marriages are arranged within the kin group *biradari*, and in certain areas different cousins are preferred. See Alavi (1972: 6) and Eglar (1960: 94). Among Mirpuris matrilateral and patrilateral cross and parallel cousins are preferred and the actual choice results from the quality and quantity of relationships that exist at the particular time.

4. These 'rules' of the *purdah* system are of my own construction and not consciously verbalized by the participants. They are intended to clarify the main unstated rules by which behaviour is regulated.

5. This is particularly so when they are at their most attractive age, and when they are unmarried. Fuller writes of a Muslim Lebanese village: 'For the growing girl has the power to disrupt society as a temptation to men.' 'The adolescent girl has come to sexual maturity but this maturity has not yet been institutionalized. Herein lies the girl's disruptive force. No longer a child nor yet a married woman, she stands in a precarious position.' (Fuller, 1961: 51-52).

6. The country can be divided into the Pathans, the Baluch, the Punjabis and the Sindhis, each with their own distinct tongue and territory. There are also refugees from Northern and Central India, the Anglo-Indians and the Kashmiris. Mirpuris do not fit so simply into these categories however. They are essentially of Punjabi culture but (if it existed) they would be of Kashmiri nationality.

7. The main Islamic sects found in Pakistan are the Sunnis and the Shias, and there is no obvious difference in their observance of *purdah*. Two numerically smaller sects show considerable differences, however. The Ismailis or Aga Khanis are a well-organized, educated group living a modern urban life and correspondingly

Verity Saifullah-Khan

putting little emphasis on *purdah*. The Ahmadiyas founded a reform movement to 'purify' existing beliefs at the beginning of the twentieth century. *Purdah* is observed strictly.

8. Those belonging to the traditional, orthodox school of Muslims see *purdah* as an Islamic injunction, its observance demonstrating their adherence to the ideals of their religion. This school interprets 'the word' rather than 'the spirit' of the *Quran*, supporting the superiority and dominance of men, the tradition of arranged marriage, polygamy and *purdah* and opposing birth control and the education of women insofar as it will alter the *status quo* by women entering into previously male domains. An outstanding example of a proponent of this school is Abul A'la Maududi, leader of the Islamic political party, Jamat-i-Islami (see Maududi, 1972a,b).

    The more liberal school of thought is far more diffuse with many variations of interpretation. Basically it reinterprets many of the traditional beliefs to accommodate life in a more modern era (see note 9). The Muslim Family Laws Ordinance is supported (fixing the minimum age for marriage, the grounds for a woman to dissolve her marriage, restricting the practice of polygamy, etc.). They also claim that the *Quran* nowhere forbids the education of women, nowhere specifies the strict observance of *purdah* and does not forbid birth control.

9. The *Quran* covers all aspects of life (economic, political, social and private), Islam being a way of life with no obvious division between the secular and the sacred. The *Quran* remains a complete 'guide-book' for those villagers living the life that must have been known in the centuries after Muhammad, but for city dwellers the new aspects of modern life are not referred to, and an increasing amount of the *Quran* is inappropriate.

10. These figures are based on the 1971 Census. Pakistanis born in Pakistan numbered 21,000. Children born of Asian parents in Bradford numbered 9,500 and if Pakistani children number approximately 6,000 (there were only 5,965 persons born in India), the total is approximately 27,000 Pakistanis. Subtracting 2,000 Bangla Deshis (a rough estimate), leaves 25,000 West Pakistanis, of which possibly 60 to 70 per cent (15,000) are Mirpuris. The total population of Bradford in 1971 was 294,177.

11. The average annual income in Pakistan is £30.40. However, other factors such as the increasing cost of living, and a larger family in Britain, minimize what initially appears to be a phenomenal increase.

12. The earlier migrants lived in Britain without their familes but since the immigration legislation in the early 1960s the majority of married men have brought or intend to bring their wives and children to Britain.

13. Some women knit and sew at home and sell their work to the local shops. Those who work outside the home are usually found in firms with all women employees or where only non-Asian men are working.

14. Two works on Islamic societies are by Barth (1959) and Fuller (1961) and two works on non-Islamic societies which manifest any features of a *purdah* society are by Campbell (1964) and Gough (1956).

15. Robert Murphy suggests that among the Tuareg the man's veil can be explained in terms of role conflict, and the ambiguity and ambivalence of relationships (in this case resulting from living among one's consanguines and affines). 'The Tuareg veil functions to maintain a diffuse and generalized kind of distance between the actor and those who surround him socially and physically. By the symbolic removal of a portion of his identity from the interaction situation, the Tuareg is allowed to act in the presence of conflicting interests and uncertainty.' (Murphy, 1964).

16. 'The Urban Villagers' (Gans, 1962) concerns the life of Italian-Americans in an inner city neighbourhood of Boston. The Italians reaction to city life, and their orientation toward 'home' and traditions is similar to that of the Mirpuris, and Gan's evaluation of the effects 'slum' redevelopment should bear our consideration in the British situation.

Bibliography

Abrams, P. and McCulloch, A., 1976. 'Men, women and communes' in *Sexual Divisions and Society: Process and Change* (Eds. D. L. Barker and S. Allen) Tavistock.

Acker, J. 1973. 'Women and social stratification', *Am. J. Sociol.*, **78**(4).

Acker, J. and Van Houten, D. R., 1974. 'Differential recruitment and control: the sex structuring of organization', *Admin. Sci. Q.*, **19**.

Alavi, Hamza, 1972. 'Kinship in West Punjab Villages,' in *Contributions to Indian Sociology*, New Series No. 4, Dec. (Ed. T. N. Madan), Vickers Publishing House.

Allen, V. L., 1971. *The Sociology of Industrial Relations*, Longman.

Anon. 1854. *The Home Book of Household Economy*, London.

Annon. 1852. *Home Truths for Home Peace, or 'Muddle' Defeated*, Edinburgh.

Archibald, K., 1947. *Wartime Shipyard*, Univ. Calif. P.

Armstrong, A., 1974. *Stability and Change in an English County Town*, C.U.P.

Bain, G. S., 1970. *The Growth of White-Collar Unionism*, O.U.P.

Bain, G. S. and Price, R., 1972. 'Union growth and employment trends in the United Kingdom, 1964-70', *Br. J. Ind. Relat.* **10**.

Banks, O., 1960. *The Attitudes of Steelworkers to Technical Change*, Liv. U.P.

Barker, D., 1972. 'Young people, and their homes: Spoiling and "keeping close" in a South Wales town', *Sociolog. Rev.*, **20**(4).

Barron, R. D. and Norris, G. M., 1976. 'Sexual divisions and the dual labour market', this volume.

Barth, F., 1959. 'Political leadership among the Swat Pathans', *London School of Economics Monographs on Social Anthropology*, No. 19, Univ. Lond., Athlone Press.

Battiscombe, G., 1951. *English Picnic*. Country Book Club.

Bayne-Powell, R., 1956. *Housekeeping in the Eighteenth Century*, John Murray.

Becker, H. S. and Strauss, A. L., 1965. 'Careers, personality and adult socialization', *Am. J. Sociol.*, **62**.

Bedford, Duke of, 1959. *A Silver-Plated Spoon*, Cassell.

Mrs. Beeton, 1859-60. *Household Management*, Beeton, London.

Belbin, B and Belbin, R., 1972. *Problems in Adult Retraining*, Heinemann.

Bell, C., 1968. *Middle Class Families*, Routledge and Kegan Paul.

Bell, C. and Healey, P., 1973. 'The family and leisure', in *Society and Leisure in Modern Britain* (Eds.S. Parker, M. Smith, and C. Smith), Allen Lane.

Bell, C., and Newby, H., 1973. 'The sources of social imagery of agricultural workers', *Sociolog. Rev.*, **21**(2).

Bell, C., and Newby, H., 1976. 'Husbands and wives: The dynamics of the deferential dialectic', this volume.

Benston, M., 1969. 'The political economy of women's liberation,' *Monthly Rev.*, **21**(4) (reprinted in *Voices from Women's Liberation*, 1971 (Ed. Leslie B. Tanner), Signet, New York).

Berger, P., and Kellner, H., 1964. 'Marriage and the construction of reality', *Diogenes*, **46**.

Bernard, J., 1964. *Academic Women*, Penn. State U.P.

Bernstein, B., 1973. 'On the classification and framing of educational knowledge', in *Knowledge, Education and Cultural Change* (Ed. R. Brown) Br. Sociolog. Assoc., Tavistock.

Bettelheim, B., 1943. 'Individual and mass behaviour in extreme situations', *J. Abnormal Psychol.*, **38**(4).

Beynon, H., and Blackburn, R. M., 1972. *Perceptions of Work*, C.U.P.

Black, C., 1907. *Sweated Industry and the Minimum Wage*, Duckworth.

Black, C., 1915. *Married Women's Work*, Women's Industrial Council, London.

Blackburn, R. M., 1967. *Union Character and Social Class*, Batsford.

Blau, P., 1959-60. 'Social integration, social rank and processes of interaction', *Human Org.*, **12**(4).

Blau, P., 1964. *Exchange and Power in Social Life*, Wiley.

Blood, R. O. and Wolfe, D. M., 1960. *Husbands and Wives: The Dynamics of Family Living*, Free Press (Glencoe).

Bluestone, B., 1970. 'The tripartite economy: labour markets and the working poor', *Poverty and Human Resources Abstracts*, July.

Booth, C., 1889. *Life and Labour of the People of London*, Vol. I, Williams and Norgate.

Bott, E., 1957. *Family and Social Network*, Tavistock.

Bourdieu, P., 1971. 'Reproduction culturelle et reproduction sociale', *Inform. Sciences Sociales*, **10**(2).

Bourdieu, P., and Darbel, A., 1966. 'La fin d'un Malthusianisme?', in Darras,? *Le Partage des Bénéfices*, Editions de Minuit (Paris).

Bourdieu, P., and Passeron, J-C., 1970. *La Reproduction: Eléments pour une Théorie du Système d'Enseignement*, Editions de Minuit (Paris).

Bourdieu, P., *et al.*, 1973. 'Les stratégies de reconversion', *Inform. Sciences Sociales*, **12**(5).

Boyd-Barrett, O., 1970. 'Journalism recruitment and training: problems in professionalisation', *Media Sociology* (Ed. J. Tunstall) Constable.

Bracer, G. and Michael, J., 1969. 'The sex distribution in social work: causes and consequences', *Social Casework*, **50**.

Brake, M., 1974. 'I may be queer but at least I'm a man,' in *Sexual Divisions and Society: Process and Change* (Eds. D. L. Barker and S. Allen), Tavistock.

Brett, J., John Brett (1831-1902), *Dictionary of National Biography*, Twentieth Century Supplement.

Brown, J., 1970. 'A note on the division of labour by sex', *Am. Anthrop.*, p. 1073.

Bibliography

Brown, M., 1974. *Sweated Labour*, Low Pay Pamphlet No. 1, Low Pay Unit (London).

Brown, R., 1976. 'Women as employees', this volume.

Brown, R. K., 1973. 'Sources of objectives in work and employment' in *Man and Organization* (Ed. J. Child), Allen & Unwin.

Brown, R. K., Brannen, P., Cousins, J. M., and Samphier, M. L., 1972. 'The contours of solidarity — social stratification and industrial relations in shipbuilding', *Br. J. Indusl. Relat.*, **10**.

Brown, R. K., Kirkby, J. M., and Taylor, K. F., 1964. 'The employment of married women and the supervisory role', *Br. J. Indusl. Relat.*, **2**.

Brown, W., 1973. *Piecework Bargaining*, Heinemann.

Bulmer, M. (Ed.), 1974. *Working Class Imagery*, Routledge and Kegan Paul.

Campbell, J. K., 1964. *Honour, Family and Patronage: A Study of Institutions and Moral Values in a Greek Mountain Community*, Clarendon Press.

Cannon, I. C., 1967. 'Ideology and occupational community: a study of compositors', *Sociology*, **1**.

Caplow, T., 1954. *The Sociology of Work*, McGraw-Hill (New York).

Carpenter, E., 1916. *My Days and Dreams: Being Autobiographical Notes*, Allen & Unwin.

Carré J. J., Dubois, P., and Malinvaud, E., 1972. *La Croissance Française*, Editions de Seuil (Paris).

Carter, M. P., 1963. *Education, Employment and Leisure*, Pergamon.

Castles, S. and Kosack, G., 1973. *Immigrant Workers and Class Structure in Western Europe*, Institute of Race Relations.

Census of Population and Occupations, *General Report*, c. 2174, Vol. CVIII, 1904.

Chase Manhattan Bank, *What is a wife worth?*

Clark, A., 1968. *Working Life of Women in the Seventeenth Century*, Frank Cass.

Clegg, H. A., Fox, A., and Thompson, A. F., 1964. *A History of British Trade Unions since 1889*, Vol. I. O.U.P.

Cobbett, W., 1829. 'Advice to young men,' in *Cobbett's England*, (Ed. J. Derry) Folio Society, 1968.

Coch, L., French, J. R. P., Jr., 1948. 'Overcoming resistance to change', *Human Relat.*, **4**.

Colburn-Mayne, E., 1929. *The Life and Letters of Anne Isabella, Lady Noel Byron*, Constable.

Comer, L., 1974. *Wedlocked Women*, Feminist Books.

Commission on Industrial Relations, 1973. *Pin, Hook and Eye and Snap Fastener Wages Council*, CIR Report No. 49, HMSO.

Commission on Industrial Relations, 1974. *Clothing Wages Councils*, CIR Report No. 77, HMSO.

Costa, M. D., 1972. 'Women and the subversion of the community' in *The Power of Women and the Subversion of the Community*, Falling Wall Press Pamphlet, (Bristol).

Cunnison, S., 1966. *Wages and Work Allocation*, Tavistock.

Daniel, W. W., 1972. *Whatever Happened to the Workers in Woolwich?* P.E.P. Broadsheet, Political and Economic Planning.

Daniel, W. W., 1973. 'Understanding employee behaviour in its context' in *Man and Organization* (Ed. J. Child), Allen & Unwin.

Davidoff, L., 1973. *The Best Circles: 'Society', Etiquette and the Season*, Croom-Helm.

Davidoff, L., 1974. 'Mastered for life: servant and wife in Victorian and Edwardian England', *J. Soc. Hist.*, Summer.

Davidoff, 1976. 'The rationalization of housework', this volume.

Davidoff, L., L'Esperance, J., and Newby, H., 1976. 'Landscape with figures: home and community in English society' in *Women and Change* (Eds. J. Mitchell and A. Oakley), Penguin. Page reference is to mimeod copy.

Davin, A., 1972. 'Imperialism and the Myth of Motherhood'. Paper presented to the Ruskin History Conference, Oxford.

Davis, J., 1973. *Land and Family in Pisticci*, Athlone Press.

Delphy, C., 1970. 'L'Ennemi principale', *Partisans*, No. 54-5.

Delphy, C., 1976. 'Continuities and discontinuities in marriage and divorce', *Sexual Divisions and Society: Process and Change* (Eds. D. L. Barker and S. Allen), Tavistock.

Delphy, C., and Barker, D. L. (forthcoming), *Women and the Family*, Tavistock.

Dennis, N., Henriques, F., and Slaughter, C., 1956. *Coal is Our Life*, Eyre and Spottiswoode.

Department of Employment, *Gazette* (1948-1971), HMSO.

Department of Employment, 1969. *New Earnings Survey 1968*, HMSO.

Department of Employment, 1973. *New Earnings Survey 1972*, HMSO.

Department of Employment, 1973. (Wages Inspectorate) *Note on Homeworkers in the Clothing Industry*, HMSO, January.

Department of Employment, 1974. *Gazette*, January, HMSO.

Department of Employment, 1975. *Women and Work: A Statistical Survey.* Department of Employment Manpower Paper No. 9, HMSO.

Diamond, J. D., 1946. *The Law of Master and Servant*, Stevens and Son.

Dony, J. G., 1942. *A History of the Straw Hat Industry*, Gibbs, Banforth and Co.

Dore, R. P., 1973. *British Factory — Japanese Factory*, Univ. Calif. P.

Douglas, M., 1968. 'The social control of cognition: some factors in joke perception', *Man*, 3(3).

Douglas, M., 1966. *Purity and Danger, An Analysis of Concepts of Pollution and Taboo*, Routledge and Kegan Paul/Penguin.

Douglas, M., 1972. 'Deciphering a meal', *Daedalus*, 101.

Dreitzel, H., 1972. 'Family, Marriage and the Struggle of the Sexes', *Recent Sociology No. 4*, Collier-MacMillan.

Dubin, R., 1956. 'Industrial workers worlds: A study of the "central life interests" of industrial workers', *Social Problems*, 3.

Dumont, L., 1972. *Homo Hierarchicus, The Caste System and Its Implications*, Paladin.

Durkheim, E., 1964. *The Division of Labour in Society*, Free Press (Glencoe).

Dyos, H. J., and Wolff, M., 1973. *The Victorian City: Images and Realities*, Routledge and Kegan Paul.

Edmonds, J. and Radice, G., 1968. *Low Pay*, Fabian Research Series.

Bibliography

Eglar, Z., 1960. *A Punjabi Village in Pakistan,* Columbia Univ. P.
Eldridge, J. E. T., 1971. *Sociology and Industrial Life,* Nelson.
Eliade, M., 1958. 'Water and water symbolism' in *Patterns in Comparative Religion,* Sheed and Ward.
Elkins, S., 1959, *Slavery,* Univ. Chicago P.
Employment and Productivity Gazette, The, 1968-72. HMSO.
Epstein, C. F., 1970. *Woman's Place,* Univ. of Calif. P.

Fabian Society, 1902. *Life in the Laundry,* Fabian Tract No. 112, July.
Fallding, H., 1961. 'Family and the idea of a cardinal role', *Human Relat.,* 14.
Field, F. (Ed), 1973. *Low Pay,* Arrow Books.
Firestone, S., 1971. *The Dialectic of Sex,* Cape.
Firth, R., Hubert, J., and Forge, A., 1969. *Families and Their Relatives,* Routledge and Kegan Paul.
Florence, P. S., 1964. *Economics and Sociology of Industry,* Watts.
Fogarty, M., Allen, I., Allen, J., and Walters, P., 1971. *Women in Top Jobs,* Allen and Unwin.
Fogarty, M. P., Rapoport, R., and Rapoport, R. N., 1967. *Women and Top Jobs,* P.E.P.
Fogarty, M., Rapoport, R., and Rapoport, R. N., 1971. *Sex, Career and Family,* Allen and Unwin.
Fox, A., 1971. *A Sociology of Work in Industry,* Collier-MacMillan.
Frankenberg, R., 1957. *Village on the Border,* Cohen and West.
Frankenberg, R., 1966. *Communities in Britain,* Penguin.
Frankenberg, R., 1974. 'Community Life and the Interaction of Production Systems.' Paper presented to the BSA conference.
Frankenberg, R., 1976. 'In the production of their lives, men (?) . . .: Sex and Gender in British Community Studies', *Sexual Divisions and Society: Process and Change* (Eds. D. L. Barker and S. Allen), Tavistock.
Frederick, C., 1920. *Scientific Management in the Home,* Routledge.
Freeman, C., 1953. *Luton and the Hat Industry,* The Corporation of Luton Museum and Art Gallery.
Freund, J., 1968. *The Sociology of Max Weber,* Allen and Unwin.
Fricke, P. H., 1974. *The Social Structure of the Crews of British Dry Cargo Merchant Ships,* Univ. Durham (Ph.D. thesis).
Friedan, B., 1963. *The Feminine Mystique* : Gollancz.
Fuller, A. H., 1961, *Buarij Portrait of a Lebanese Muslim Village,* Harvard Middle Eastern Monograph Series for Center of Middle Eastern Studies, Harvard Univ. P.
Furnivall, F. S., 1888. 'For to Serve a Lord' from John Russell's *Boke of Nurture,* London.
Fyzee, Asaf, A. A., 1949, *Outlines of Muhammedan Law,* O.U.P.

Gail, S., 1968. 'The housewife' in *Work: Twenty Personal Accounts* (Ed. R. Frazer), Penguin.
Galbraith, J., 1973. *Economics and the Public Purpose,* Houghton Mifflin.
Gans, H. J., 1962. *The Urban Villagers,* Free Press (New York) and Collier-MacMillan.
Gardiner, J., 1976. 'Political Economy of Domestic Labour in Capitalist Society', this volume.

Gardiner, J., 1974. 'Women's Employment since the sixties', *Spare Rib*, No. 27, **19**.

Genovese, E. D., 1971. *In Red and Black*, Allen Lane.

Gerbner, G., 1969. 'Institutional pressures upon mass communicators' in *The Sociology of Mass Media Communicators* (Ed. P. Halmos), Sociolog. Rev. Monograph **13**.

Gillespie, D., 1972. 'Who has the Power? The Marital Struggle' in *Family, Marriage and the Struggle of the Sexes* (Ed. H. P. Dreitzel). Collier-MacMillan.

Glasse, H., 1748. *The Art of Cookery Made Plain and Easy*, London.

Goffman, E., 1961. *Encounters: Two Studies in the Sociology of Interactions*, Bobbs-Merrill.

Goffman, E., 1968. *Asylums*, Penguin.

Goffman, E., 1969. *The Presentation of Self in Everyday Life*, Allen Lane.

Goffman, E., 1972. 'The Nature of Deference and Demeanour', *Interaction Ritual*, Penguin.

Goldthorpe, J. H., Lockwood, D., Bechhofer, F., and Platt, J., 1968. *The Affluent Worker: Industrial Attitudes and Behaviour*, C.U.P.

Goldthorpe, J., Lockwood, D., Bechhofer, F., and Platt, J., 1969. *The Affluent Worker and the Class Structure*, C.U.P.

Goode, W. J., 1962. *The Family*, Prentice-Hall (New York).

Gordon, D. M., 1972. *Theories of Poverty and Underemployment*, Lexington.

Goslett, D., 1971. *The Professional Practice of Design*, Batsford.

Gough, I., 1972. 'Marx's theory of productive and unproductive labour', *New Left Review*, December.

Gough, K., 1956. 'Brahmin kinship in a Tamil village', *Am. Anthrop.*, **58**.

Gouldner, A. W., 1959. 'Organizational analysis' in *Sociology Today* (Eds. R. K. Merton *et al.*), Basic Books (New York).

Gouldner, A. W., 1960. 'The norm of reciprocity: a preliminary statement', *Am. Sociolog. Rev.*, **25**.

Government Statistical Office, 1973. *Social Trends*, No. 4., London, HMSO.

Grant, B. (Ed.), 1924. *The Receipt Book of Elizabeth Roper* (and a portion of her Cipher Journal 1756-1770), Nonesuch Press.

Gray, R. Q., 1973. 'Styles of life; the "labour aristocracy" and class relations in later 19th-century Edinburgh', *Int. Rev. of Social History*, XVIII.

Griffin, S. A., 1973. *Women in Top Financial Jobs*, H. E. Griffin (Oxford).

Gronseth, E., 1970. 'The Dysfunctions of the Husband-Provider Role', paper at the XI International Family Conference, London.

Gross, E., 1968. 'Plus ca change? the sexual structure of occupations over time', *Social Problems*, **16**.

Hall, C., 1974. 'The History of the Housewife', *Spare Rib*, **26**.

Harris, A., 1970. 'The second sex in academe', *Am. Assoc. Univ. Professors Bull.*

Harris, A. and Clausen, R., 1966. *Labour Mobility in Great Britain, 1953-1963*, HMSO.

Harrison, B., 1965-6. 'Philanthropy and the Victorians', *Victorian Studies*, **9**.

Bibliography

Harrison, J., 1973. 'Productive and unproductive labour in Marx's political economy' in *Bulletin of the conference of Socialist Economists*, Autumn.

Harrison, J., 1973. 'The political economy of housework' *Bulletin of the conference of Socialist Economists*, Winter.

Heer, D., 1963. 'The measurement and bases of family power; an overview', *Marriage and Family Living*, 25(2).

Henderson, W., 1795. *The Housekeeper's Instructor or Universal Family Cook*, London.

Higgins, R., 1974. *Observer Magazine*, 13 October.

Himmelfarb, G., 1971. 'Mayhew's poor: a problem of identity', *Victorian Studies*, March.

Hobsbawm, E., 1964. *Labouring Men: Studies in the History of Labour*, Weidenfeld and Nicolson.

Hoffman, L., 1963. 'The decision to work', in *The Employed Mother in America*, (Eds. F. Nye and L. Hoffman), Rand McNally.

Hole, C., 1953. *The English Housewife in the Seventeenth Century*, Chatto & Windus.

Hollowell, P. G., 1968. *The Lorry Driver*, Routledge & Kegan Paul.

Holter, H., 1970. *Sex Roles and Social Structure*, Oslo Univ. P.

Homans, G. C., 1960. *English Villages in the Thirteenth Century*, Russell and Russell. (New York).

Hope, E., Kennedy, M. and de Winter, A., 1976. 'Homeworkers in North London', this volume.

Hudson, D., 1972. *Munby, Man of Two Worlds: The Life and Diaries of Arthur J. Munby, 1828-1910*, John Murray.

Hughes, E. C., 1958. *Men and their Work*, Free Press (Glencoe).

Hunt, A., 1968. *A Survey of Women's Employment*, Vols. I & II, HMSO.

Hutt, C., 1972. *Males and Females*, Penguin.

Hyman, R., 1972. *Strikes*, Fontana.

Inchfawn, F., 1920. *The Verse Book of a Homely Woman*, Girls' Own Paper, (London).

Informations Sociales, No. 4, 1973. 'Où va la famille française?'.

Ingham, G., 1970. *Size of Industrial Organisation and Worker Behaviour*, C.U.P.

Irwin, M., 1907. *The Problem of Homework*, Glasgow.

Jephcott, P., Seear, B. N., and Smith, J. H., 1962. *Married Women Working*, Allen and Unwin.

John, A., 1973. 'Pit-Brow Lassies, A Test Case For Female Labour', unpublished MS.

Johnson, M. B., 1971. *Household Behaviour: Consumption, Income and Wealth*, Penguin Modern Economics Texts.

Joseph, J., 1961. 'Attitudes of 600 adolescent girls to work and marriage', *Br. J. Sociol.*, 12.

Kahn, R. L., 1958. 'Human relations on the shop floor', in *Human Relations and Modern Management* (Ed. E. M. Hugh-Jones). North-Holland.

Kapferer, B. and Handelmen, D., 1972. 'Forms of joking activity: a comparative approach'. *Am. Anthrop.*, **74**.

Kavanagh, D., 1971. 'The deferential English: a comparative critique', *Government and Opposition*, May.

Kerr, C., and Siegel, A., 1954. 'The interindustry propensity to strike — an international comparison', in *Industrial Conflict* (Eds. A. Kornhauser, *et al.*), McGraw-Hill (New York).

Kitchiner, W., 1823. *The Cook's Oracle: Containing Receipts for Plain Cookery on the most Economical Plan for Private Families, the Quantity of each Article is Accurately stated by Weight and Measure; being the Actual Experiments Investigated in the Kitchen of Wm. Kitchener, M.D.*, Whittaker.

Kitchiner, W., 1825. *The Housekeeper's Oracle: A Plain and Easy Plan of Keeping Accurate Accounts of the Expenses of Housekeeping*, Whittaker.

Klein, J., 1965. *Samples from English Culture*, Routledge and Kegan Paul.

Klein, L., 1964. *'Multiproducts Ltd.'*, HMSO.

Klein, V., 1960. *Working Wives*, Institute of Personnel Management, Occasional Paper 15.

Klein, V., 1961. *Employing Married Women*, Institute of Personnel Management, Occasional Paper 17.

Klein, V., 1965a. *Women Workers: Working Hours and Services*, OECD (Paris).

Klein, V., 1965b. *Britain's Married Women Workers*, Routledge & Kegan Paul. (Includes Klein, 1960 and Klein, 1961).

Knowles, K. G. J. C., 1952. *Strikes*, Blackwell.

Koedt, A., 1970. 'The myth of the vaginal orgasm' in *Voices from Women's Liberation* (Ed. L. B. Tanner). Bantam (New York).

Komarovsky, M., 1962. *Blue Collar Marriage*, Random House (New York).

Lady, A., 1829. *The Home Book*, London.

Land, H., 1976. 'Women: supporters or supported?' in *Sexual Divisions and Society: Process and Change* (Eds. D. L. Barker and S. Allen), Tavistock.

Landsberger, H. A., 1958. *Hawthorne Revisited*, Cornell Univ.

Larguia, I. and Dumoulin, J., 1973. *Towards a Science of Women's Liberation*, Red Rag Pamphlet, No. 1, London.

Laslett, P., 1965. *The World We Have Lost*, Methuen.

Le Gros Clark, F., 1962. *Women, Work and Age*. The Nuffield Foundation.

Legman, C., 1969. *The Rationale of the Dirty Joke: An Analysis of Sexual Humour*, Jonathan Cape (Panther, 1972).

Lenin, V. I., 1969. 'A great beginning', *Selected Works*, Lawrence and Wishart.

Lenski, G. H., 1954. 'Status crystallization: a non-vertical dimension of social status', *Am. Sociolog. Rev.*, **19**.

Lenski, G. H., 1966. *Power and Privilege*, McGraw-Hill.

Leser, C. E. V., 1959. 'Trends in women's work participation', *Population Studies*, **12**.

Levi-Strauss, C., 1965. 'The norm of reciprocity' in *Sociological Theory: A Book of Readings* (Eds. L. Coser and B. Rosenberg). Macmillan.

254

Bibliography

Liberal Party Report on Nottingham Lace Workers, 1972. Unpublished.
Liebow, E., 1967. *Tally's Corner,* Little, Brown (Boston).
Littlejohn, J., 1963. *Westrigg: The Sociology of a Cheviot Parish,* Routledge.
Lockwood, D., 1958. *The Blackcoated Worker,* Allen & Unwin.
Lopata, H. Z., 1971. *Occupation: Housewife,* O.U.P.
Loudon, J., 1845. *The Ladies Country Companion; or how to enjoy a country life rationally,* London.
Loudon, J. B., 1970. 'Teasing and socialization on Tristan da Cunha' in *Socialization: The Approach from Social Anthropology* (Ed. P. Mayer). Tavistock (for the A.S.A.).
Lupri, E., 1969. 'Contemporary authority patterns in the West German family: a study in cross-national validation', *Journal of Marriage and the Family,* **31**(1).
Lupton, T., 1961. *Money for Effort,* HMSO.
Lupton, T., 1963. *On the Shop Floor,* Pergamon.
Lydall, H. F., 1968. *The Structure of Earnings,* O.U.P.

Macdonald, D., 1973. 'Hotel cowboys', *New Society,* 31 May.
Mackay, D., Boddy, D., Brack, J., Diack, J. A., and **Jones, N.,** 1971. *Labour Markets under Different Employment Conditions,* Allen and Unwin.
Maher, V., 1976. 'Kin, clients and accomplices: relationships among women in Morocco', *Sexual Divisions and Society: Process and Change* (Eds. D. L. Barker and S. Allen), Tavistock.
Mainardi, P., 1971. *The Politics of Housework,* Agitprop Information.
Maizels, J., 1970. *Adolescent Needs and the Transition from School to Work,* Athlone Press.
Mann, M., 1973. *Workers on the Move,* C.U.P.
Marceau, F. J., 1976. 'Marriage, role division and social cohesion', this volume.
Marsden, D., 1969. *Mothers Alone,* Allen Lane.
Marsden, D., 1975, *Workless,* Penguin.
Marx, K., 1961. *Capital,* vol. I, Moscow. (1887 edition).
Marx, K., 1969. *Theories of Surplus Value,* Part I, Lawrence and Wishart.
Mattfeld, J. A. and **Van Aken, C. G.,** 1965. *Women and the Scientific Professions,* M.I.T. Press.
Maududi, S. A. A., 1972a. *Towards Understanding Islam* (13th edn) Islamic Publications Ltd. Lahore.
Maududi, S. A. A., 1972b. *Purdah and the Status of Women in Islam,* Islamic Publications Ltd., Lahore.
Mauss, M., 1970. *The Gift,* Cohen and West.
Mead, M., 1970. *Male and Female,* Penguin.
Mehta, Aban, 1950. *The Domestic Servant Class,* Bombay.
Merton, R. K., 1970. *Science, Technology and Society in Seventeenth-Century England,* Howard Fertig (New York).
Michel, A., 1972. *Statut professionnel feminin et structure du couple Français Urbain.* CNRS-CORDES (Paris).
Middleton, C., 1974. 'Sexual inequality and stratification theory', in *The Social Analysis of Class Structure* (Ed. F. Parkin), Tavistock.
Mill, J. S., 1869. *On the Subjection of Women,* London.

Miller, D. C., and Form, W. H., 1964. *Industrial Sociology*, Harper (New York).
Millward, N., 1968. 'Family status and behaviour at work', *Sociolog. Rev.* **16**.
Ministry of Labour *Gazette*, 1920-39 and 1946-67.
Morgan, D. H. J., 1969. 'Who confronts whom? — the case of the Rectifier Department' in *Social Stratification and Industrial Relations* (Eds. J. H. Goldthorpe and M. Mann). Proceedings of an SSRC Conference, Cambridge.
Morse, N., and Reimer, E., 1956. 'The experimental change of a major organizational variable', *J. Abnormal and Social Psychol.*, **52**.
Morton, P., 1970. 'Womens' work is never done', *Leviathan*, May.
Mumford, E., and Banks, O., 1967. *The Computer and the Clerk*, Routledge & Kegan Paul.
Murphy, R., 1964. 'Social distance and the veil', *Am. Anthrop.*, **66**.
Myrdal, A., and Klein, V., 1956. *Women's Two Roles*, Routledge & Kegan Paul.

National Board for Prices and Incomes, 1969. *Pay and Conditions in the Clothing Manufacturing Industries*. NBPI Report No. 110, HMSO. April.
National Board for Prices and Incomes, 1971. *General Report on Low Pay*, NBPI Report No. 169, HMSO.
National Manpower Council, 1957. *Womanpower*, Columbia U.P.
National Union of Journalists, 1974. *Annual Report 1973-4*, NUJ, Acorn House, 314 Grays Inn Road, London WC1.
Newby, H., 1972. 'Agricultural workers in the class structure', *Sociolog. Rev.*, **20**.
Newby, H., 1975. 'The deferential dialectic', *Comparative Studies in Society and History*.
Newson, J., and Newson, E., 1963. *Infant Care in An Urban Community*, Allen and Unwin.
Nisbet, R. A., 1967. *The Sociological Tradition*, Heinemann.

Opie, I, and Opie, P., 1952. *The Oxford Dictionary of Nursery Rhymes*, O.U.P.
Oakley, A., 1974a. *Housewife*, Allen Lane.
Oakley, A., 1974b. *Housework: stereotypes and realities*, unpublished MS.
Oren, L., 1973. 'The welfare of women in laboring families in England 1860-1950', *Feminist Studies*, Winter-Spring, **1**(3-4).
Ortner, S., 1974. 'Is female to male as nature is to culture?' in *Women, Culture and Society* (Eds. M. Z. Rosaldo and L. Lamphere), Stanford U.P.
Orwell, G., 1959. *The Road to Wigan Pier*, Secker and Warburg.
Owen, C., 1974. 'The outwork outrage', *The Guardian*.

Pahl, J. M., and Pahl, R. E., 1972. *Managers and their Wives*, Penguin.
Papanek, H., 1964. 'The woman field worker in a purdah society', *Human Org.*, **23**, No. 2, Summer.
Papanek, H., 1971. 'Purdah in Pakistan: Seclusion and Modern Occupations for Women', *J. Marriage and the Family*, August.

Bibliography

Parker, S., 1973. 'Relations between work and leisure', in *Leisure and Society in Britain* (Eds. M. Smith, S. Parker and C. Smith), Allen Lane.

Parker, S. R., Brown, R. K., Child, J., and Smith, M. A., 1972. *The Sociology of Industry*, Allen & Unwin.

Parkin, F., 1971. *Class Inequality and Political Order*, MacGibbon and Kee.

Perkin, H., 1969. *The Origins of Modern English Society, 1780-1880*, Routledge.

Phelps, C. E., 1968. 'Women in American Medicine', *J. Med. Educ.*, **43**.

Phelps Brown, E. H., 1962. *The Economics of Labor*, Yale U.P.

Pinder, P., 1969. *Women at Work*, Political and Economic Planning.

Piore, M., 1972. 'On the technological foundations of economic dualism,' *M.I.T. Working Paper*, Mass. Inst. Tech., Econ. Dept.

Pitrou, A., 1972. *La famille dans la vie de tous les jours*, Privat, Paris.

Pizzey, E., 1974. *Scream Quietly or the Neighbours Will Hear*, Penguin.

Pleck, J., and Sawyer, J. (Eds), 1974. *Men and Masculinity*, Prentice-Hall Spectrum (New York).

Political and Economic Planning, 1945. *The Market for Household Appliances* (Wartime social survey, Heating of Dwellings Inquiry), O.U.P.

Poloma, M., and Garland, T., 1971. 'Jobs or careers? the case of the professionally employed married woman', in *Family Issues of Employed Women in Europe and America* (Ed. A. Michel) Brill (Leiden).

The Queen, 1919. 'Le Menage', March 29.

The Queen, 1932. 'Sunday Night Supper', Oct. 26.

Radcliffe-Brown, A. R., 1952. 'On joking relationships', *Structure and Function in Primitive Society*, Cohen and West.

Rainwater, L., 1974. *Behind Ghetto Walls*, Penguin.

Rapoport, R., and Rapoport, R. N., 1969. 'The dual-career family: a variant pattern and social change', *Human Relat.*, **22**(1).

Rapoport, R., and Rapoport, R. N., 1971a. *Dual Career Families*, Penguin.

Rapoport, R., and Rapoport, R. N., 1971b. 'Further considerations on the dual career family', *Human Relat.*, **24**.

Rapoport, R., and Rapoport, R. N., 1971c. 'Early and late experiences as determinants of adult behaviour: married women's family and career patterns', *Br. J. Sociol.*, **22**(1).

Ravetz, A., 1965. 'Modern technology and an ancient occupation: housework in present day society', *Technology and Culture*, vol. VI, Society for the History of Technology, (privately printed) U.S.A.

Ravetz, A., 1968. 'The Victorian coal kitchen and its reformers', *Victorian Studies*, June.

Red Rag, 1973. 'Striking progress, 1972-1973', vol. 5. (anon.)

Rees, A. D., 1950. *Life in a Welsh Countryside*. Univ. Wales P.

Rennie, J., 1955. *Every Other Sunday — The Autobiography of a Kitchen Maid*, Arthur Barker.

The Report of the Committee Appointed to Consider the Position of Outworkers in Relation to Unemployment Insurance, 1923. HMSO.

Robbins Report (Committee on Higher Education), 1963. HMSO.

Rodman, H., 1967. 'Marital power in France, Greece, Yugoslavia: a cross-national discussion, *J. Marr. and Fam.*, **29**(2).

Roethlisberger, F. J., and Dickson, W. J., 1939. *Management and the Worker*, Harvard U.P.

Rosen, G., 1974. 'Disease, debility and death' in *The Victorian City, Images and Realities* (Eds. M. Wolff and H. Dyos), Vol. II, Routledge.

Rosser, C., and Harris, C., 1965. *The Family and Social Change*, Routledge and Kegan Paul.

Rossi, A. C., 1965. 'Barriers to career choice of engineering, medicine or science among American women' in *Women and the Scientific Professions* (Eds. J. A. Mattfeld and C. Van Aken) Mass.Inst.Tech.P. (London).

Rossi, A. C., 1970. 'Status of women in graduate departments of sociology', *Am. Sociolog.*, **5**.

Rowbotham, S., 1972. *Women, Resistance and Revolution*, Allen Lane.

Rowbotham, S., 1973a. *Hidden From History*, Pluto Press.

Rowbotham, S., 1973b. *Woman's Consciousness, Man's World*, Penguin.

Rowntree, B. S., 1901. *Poverty. A Study of Town Life*, Macmillan.

Rowntree, B. S., 1941. *Poverty and Progress*, Longmans.

Rowthorn, B., 1974. 'Skilled labour in the Marxist system', *Bulletin of the Conference of Socialist Economists*, Spring.

Rundell, Mrs (A Lady) 1845. *A New System of Domestic Cookery*, London.

Safilios-Rothschild, C., 1967. 'A comparison of power structures and marital satisfaction in urban Greek and French families', *J. Marr. and Fam.*, **29**(2).

Safilios-Rothschild, C., 1969. 'Family sociology or wives' family sociology', *J. Marr. and Fam.*, **31**(2).

Saifullah-Khan, S. (1975). 'Pakistani Villagers in a British City' (Ph.D. thesis), Univ. Bradford.

Saifullah-Khan, V., 1976. 'Purdah in the British Situation', this volume.

Sathyamurthy, C., 1974. 'Women's Occupations and Social Change: the Case of Social Work', Paper given at BSA Conference.

Sayle, M., 1973. 'Jayant Naik's new job for the new year', *Sunday Times*, 24 December.

Sayles, L. R., 1958. *Behavior of Industrial Work Groups*, Wiley (New York).

Scanzoni, J., 1972. *Sexual Bargaining*, Prentice Hall (New Jersey).

Schein, E. H., 1965. *Organizational Psychology*, Prentice-Hall (New Jersey).

Schneider, E. V., 1957. *Industrial Sociology*, McGraw-Hill (New York).

Schoenwald, R. L., 1974. 'Training urban man: a hypothesis about the sanitary movement' in *The Victorian City, Images and Realities* (Eds. M. Wolff and H. Dyos), Vol. II, Routledge.

Scott, W. H., Banks, J. A., Lupton, T., and Halsey, A. H., 1956. *Technical Change and Industrial Relations*, Liverpool U.P.

Scott, W. H., Mumford, E., McGivering, I. C., and Kirkby, J. M., 1963. *Coal and Conflict*, Liverpool U.P.

Bibliography

Secombe, W., 1974. 'The housewife and her labour under capitalism', *New Left Review*, Jan-Feb.

Seear, B. N., 1968. 'The position of women in industry' in Royal Commission on Trade Unions and Employers' Associations, *Research Papers*, 11, HMSO.

Shaw, J., 1976. 'Some implications of sex segregated education', *Sexual Division and Society: Progress and Change* (Eds. D. L. Barker and S. Allen), Tavistock.

Shipley, S. (N.D.). *Club Life and Socialism in Mid-Victorian London*, Ruskin History Workshop Pamphlet, No. 5. (London).

Shirtmaking Wages Council, 1971. *Proposals for Statutory Minimum Remuneration and Holidays and Holiday Remuneration, 12 October, 1971.* HMSO.

Sigal, C., 1962. *Weekend in Dinlock*, Penguin.

Simmel, G., 1971. *Georg Simmel on Individuality and Social Forms* (Ed. D. Levine), Univ. Chicago P.

Simmel, G., 1950. *The Sociology of Georg Simmel* (Ed. K. Wolff), Free Press (Glencoe).

Simpson, R. L., and Simpson, I. H., 1969. 'Women and bureaucracy in the semi-professions', in *The Semi-Professions and their Organisation* (Ed. A. Etzioni), Free Press (New York).

Sinfield, A., and Twine, F., 1970. 'The working poor', *Poverty*, Winter.

Smith, D. E., 1973. 'Women, the family and corporate capitalism' in *Women in Canada* (Ed. M. Stephenson), New Press (Toronto).

Smith, J. H., 1961. 'Managers and married women workers', *Br. J. Sociol.*, 12.

Smith, R. F., 1971. 'Science and the Second Sex' (Unpub. M.Sc. thesis), Univ. Bath.

Social Trends, 1973. HMSO.

Sombart, W., 1916. 'Medieval and modern commercial enterprise' in *Enterprise and Secular Change* (Ed. F. C. Lane), Allen & Unwin, 1953.

Sombart, W., 1914. 'Middle class virtues' in *The Quintessence of Capitalism: A Study of the History and Psychology of the Modern Business Man* (Trans. M. Epstein), Howard Fertig (New York), 1967.

Srinivas, M. N., 1965. *Religion and Society Among the Coorgs of South India*, Asia Publishing House.

Stacey, M., 1960. *Tradition and Change: A Study of Banbury*. O.U.P.

Stedman Jones, G., 1971, *Outcast London: A Study in the Relationship Between Classes in Victorian Society*, Clarendon Press.

Stewart, C. M., 1961. 'Future trends in the employment of married women', *Br. J. Sociol.*, 12.

Stone, L., 1967. *The Crisis of the Aristocracy, 1558-1641*, O.U.P. (abridged).

Streatfield, N., 1956. *The Day Before Yesterday; First Hand Stories of Fifty Years Ago*, Collins.

Syfers, J., 1971. 'Why I want a Wife', *Mother Lode*. Reprinted by KNOW, Pittsburgh, Pennsylvania.

Sykes, A. J. M., 1966. 'Joking relationships in an industrial setting', *Am. Anthrop.*, 68.

Sykes, A. J. M., 1969. 'Navvies: their work attitudes'; and 'Navvies: their social relations', *Sociology*, 3.

Syson, L., and Young, M., 1974. 'Poverty in Bethnal Green' in *Poverty Report 1974* (Ed. M. Young), Temple Smith.

Szwed, J. F., 1966. *Private Cultures and Public Imagery*, Newfoundland Social and Economic Studies, No. 2.

Tambiah, S. J., 1973. 'From varna to caste through mixed unions' in *The Character of Kinship* (Ed. J. Goody), C.U.P.

Tannahill, J. A., 1958. *European Volunteer Workers in Britain*, Manchester University Press.

Tannenbaum, A. S., 1966. *Social Psychology of the Work Organization*, Tavistock.

Teale, T. P., 1883. *Economy of Coal in House Fires*, London.

Thatcher, A. R., 1968. 'The distribution of earnings of employees in Great Britain', *J. Roy. Stat. Soc.*

Thomas, G., 1948. *Women and Industry*, The Social Survey.

Thompson, B., and Finlayson, A., 1963. 'Married women who work in early motherhood', *Br. J. Sociol.*, **14**.

Thompson, E. P., 1964. *The Making of the English Working Class*, Gollancz.

Townsend, P., 1963. *The Family Life of Old People*, Penguin.

Trist, E., Higgin, G. W., Murray, H., and Pollock, A. B., 1963. *Organizational Choice*, Tavistock.

Tunstall, J., 1962. *The Fishermen*, MacGibbon & Kee.

Tunstall, J., 1971. *Journalists at Work*, Constable.

Turner, H. A., 1962. *Trade Union Growth, Structure and Policy*, Allen & Unwin.

Turner, H. A., Clack, G., and Roberts, G., 1967. *Labour Relations in the Motor Industry*, Allen & Unwin.

University of Liverpool, Department of Social Science, 1956. *The Dock Worker*, Liverpool U.P.

Veness, T., 1962. *School Leavers*, Methuen.

Vernon, A., 1966. *Three Generations: The Fortunes of a Yorkshire Family*, Jarrolds.

Viteles, M. S., 1954. *Motivation and Morale in Industry*, Staples.

Wainwright, D., 1972. *Journalism Made Simple*, W. H. Allen.

Webb, S. and Webb, B., 1910. *English Poor Law Policy*, Longman Green.

Weber, M., 1964. *The Theory of Social and Economic Organization*. The Free Press (Glencoe, Ill.).

Weber, M., 1966. *General Economic History*, Collier-MacMillan.

Weber, M., 1968. *Economy and Society: An Outline of Interpretive Sociology*, vol. I. (Eds. G. Roth and C. Wittich), Bedminster Press (New York).

Weber, M., 1971. *The Protestant Ethic and the Spirit of Capitalism*, Unwin University Books.

Wedderburn, D., and Craig, C., 1974. 'Relative deprivation in work' in *Poverty, Inequality and Class Structure* (Ed. D. Wedderburn), C.U.P.

Bibliography

Wedderburn, D., and Crompton, R., 1972. *Workers' Attitudes and Technology*, C.U.P.

White, J. J., 1967. 'Women in the law' *Michigan Law Rev.*, **65**.

Whitehead, A., 1971. 'Social Fields and Social Networks in an English Rural Area' (unpublished PhD thesis), Univ. Wales.

Whitehead, A., 1976. 'Sexual antagonism in Herefordshire', this volume.

Wilensky, H. L., 1969. 'Work, careers and social integration', in *Industrial Man* (Ed. T. Burns), Penguin.

Williams, R., 1973. *The Country and the City*, Chatto.

Williams, W. M., 1956. *The Sociology of an English Village: Gosforth*, Routledge and Kegan Paul.

Williams, W. M., 1963. *A West Country Village: Ashworthy*, Routledge and Kegan Paul.

Young, G., 1936. *Victorian England: Portrait of An Age*, Oxford Paperback, 1966.

Young, M., Common Place Book, 1828-1840, 300.01; 48. 85/3 London Museum Library.

Young, M., 1952. 'The distribution of income within the family', *Br. J. Sociol.*

Young, M. and Willmott, P., 1957. *Family and Kinship in East London*, Routledge and Kegan Paul.

Young, M., and Willmott, P., 1973. *The Symmetrical Family*, Routledge and Kegan Paul.

Young, M., and Syson, L., 1974. 'Women: the new poor', *Observer*, 20, Jan.

Yudkin, S., and Holme, A., 1963. *Working Mothers and Their Children*, Michael Joseph.

Index

Index

264

Index